"African - Americans Are The American Indians"

THE MISEDUCATION OF THE AFRICAN - AMERICAN

What Every African – American Needs To Know

Benz Veal

Legacy Footprints
An Imprint of Legacy Footprints Publishing

ACKNOWLEDGMENTS

First, I would like to thank my grandmothers on my mother and father's side of the family. These two wonderful women made sure that I knew who I was in regards to ethnicity. I want to thank my Great Aunt on my father's mother's side for giving me in-depth information about the American Indian heritage of the family and giving me gifts from the tribe she has been affiliated with throughout her life. I love all of you beautiful matriarchs. I am happy that you saw my sincerity, shared the information, and I won't let it perish. Thank you Toni V. Morrison for listening to me for countless hours throughout the years, ranting about the subject matter of this book, and assisting me with the title, much love.

Secondly, I would like to thank a Youtube user by the name of "1000gohead". If it weren't for me navigating Youtube and stumbling across your Youtube video titled "UNDENIABLE pt.1 African Americans Ain't African" at the beginning of 2015, I wouldn't have been inspired to learn more about my family's history. I probably wouldn't have joined in the fight to help inform the people labeled African-Americans throughout the years or wrote this book.

Lastly, I would like to thank Kerry Davis for creating a platform on Facebook with the group "African Americans Ain't African." There are so many intelligent, beautiful, and talented people in that group that has brought forth valuable information to help aid the American people in finding their truth. Thank you to everyone in that group. Thank you to the advocates before me and those who came after me, spreading this truth. Thank you to every source in this book, your contributions are very much appreciated and invaluable. Thank you to everyone who asked for my assistance, listened to me, and researched their family. You gave me a purpose, and I'm forever grateful.

ISBN: 978-1-7337008-2-5

Copyright © 2019 Benz Veal all rights reserved. No part of this publication may be reproduced, distributed or transmitted in any form or by any means, including photocopying, recording or other electronic or mechanical methods, without the prior written permission of the publisher, except in the case of brief quotations embodied in reviews and certain other non-commercial uses permitted by copyright law.

CONTENTS

Preface
1

SECTION 1:
Transatlantic Slave Trade
5

SECTION 2:
Indian Descriptions Match African Americans
75

SECTION 3:
They Tried To Tell You That You're Indian
111

SECTION 4:
African Americans Look Like Past Indians
151

SECTION 5:
Paper Genocide Of The American Indian
181

SECTION 6:
Other Miscellaneous Facts
211

SECTION 7
Let's Clear Up Some Things
229

SECTION 8
Where Do We Go From Here
277

PREFACE

When I was young, my grandmother told me about my heritage. I remember asking her about our family name, and she explained it to me. She never once said that I was African or had any African blood. I hiked on trails, collected arrowheads, and kept a dream catcher hanging over my bed.

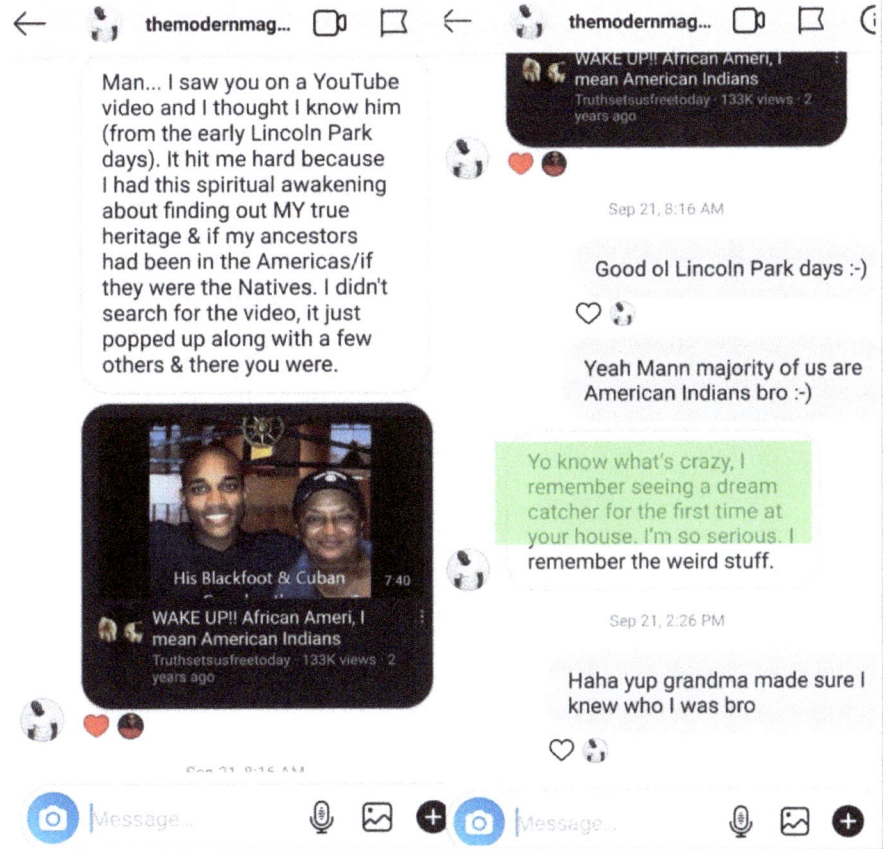

Many people labeled as African Americans share the same story. If you were to ask 95 % of the people labeled black/African American if they have Indian blood, they'll say yes and name the specific tribe. Their elders and matriarchs taught many of them about their heritage, but they still went astray. For many years, I didn't care about the ancestry and was more concerned with living my life and making money. The first time the ancestors reached out to me was in high school. I was in an African American literature class, and I almost failed because I was infuriated with the curriculum. They were teaching that everyone in the United States listed as African American, were descendants of slaves that came from Africa. There was something suspicious about that story, and I didn't believe it. I went on with my life, and in 2015, the ancestors grabbed my attention.

I stumbled across a video on Youtube that was showing comparisons of American Indians of the past and people labeled as African Americans that resembled those ancient Indians. When I saw that video, it brought back memories from my childhood. It also made me want to research and find out if any of my people were slaves and Africans. I began my intensive research on American history, my family history and concluded that the people labeled as African Americans are the American Indians. They didn't die off through diseases like the books teach everyone. They died off by paper genocide through constant reclassification. The victor writes the history, and they chose to write an account that they decimated the indigenous population, and a new batch of Africans was brought to replenish the country and build the most powerful nation that we have today. However, it was an exaggeration, and we are going to find the underlying cause of it.

Why did I write this book?

For many years, I researched, taught, dedicated a YouTube channel and Instagram page to help spread the message and wake my people up. I have helped people find their relatives on the Dawes rolls and census records. I stop teaching for the past two years because I lost the desire until 2019. I kept getting into altercations with my American brothers and sisters who were still regurgitating the same lies taught in school about the African transatlantic slave trade, African Diaspora, and that we are the descendants of those people. Each individual that I encountered all shared the same story of someone in their family was American Indian, but somehow, they still believed that they were African. One young woman told me that her granddad was Seminole, and she used to sit on the porch with him while he smoked his peace pipe with two long braids. She still considered herself African American.

I had another conversation with a man whose grandma was on an Indian reservation, and he was fascinated with Egypt and knew nothing about the Americas or its history. I have such a strong love for my people that I want them to wake up and claim their rightful identity and birthright. The continuous lies agitate me, and I want the youth to have a book that they can read to provide them with some insight. I became tired of explaining myself to people about my heritage and who the real American Indians are in America. Finally, my ancestors wouldn't let me sleep until I started writing this book. We are on a speedy course to extinction, and I want to prevent that.

"The world will not be destroyed by those who do evil, but by those who watch them without doing anything." – Albert Einstein

What is my objective?

To inform the people in America labeled as Black/African American. I hope to restore their identity and align them with their American ancestors. I want to expose the myths and lies taught in school about our history in America. I want to disprove that all the people mislabeled as African Americans were kidnapped or sold Africans from Africa. I want to prove beyond any doubt that the people classified as black/African American are the American Indians that were found here by Christopher Columbus and other explorers. I want to inspire our collective to start working together again and build great things as our ancestors did.

I want this book to be given to the youth so that they can learn about the truth after we've perished so that our history won't be lost. I want to unite all of the American Indian nations so that we can stop the oppression, abuse, and exploitation that we continually receive from the foreign rulers of this land and the immigrants that are coming here seeking a better life off our ignorance. So let's get started, and I hope you enjoy this journey, and it brings enlightenment.

"If you don't know history, then you don't know anything. You are a leaf that doesn't know it is part of a tree." – Michael Chrichton

HOW TO SOURCE THIS BOOK

Throughout this book there are hyperlinks, book titles, and photos as sources. You can double-check everything listed in this book. I want you to be interactive with this work. It's one thing to read someone's work, but it's better if you do the labor and see it with your own eyes.

1. Click The Hyperlink (Ebook) Or Type The Url Into The Browser.
2. Type The Title Or Portion Of The Information Into A Browser.
3. Save The Photo (Ebook) & Insert It Into Google Images & Search

BEFORE YOU READ THIS BOOK

There is potentially offensive material in this book. However, it applies to a collective of a group and not the individual. I am aware that not all Caucasian people and other ethnicities are treacherous, malicious, and manipulative. Some of you are very caring and helpful towards the people labeled as African Americans. I have many friends and relatives who are Caucasian, partial Caucasian, and various ethnic descents, and they are the most supportive, loving people that I know. If anything negative about your ethnic group is mentioned and doesn't apply to you, ignore it.

Dear U.S Government,

DO NOT KILL ME! don't drone strike me, make my death look like a suicide, or place me on a terrorist list. I have no intention of starting a revolution or trying to overthrow your well running system here. Besides, if the stereotype is true, then many African-Americans probably won't read this book, but if they do, I'll receive some attacks from the community, so don't waste your time on me.

SECTION 1: TRANSATLANTIC SLAVE TRADE

Chapter 1

CHRISTOPHER COLUMBUS

The world knows Christopher Columbus (Colon) as the discoverer of America. It's taught that he accidentally discovered America because he was sent to find new resources because Spain admonished theirs during the war with the African moors. What if I told you that finding America by accident was a lie, he knew where he was going, about the people in the Americas before setting sail in 1492 and that he was an informant exposing what was already known? Let's look at the definition of discover and what proves that Columbus knew about the people in America.

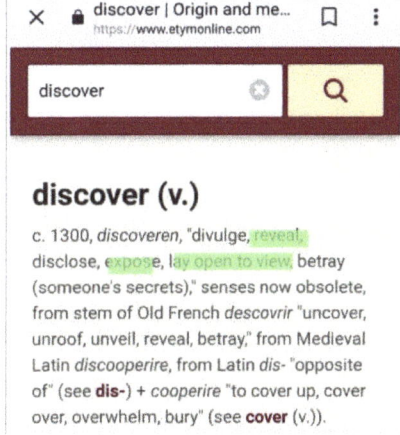

AFRICAN-AMERICANS ARE THE AMERICAN INDIANS

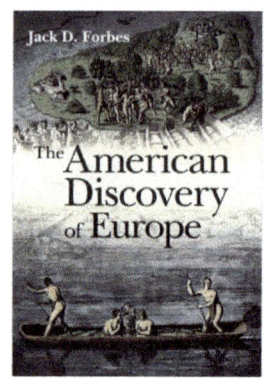

Introduction

PICTURE GIANT TURTLES from the Caribbean following the Gulf Stream to the coasts of Cornwall and other parts of Europe, diving occasionally to feed upon jellyfish as they make their epic journeys. Picture also Ancient American mariners, perhaps from the Caribbean or the east coast of North America, also following the Gulf Stream in dugout boats, large and small, reaching places as diverse as Ireland, Holland, and Iberia. Visualize the surprise of Christopher Columbus when he actually met two such Americans, a man and a woman, at Galway, Ireland, some fifteen years before making his famous voyage of 1492.

The story of Ancient Americans as seafarers, mariners, and navigators is, for me, a fascinating although often overlooked aspect of history. Evidence presented here will show that American Indians were builders of great boats, up to almost one hundred feet in length in the Caribbean, and were outstanding students of the ocean's currents, storms, winds, and resources. The epic story of American seafaring includes maritime cultures of northeastern North America, fishing at sea for challenging prey such as swordfish, developing advanced toggling harpoons as early as 7,500 years ago, and evolving the "Red Earth" culture that may have spread as far as Europe.

The story of ancient seafaring also includes the daring voyages of Eskimo (Inuit) groups from Greenland and Labrador using ingeniously designed kayaks and larger umiaks, voyages that took them along the coasts of Greenland, sometimes passing underneath huge ice mountains arching over the coastline and always facing terrible obstacles from storms and drifting ice. Unbelievably perhaps, intrepid Inuit kayakers show up in the waters of England, Scotland, and elsewhere, whether arriving directly from America or escaping from European whaling vessels.

https://books.google.com/books/about/The_American_Discovery_of_Europe.html?id=09tmdIA6cDoC&printsec=frontcover&source=kp_read_button

INDIA DIDN'T EXIST IN 1492

It's taught that Columbus called the indigenous American people Indians because he thought he was in India. What if I told you that was also a lie and that India didn't exist back in 1492? Instead, the country was named Hindustan/Bharat and was changed to India to confuse the indigenous people of the Americas. Let us take a look into his journal calling the indigenous people Indians and look at India's history.

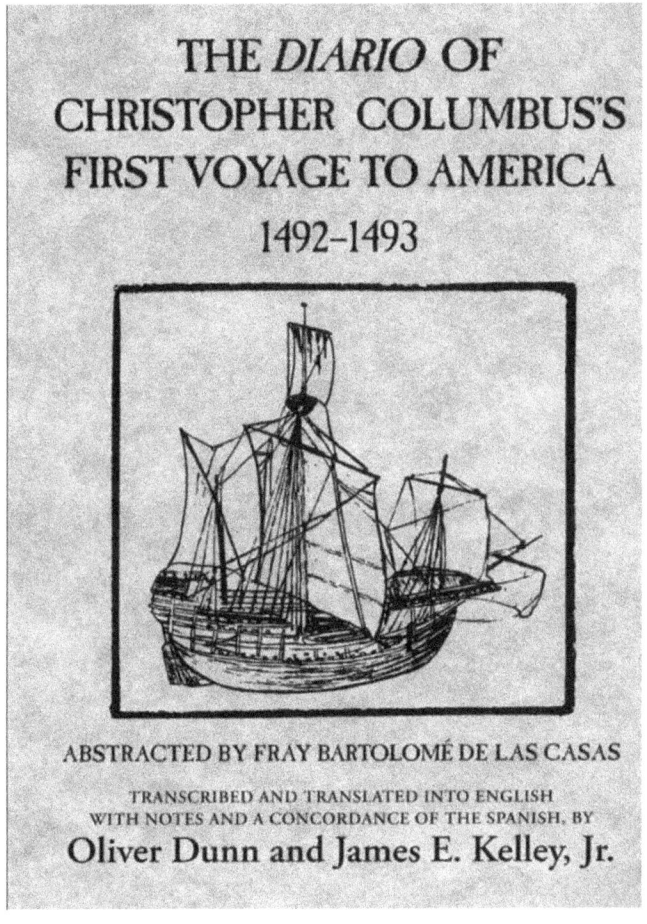

q̃ la acostūbrā dezir e cantar a su mařa
                                          rogo y
todos los marineros y se hallan todos : ∧a
monestolos el almi^e q̃ hiziesen buena guar
15 da al castillo de proa y mirasen bien por la
tr̄r̄a : y q̃ al q̃ le dixese primero q̃ via tr̄r̄a
le daria luego vn Jubon de ——[?] seda : sin
las otras m[erce]d[e]s que los reyes avian prome
tido que erā diez mill m[araved]īs de juro a quien
20 primero la viese /. a las dos oras despues
de media noche pareçio la tr̄r̄a dla qual esta
rian dos leguas /. amaynarō todas las velas
y quedarō con el treo que es la vela grade
sin bonetas y pusierōse a la Corda tempo
                        viernes
25 rizādo hasta el dia ∧q̃ llegarō a vna Isleta
dlos lucayos q̃ se llamava en lengua de
yndios guanahani /. luego vierō gente ds

Salio el almirate
y los demas [e?]n   nuda : y el almi^e salio a tr̄r̄a en la barca arma
la primera tr̄r̄a de   da : y martin alonso pincon y viçeynte anes
las yndias vier   su hr^o q̃ era capitan dla niña /. Saco el almi^e
nes de mañana
a .12. de otubre   la vandera real : y los capitanes con dos
de 1492   vanderas dla cruz verde : q̃ llevava el al
                     mirāte en todos los navios por seña : co
                     vna .f. y vna .y. ençima ~~su~~ de cada letra
35 su corona vna de vn cabo dla .✝. y otra
            [asi?]   vieron
de otro /. puestos en tr̄r̄a ~~llegarō a vnos~~
arboles mỹ verdes : y aguas mūchas
y frutas de diversas mařas /. El almi^e
llamo a los dos capitanes y a los demas
40 q̃ saltarō en tr̄r̄a y a Rodrigo descobedo
escrivano de toda el armada y a Rodrigo

Thursday 11 October   Transcription and Translation   63

Salve, which sailors in their own way are
accustomed to recite and sing, all being present, the Admiral entreated and admonished
them to keep a good lookout on the forecastle
and to watch carefully for land; and that to
the man who first told him that he saw land he
would later give a silk jacket in addition to
the other rewards that the sovereigns had
promised, which were ten thousand *maravedis*[1]
as an annuity to whoever should see it first.
At two hours after midnight the land appeared,
from which they were about two leagues distant. They hauled down[2] all the sails and
kept only the *treo*, which is the mainsail
without bonnets, and jogged on and off,[3] passing time until daylight Friday, when they
reached an islet of the Lucayas, which was
called Guanahani in the language of the Indians. Soon they saw naked people; and the
Admiral went ashore in the armed launch, and
Martín Alonso Pinzón and his brother Vicente
Anes,[4] who was captain of the *Niña*. The Admiral brought out the royal banner and the
captains two flags with the green cross, which
the Admiral carried on all the ships as a
standard, with an F and a Y, and over each
letter a crown, one on one side of the ✝ and
the other on the other. Thus put ashore they
saw very green trees and many ponds and
fruits of various kinds. The Admiral called
to the two captains and to the others who had
jumped ashore and to Rodrigo Descobedo, the
escrivano[5] of the whole fleet, and to Rodrigo

---

1. (8v19) A *maravedi* was a copper coin valued at two *blancas*, or 375 to the gold ducat.
2. (8v22) The Elizabethan English mariners' equivalent to *amaynarvn* (hauled down) was *amaine*, which expressed a sense of urgency: "Lower as fast as you can." (Smith 1970, 50).
3. (8v24) *Pusieronse a la Corda* (jogging on and off) means tacking back and forth, intentionally making no headway. See Las Casas's definition at 23v23–25.
4. (8v29) *Anes*. Columbus uses the form "Anes" in every mention of Vicente except one, when the name is spelled "Yanes." Morison spells the name "Yáñez" and "Yáñes."
5. (8v41) Jane-Vigneras (1960) and Morison (1963) translate *escrivano* as "secretary." Jados (1975, 33ff.) translates the Italian equivalent term, *scrivano*, as

https://books.google.com/books?id=nS6kRnXJgCEC&printsec=frontcover#v=onepage&q&f=false

Google

Q when was india founded

ALL   NEWS   IMAGES   MAPS   VIDEOS

India / Founded

August 15, 1947

On **15 August 1947**, British Indian Empire was partitioned into two countries, India (Hindustan) and Pakistan. With this the British Raj in the Indian subcontinent ended. On 26 January 1950, Hindustan adopted a constitution.

History of India - Simple English Wikipedia, the free encyclopedia
Wikipedia › simple › wiki › History_of_...

∧ Republic of India

Emblem of India

On 15 August 1947, British Indian Empire was partitioned into two countries, India (Hindustan) and Pakistan. With this the British Raj in the Indian subcontinent ended. On 26 January 1950, Hindustan adopted a constitution. From that day, Hindustanis became the Republic of India or Indians.

Partition of India

The 1940 Lahore Resolution of the All-India Muslim League demanded sovereignty for the Muslim-majority areas in the northwest and northeast of India, which came to be called 'Pakistan' in popular parlance and the remaining India came to be called 'Hindustan'.[39] The British officials too picked up the two terms and started using them officially.[16]

However, this naming did not meet the approval of Indian leaders due to the implied meaning of 'Hindustan' as the land of Hindus. They insisted that the new Dominion of India should be called 'India', not 'Hindustan'.[40] Probably for the same reason, the name 'Hindustan' did not receive official sanction of the Constituent Assembly of India, whereas 'Bharat' was adopted as an official name.[41] It was recognised however that 'Hindustan' would continue to be used unofficially.[42]

North India

With the Turko-Persian conquests starting in the 11th century, a narrower meaning of *Hindustan* also took shape. The conqueres were liable to call the lands under their control as "*Hindustan*" ignoring the rest of the subcontinent.[24] In the early 11th century a satellite state of the Ghaznavids in the Punjab with its capital at Lahore was called "Hindustan".[25] After the Delhi Sultanate was established, north India, especially the Gangetic plains, came to be called "Hindustan".[24][26][27][28] Scholar Bratindra Nath Mukherjee states that this narrow menaing of *Hindustan* existed side by side with the wider meaning, and some of the authors used both of them simultaneously.[29]

The Mughal Empire (1526–1857) called its lands 'Hindustan'. The term 'Mughal' itself was never used to refer to the land. As the empire expanded, so too did 'Hindustan'. At the same time, the meaning of 'Hindustan' as the entire Indian subcontinent is also found in *Baburnama* and *Ain-i-Akbari*.[30]

https://en.m.wikipedia.org/wiki/Hindustan

A map of the provinces of Delhi, Agrah, Oude, and Ellahabad: comprehending the countries lying between Delhi and the Bengal-provinces, 1786

Rennell's map of 1777 was republished by Robert Sayer in 1786, exhibited here. It is also available in an electronic version (the bottom half only) via the Internet at: http://nla.gov.au/nla.map-rm183.

Memoir of a map of Hindoostan; or, The Mogul empire: with an introduction, illustrative of the geography and present division of that country: and a map of the countries situated between the heads of the Indian rivers, and the Caspian Sea, 1792

This was written to accompany his very large map, *Hindoostan*. Rennell describes the critical editing and the many corrections that he made for this new map of India. He relied on native sources of geographic information to update the Punjab region. This a later

https://www.lib.umich.edu/online-exhibits/exhibits/show/india-maps/rennell

Chapter 2

THE TRANSATLANTIC SLAVE TRADE EXAGGERATION

The transatlantic slave trade is a big topic among the people labeled as African Americans. They believe that **MILLIONS** of Africans were brought across the Atlantic Ocean from Africa as slaves. They also believe that every person that has a chocolate brown complexion or labeled as black came from Africa. The majority of these people accepted the story and never researched any of the information. What if I told you that the African slave trade story is an extreme exaggeration? In this chapter, we will expose this great deception. We will discuss the total number of slaves that were transported, died, made it to the shores of the U.S, Slave boat drawings, and various other material. Let's begin with the total number of slaves brought and perished on the journey. ***PAY ATTENTION TO THE INCONSISTENCIES.***

How to know if someone is lying to you | ...
2KnowMySelf › Liar_detection_sings

Inconsistencies in the Story: If the person is lying then the story he tells might change a bit every time it is discussed. The liar will forget a ...

> **The Middle Passage - Digital History**
> University of Houston › digitalhistory › ...
>
> At least 2 million Africans--10 to 15 percent-- died during the infamous "Middle Passage" across the Atlantic. Another 15 to 30 percent ...
>
> Missing: ~~imaginable 60~~

Nine million Africans made the passage, and one million of them (c. 11%) died en route. So says John Reader in *Africa: A Biography of the Continent*.

15% to 25% of the slaves died in the Middle Passage. So says Dale Taylor in *The Writer's Guide to Everyday Life in Colonial America*.

24 million Africans made the Middle Passage, and 9 million (c. 38%) died en route. So says Richard Armstrong in *The Merchantmen*.

25 to 50 million Africans died in the Middle Passage. So says The Middle Passage Institute.

30 to 60 million Africans made the Middle Passage, and 67% (20 to 40 million) died en route. So says Dr. John Henrick Clarke.

> **How many slaves made the Middle Passage? How many died? - Straight ..**
> boards.straightdope.com › showthread
> Sep 2, 2001 - 27 posts - 14 authors
> 30 to **60 million** Africans made the **Middle Passage**, and 67%(20 to 40 **million**) **died** en route. So says ...

them to Christianity? Martin Luther King said that 75 million Black people lost their lives as a result of the Transatlantic Slave Trade. (See <u>Death of a King, by Tavis Smiley</u>.)

> Conspiracy theories and Blacks - Bristol ...
> www.sullivan-county.com › freemasons_...
>
> Mobile-friendly - A columnist calls these "the life blood of the **African**-American community," and a .... **Jesse Jackson** accused the government, through the CIA, of being ... They carried out the transatlantic **slave trade** that he claims **killed 100 million Africans.**

You can see the inconsistencies in the sources above dealing with the number of slaves and how many died. It doesn't stop there. Let's take a look at the number of African Slaves supposedly made it to the U.S.A. ***PAY ATTENTION TO THE INCONSISTENCIES.***

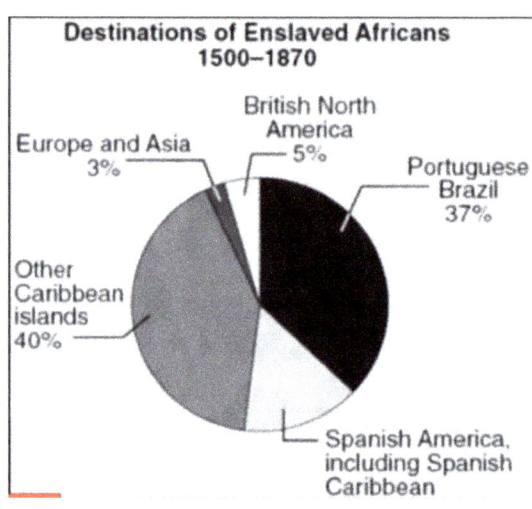

African Slavery in the Americas

Slave Traffic Out of Africa	
1450-1600	250,000
1601-1700	1,300,000
1701-1811	6,000,000
1811-1870	2,000,000
Into the Americas	
Carribean Islands	40%
Brazil	38%
Spanish America	17%
British North America	6%

Atlas of the Transatlantic Slave Trade | Africans, Maps and Voyage

Country	Voyages	Slaves Transported	% Slaves Transported
Portugal (including Brazil)	30,000	4,650,000	42.3
Spain (including Cuba)	4,000	1,600,000	14.5
France (including West Indies)	4,200	1,250,000	11.4
Holland	2,000	500,000	4.5
Britain	12,000	2,600,000	23.6
British North America, US	1,500	300,000	2.7
Denmark	250	50,000	0.5
Other	250	50,000	0.5
Total	54,200	11,000,000	100.0

The Atlantic Slave Trade
www.whitneyplantation.com

	Europe	Mainland North America	Caribbean	Spanish American Mainland	Brazil	Africa	Other	Totals
1514-1525	624		300					924
1526-1550			1,209	361			1,131	2,701
1551-1575			1,319	2,176	388		404	4,287
1576-1600	266		3,394	52,758	931	236	16,280	73,865
1601-1625	120		7,935	112,183	1,200		8,169	129,607
1626-1650		141	10,782	56,004	40,265	240	3,909	111,341
1651-1675	3,582	2,083	123,152	20,290	7,063	1,282	1,796	162,228
1676-1700	1,437	10,523	317,019	13,071	79,380	207		421,637
1701-1725	377	39,536	453,642	38,519	240,377	1,063		773,514
1726-1750	3,860	99,002	683,748	15,905	424,141	473	963	1,228,092
1751-1775	1,151	122,578	1,117,594	1,806	353,398	1,297	1,056	1,598,886
1776-1800	18	23,535	1,158,452	11,285	453,561	1,680	1,195	1,649,726
1801-1825		65,722	497,616	26,004	1,044,426	34,462	644	1,670,874
1826-1850		585	363,804	3,849	892,082	106,179		1,356,499
1851-1866			2,272	190,423		9,798	18,603	221,096
Totals	11,435	365,977	4,530,389	359,211	3,537,010	165,702	35,547	9,405,271

Fascinating Database about the Trans-Atlantic Slave Trade ...
thesocietypages.org

AFRICAN-AMERICANS ARE THE AMERICAN INDIANS

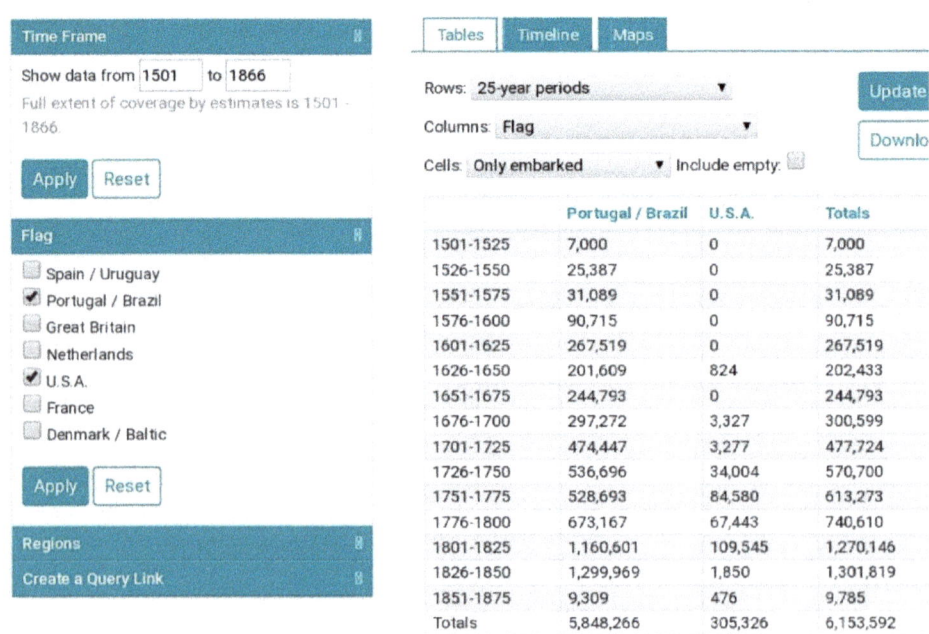

https://www.slavevoyages.org/assessment/estimates

AFRICAN-AMERICANS ARE THE AMERICAN INDIANS

There are many inconsistencies with the number of African slaves that made it to the U.S.A. I want you to look at the last picture you just saw dealing with the U.S.A. Only 111,871 Africans were imported into the United States between 1801-1866.

Regions				
Create a Query Link				
	1801-1825	1,160,601	109,545	1,270,146
	1826-1850	1,299,969	1,850	1,301,819
	1851-1875	9,309	476	9,785
	Totals	5,848,266	305,326	6,153,592

On the diagram below, they started with 900,000 slaves at 1800 with only 193,455 of them being African (who were the other 700,000?) and ended with 4,000,000 slaves by 1860 with 111,871 Africans? (Who were the other 3+ million slaves?) Things that make you go hmm. Someone is lying.

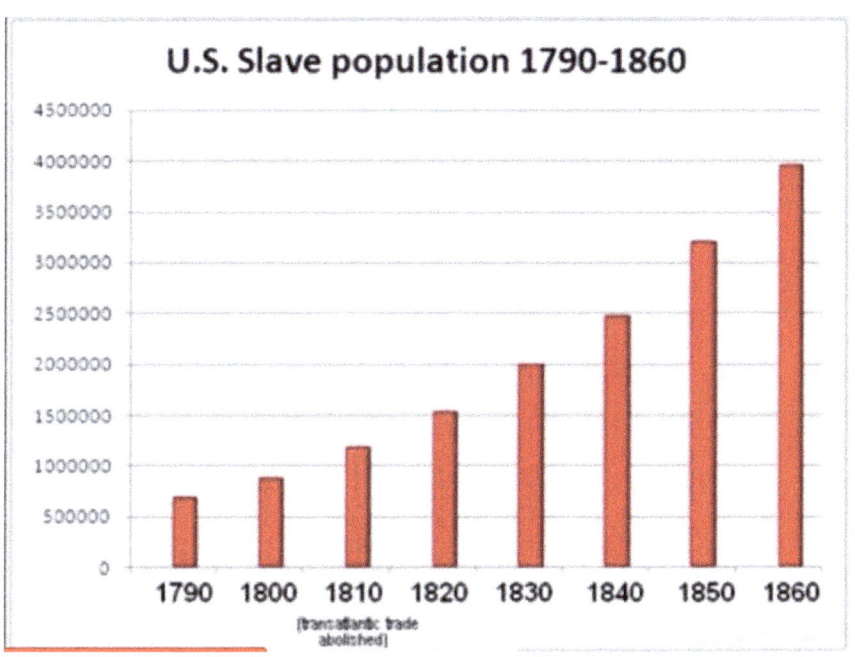

https://civilwartalk.com/threads/was-slavery-dying-out-copied-from-h-k-edgerton-video-challenge-thread.134229/

THE GIANT SLAVE BOAT THAT COULDN'T

Every transatlantic slave trade enthusiast loves talking about the giant slave ships (that never existed) that transported 400+ African slaves across the Atlantic Ocean stacked like sardines in the belly of the boat. These people couldn't move, use the restroom or eat on the ship for extended periods in this position. Many African Americans believe in this story. Let's take a look at the infamous Brookes slave ship. ***PAY ATTENTION TO PROPAGANDA.***

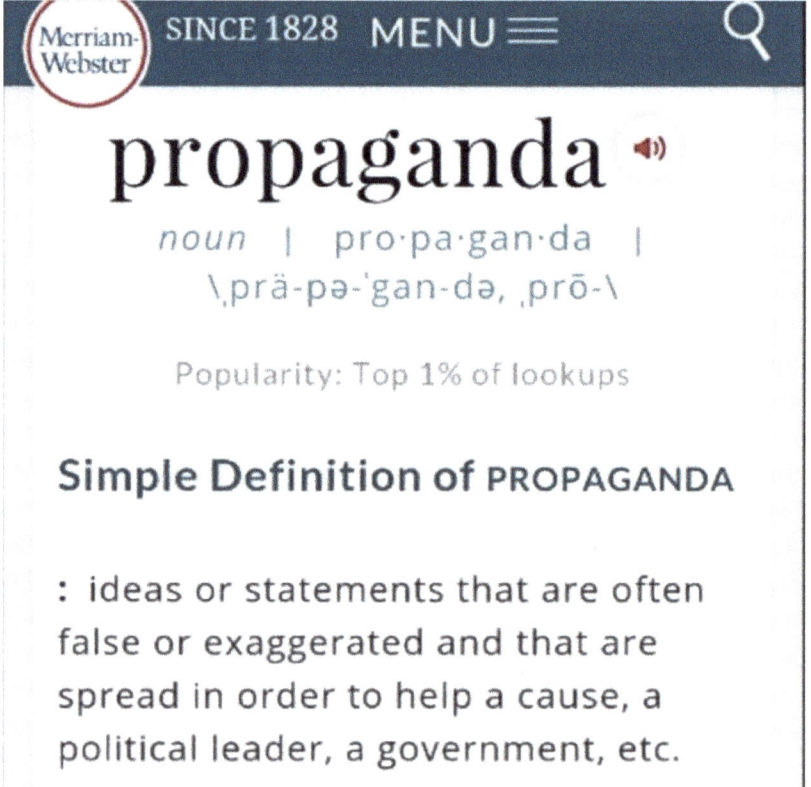

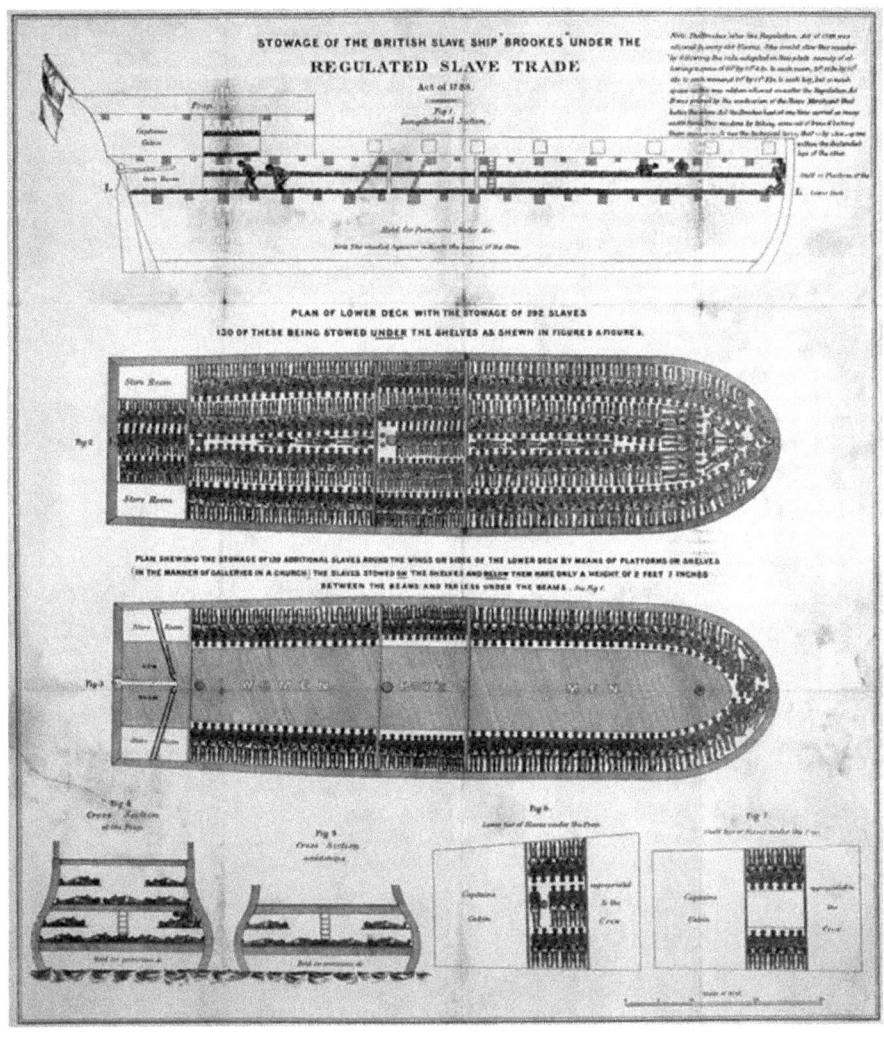

AFRICAN-AMERICANS ARE THE AMERICAN INDIANS

Diagram of the 'Brookes' Slave Ship

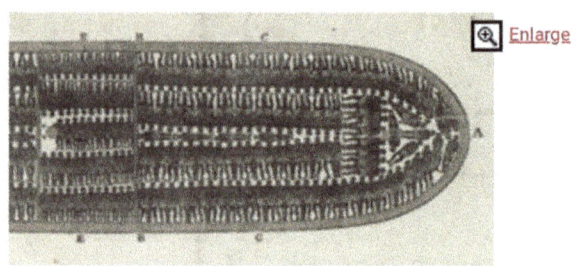 Enlarge

This diagram of the 'Brookes' slave ship is probably the most widely copied and powerful image used by the abolitionist campaigners. It depicts the ship loaded to its full capacity - 454 people crammed into the hold. The 'Brookes' sailed the passage from Liverpool via the Gold Coast in Africa to Jamaica in the West Indies.

The diagram was a very useful piece of propaganda. Thomas Clarkson commented in his *History of the Rise, Progress, and Accomplishment of the Abolition of the African Slave Trade* (1808) that the 'print seemed to make an instantaneous impression of horror upon all who saw it, and was therefore instrumental, in consequence of the wide circulation given it, in serving the cause of the injured Africans'.

By April 1787, the diagram was widely known across the UK, appearing in newspapers, pamphlets, books and even posters in coffee houses and pubs. An image had rarely been used as a propaganda tool in this way before.

Visit Campaign for Abolition to view more sources related to the campaign.

Taken from: Description of a Slave Ship
Publisher: James Phillips, George Yard, Lombard Street, London
Date: 1787
Copyright: By permission of the British Library Board
Shelfmark: 1881.d.8 (46)

 ShareThis

Page | 24

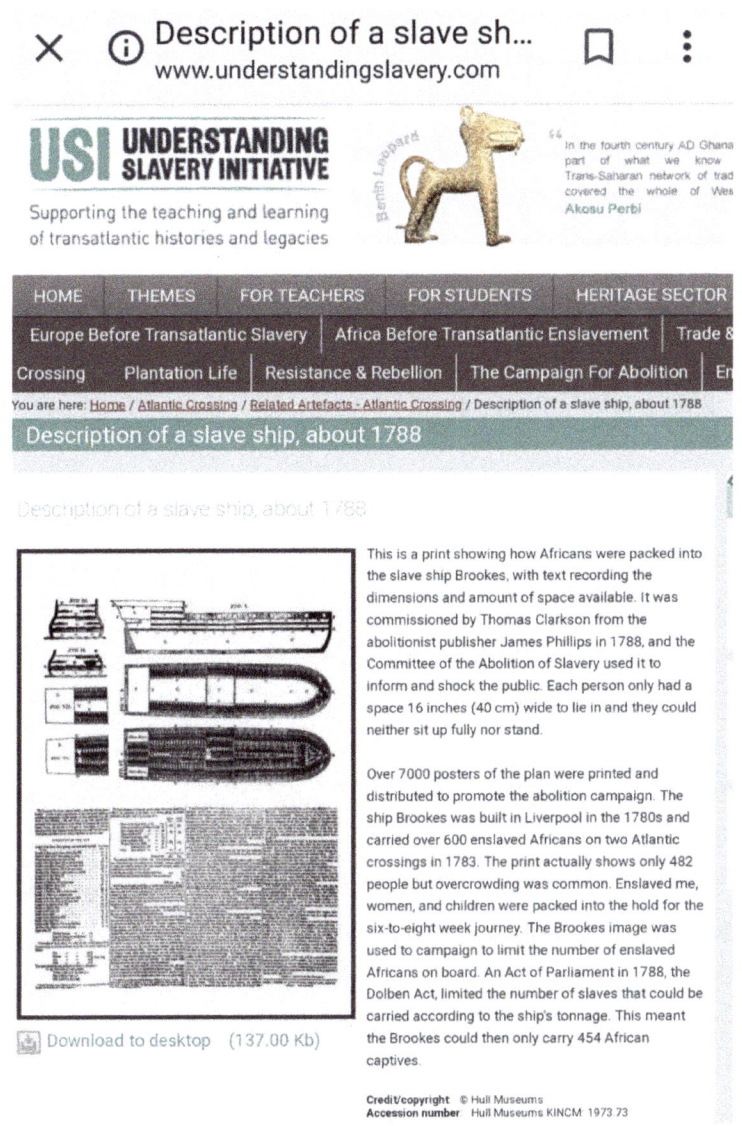

The Brookes was a drawing of a hypothetical situation to show the possibility of what it would look like to transport a mass amount of Africans. It was used to aid in abolishing slavery. It claims to have made two trips, but that hasn't been proven. There isn't any archaeological evidence of a ship that size ever existing.

REASONS WHY MASS AMOUNT OF AFRICANS WEREN'T TRANSPORTED AT ONE TIME

1. Medically Impossible

When you have a mass amount of people stacked like sardines, where they only can lie in one position, you start asking several questions like; how long is the trip, how long are they going without food and water? Below are some reasons that it was medically impossible for it to have happened.

How long did it take to cross the Atlantic in 1492?

Columbus's first voyage across the Atlantic to the New World in 1492 took more than **two months**. That famous trip launched a centuries-long effort to decrease the amount of time needed to get from Europe to America and vice versa. By the 1700s, sailing ships still needed **six weeks** or more to make the crossing.Nov 27, 2015

Time to cross the Atlantic – 500 year history | Outrun Change
https://outrunchange.com › 2015/11/27

about six weeks

In the early 19th century sailing ships took **about six weeks** to cross the Atlantic. With adverse winds or bad weather the journey could take as long as fourteen weeks.

Journey to America - Spartacus Educational
Spartacus Educational › USAEjourney

These studies have uncovered several observations about starvation:

- An article in Archiv Fur Kriminologie ◉ states the body can survive for 8 to 21 days without food and water and up to two months if there's access to an adequate water intake.

- Modern-day hunger strikes have provided insight into starvation. One study in the British Medical Journal ◉ cited several hunger strikes that ended after 21 to 40 days. These hunger strikes ended because of the severe, life-threatening symptoms the participants were experiencing.

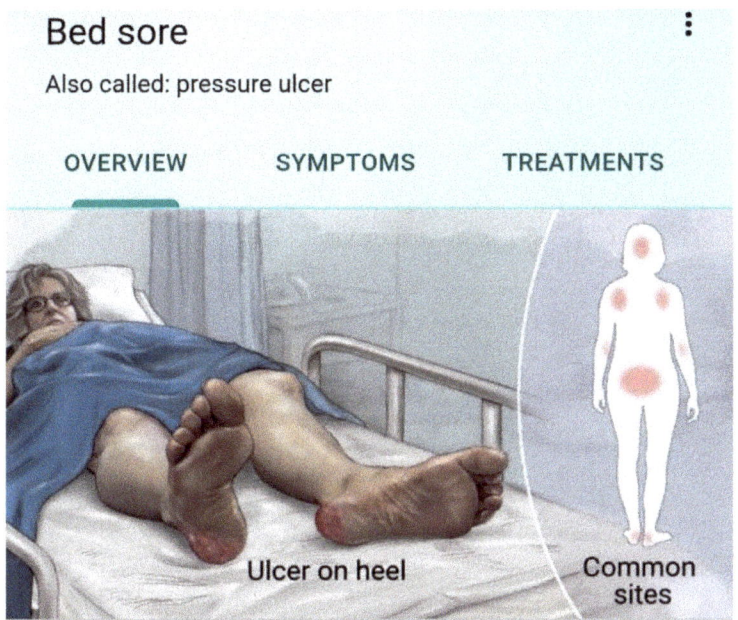

Injury to skin and underlying tissue resulting from prolonged pressure on the skin.

Common
More than **200,000** US cases per year

- Treatable by a medical professional
- Usually self-diagnosable
- Lab tests or imaging not required
- Medium-term: resolves within months

People most at risk are those with a condition that limits their ability to change positions.

What Would Happen to Your Body If You Stayed in Bed Forever? | Mental Floss
Mental Floss › article › what-would-happ...

Aug 20, 2016 · Muscles you don't use lose 10 to 15 percent of their strength every week, meaning that your body would quickly become floppy and useless. ... Your muscles and your bones will lose mass, your resting heart rate will go up, and your blood volume will go down.

Diagnosis. **Claustrophobia** is the fear of having no escape, and being closed into a small space. It is typically classified as an anxiety **disorder** and often times results in a rather severe panic attack. It is also confused sometimes with Cleithrophobia (the fear of being trapped).

Claustrophobia - Wikipedia
https://en.wikipedia.org › wiki › Claustro...

Can you die from claustrophobia?

Yes, Fear **Can** Kill **You**. People who have suffered panic attacks - and I'm one - know that fear **can** be so intense that **you** feel like **you**'re going to **die**. Your pulse races, your heart pounds, **you** find it hard to breathe. **You** might even pass out.Apr 7, 2010

Yes, Fear Can Kill You | Psychology Today
https://www.psychologytoday.com › blog

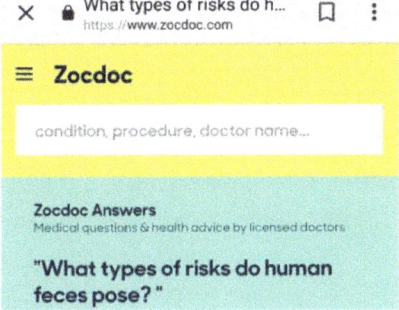

It takes six weeks to more than two months to cross the Atlantic Ocean. They can't move, sit up, eat, drink or use the restroom because of how they're stacked. The Africans would've obtained bedsores, develop claustrophobia, contract many diseases from laying and inhaling their feces and urine, or die from starvation. If they survived, their muscles would be too weak to do anything and rendering them useless for immediate plantation work.

2. The Violent Atlantic Ocean

The Atlantic Ocean is a very violent ocean with constant hurricanes and storms. The route chosen for these 400+ Africans in the belly of their ships was the middle of the South Atlantic Ocean, where most of the storms are. The Atlantic Ocean pushes modern ships underwater, so imagine what it did to wooden wind sailboats.

The Atlantic Ocean ranks the second in the catalogue of the most dangerous ocean waters in the world. This ocean water is usually affected by coastal winds, temperature of the water surface and the water currents. The ocean waters of Pacific, Mediterranean, Aegean, and Sea of Marmara are some of the other ocean waters that can be classified as deadly.

Winter storm 2018: Cruise ship passengers recall harrowing trip out at sea
⚡ CBS News

Jan 6, 2018 · ... but imagine being in the thick of it on a cruise ship in the Atlantic Ocean. ... "I flew across the room, landed in the bathroom, and then I got up, I got into ...

Why Tropical Waves Are Important During Hurricane Season | The Weather Channel
⚡ Weather.com › hurricane › news

Aug 28, 2018 · According to the National Hurricane Center, 60 tropical waves track across the Atlantic Ocean each year.

https://youtu.be/LK0um3j89a0

https://youtu.be/KKOQdZXm1Rw

https://youtu.be/5Wj2pzOVDeY

The Atlantic Ocean would've destroyed that wooden ship and kill the 400+ Africans in the belly of those ships if it ever tried to journey across. There are 60 tropical waves a year in the Atlantic, and in 2018, a metal cruise ship was being tossed around like it didn't exist. Don't believe the hype of Europeans stacking Africans like sardines to transport them across the Atlantic Ocean to be slaves in the Americas.

SLAVE PORT MYTH

People will read what I have presented them and say, "but what about the slave ports? The infamous "door of no return" surely is proof that millions of Africans were sent to America." What if it's untrue? Let's have a look at Goree Island.

President Obama looks out of the "door of no return" during a tour of Goree Island. (AP Photo/Evan Vucci)

President Obama visited one of Africa's most famous memorials to the slave trade on Thursday, the House of Slaves on Senegal's Goree Island. The official story is that millions of African slaves passed through the house's Door of No Return, which faces West across the Atlantic; countless visitors have come to contemplate the slave trade and to pay heartfelt tribute, including Nelson Mandela, Pope John Paul II and the last three U.S. presidents.

Except that the official story turns out to be largely a myth. Historians have agreed since the 1990s that the house was likely just a private residence that had nothing to do with the slave trade. Earlier, we explored this long-standing disconnect between the reality and myth of Goree Island, why it's proven so resilient and what it says about the world's struggle to deal with this dark chapter in history.

University of Chicago historical anthropologist François Richard, a West Africa scholar who has studied the slave trade, has some thoughts about that disconnect between the myth and reality of Goree. Richard emphasizes the house's value as a sort of manifestation of slavery's legacy, which is still so big today that it demands this sort of totem. He reproduces a term that seems to capture the phenomenon well: it is a "sincere fiction." Here's Richard:

1) Yes, there has been heated academic debate around Gorée, but in the mid-90s (following a controversial article written in 1996 in Le Monde). The debates have largely been on the revisionist side, and most historians today would argue that the scale of the slave trade in Gorée was likely much lower than in many other parts of western Africa (for a variety of reasons. I should note, however, that turning the question of international slavery into a statistical exercise is not the most useful way to think about it, and sadly that legacy has clouded academic debates more than it has helped). So, Gorée was a transit point, though the volume of trade there was 'fairly' low (square quotes are important here) and that it ebbed and flowed over time, probably decreasing over time, especially after the 1750s, as captives were increasingly retained in Senegal to work in food production. [**Max here: When Richard says 'fairly' low, he is referring to estimates of, for example, 33,000 slaves, a huge number by every possible standard except for the actual trans-Atlantic slave trade of several million.**]

2) Yes, there was slavery on the island, but of a much different kind than the chattel slavery that was established on plantations in the Caribbean and Americas.

3) The House of Slaves holds a huge amount of symbolic value as a 'place of memory,' a testimony to a not-so-savory part of global history. In this sense, the house was erected into a 'myth' (or perhaps, a term I'd prefer, to follow sociologist Pierre Bourdieu, a sincere fiction) and mobilized as memento.

As far as archives will go, the house was built probably in the 1770s, thus rather late in the era of the Atlantic trade, at a point when the commerce in slaves was diminishing and when the gum trade was gaining ascendance. What's more, it was a residential structure, upper floor were living quarters, lower sections were probably for merchandise and magazine. And yes, the enslaved people living there were probably attached to the house (cooks, domestics, laborers, traders, etc.).

Some people use the history/memory couplet to parse the problem of Gorée's house of slaves (i.e., history concerned with facts and memory with symbolic value and historical gravity, a mode of affective resonance absolutely central to identities in the African diaspora). It's not the most satisfying or cutting way of analyzing the phenomenon, but it has the merit of offering a point of entry. What's important to remember, though, is that while the details about the house may not be entirely exact, they do speak to a deeper historical truth - namely, the experience and infamy of turning humanity into a commodity.

A "point of entry" is a nice way to describe Goree's famous monument, which is, after all, a literal entry point – the Door of No Return. As some scholars have written, even if slaves never really exited through the Door, members of the African diaspora created by slavery have since used the site as a way to engage with that legacy, making it sort of like a Door of Return to a past that was very real even if the symbol's official history is not. President Obama, in his solemn visit there Thursday, seems to have had a similar experience, even if it was based on a small myth within a much larger truth.

💬 14 Comments

https://www.washingtonpost.com/news/worldviews/wp/2013/07/01/the-sincere-fiction-of-goree-island-africas-best-known-slave-trade-memorial/?noredirect=on&utm_term=.8cdb192a0194

It turns out that the place the slave trade enthusiasts love so much was mostly fiction. It was propaganda to tell an exaggerated story and another way to keep the American people in an enslaved immigrant mentality. Pay attention to the mind tricks that are used on the American people.

REASONS WHY THE AFRICAN TRANSATLANTIC SLAVE TRADE IS EXAGGERATED

Many people will read the above information and automatically think that I am being disrespectful and trying to say that the transatlantic slave trade never happened. That would be an ignorant statement. Of course, there is proof that Africans were sent to the Americas. You can find them on plantation records.

FIELD SLAVES – 93 INCLUDING CHILDREN

Léandre (63 yrs.) – Creole Negro field boss & driver	$500
Avril (35 yrs.) – Creole Negro teamster & laborer	$1,000
Paris (35 yrs.) – Creole Negro teamster & laborer	$1,000
Pret-à-boire "ready-to-drink" (46 yrs.) – Teamster & laborer	$500
Jack (39 yrs.) – American Negro	$800
Mars (44 yrs.) – Creole Negro teamster & laborer	$800
Mandrin (49 yrs.) – Creole Negro teamster & laborer	$900
Toni (24 yrs.) – Creole Negro teamster & laborer	$1,000
Do (21 yrs.) – Creole Negro teamster & laborer	$1,000
John (46 yrs.) – American Negro cooper (cask/barrel maker)	$1,000
Mohamet (34 yrs.) – Creole Negro teamster & laborer	$1,000
Isaac (30 yrs.) – American Negro cooper	$900
Cary (22 yrs.) – American Negro	$800
William (28 yrs.) – American Negro	$800
Madison (55 yrs.) – American Negro	$300
Anthony (49 yrs.) – American Negro	$800
Daniel (40 yrs.) – American Negro	$400
Hiram (42 yrs.) – American Negro blacksmith	$1,200
Mercury (64 yrs.) – African Negro	$100
Argus (27 yrs.) – Creole Negro mason	$1,200
Gognon (24 yrs.) – Creole Negro teamster & laborer	$800
Bacchus (36 yrs.) Creole Negro teamster & laborer	$1,000
Antoine (38 yrs.) – Creole Negro gardener/expert grafter of pecan trees	$1,000
Lovelace (23 yrs.) – Creole Negro teamster & laborer	$1,000
Prince (34 yrs.) – Mulatto carpenter	$1,500
Henry (44 yrs.) – African Negro	$500
Ellick (21 yrs.) – Creole Negro teamster & laborer	$1,000

However, as you can tell by the plantation records, there weren't that many Africans sent here. My argument is that the transatlantic slave trade is exaggerated to confuse the people labeled African Americans in the U.S. The following are a few more reasons why it's an exaggeration.

1. **Because it would've decimated Africa's population.**

People always talk about how many died in the middle passage. I showed you in the previous sections the 100 million, 75 million, 60 million, that supposedly died. However, if you check Africa's population and the Sub Saharan population during that time, then you would see that Africa wouldn't exist if those many people were taken. Instead, you see a population increase throughout the years. Even the max amount that supposedly died is higher than the whole continent of Africa around that time of abolishment, and importing African slaves was banned since 1808.

World population figures (table):

Estimated world population (millions)				
***	1800	1850	1900	1950
Europe	150	206	291	366
Russia	37	60	111	193
Africa	90	95	120	198
Asia	602	749	937	1302
North America	16	39	106	217
South America	9	20	38	111
Oceania	2	2	6	13

Source: R. Cameron, *Concise Economic History of the World* (New York: O.U.P., 1993) p. 193.

Back to top

Copyright © 2000 University of Botswana History Department
Last updated 27 August 2000

> the population of sub Saharan Africa was 34 million by 1600 44 million by 1700
> Course Hero › ... › HISTORY History 13
>
> the population of sub-Saharan Africa was 34 million; by 1600 44 million, by 1700 52 million and by 1800 African populations had grown ...
>
> Rating
> 100% ★★★★★ (1)

2. Because the Africans were too expensive

Another reason that mass amounts of Africans weren't shipped and sold to the Americas is because they were too expensive versus the American Indians and Their European brethren. The African in the 1600's were 50 sterling and only 5 sterling for the Irish slaves.

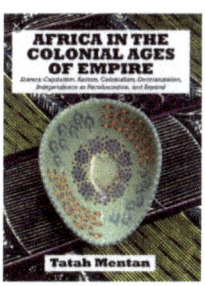

The African slave trade was just beginning during this same period. It is well recorded that African slaves, not tainted with the stain of the hated Catholic theology and more expensive to purchase, were often treated far better than their Irish counterparts. African slaves were very expensive during the late 1600s (50 Sterling). Irish slaves came cheap (no more than 5 Sterling). If a planter whipped or branded or beat an Irish slave to death, it was never a crime. A death was a monetary setback, but far cheaper than killing a more expensive African.

3. Because there are no oral stories or receipts.

I have asked several Africans about the slave trade, specifically from the areas where they supposedly obtained the slaves. No one cosigns an oral story saying that a massive amount of Africans was sold or taken from there and brought to America. I have lived in South Africa for three months for work and have talked to different Africans from different regions. They said they weren't told anything from their families about the transatlantic slave trade, kidnapping their relatives and shipping them to the Americas. There aren't any receipts from any kings or documents stating how many slaves were sent or what they received in return for trading or selling slaves to go to America. The Africans do admit that they were taught about the slave trade from European Americans and Europeans from Europe in school.

TRANSATLANTIC SLAVE TRADE CHALLENGE

SLAVESHIP CHALLENGE: For all African Americans who believe they came on slaveships, take the challenge. You might want to elicit the help of a loved one.

1. Take a 30 day vacation.
2. Turn off the heat in your home.
3. Get as close to naked as possible
4. Lie on your hardwood floor, prone or face up(whichever is most comfortable)
5. Have your loved one bind your hands and feet (use materials of your choice)
6. Have loved ones piss and shit on you for 30 days.
7. While still in the prone or supine position have loved one give you food and water(making sure the the food and water don't get mixed in with the piss and shit)

After 30 days let us know how you survived the slaveship challenge. We're all rooting for you.

Chapter 3

ARE THE EUROPEANS REALLY THE AFRICAN SLAVES?

Most people will read that title and think that I have lost my mind. However, follow me on this journey. We can't prove that millions of Africans were brought to America as slaves, but we know for sure that millions of Europeans came to America while slavery was happening.

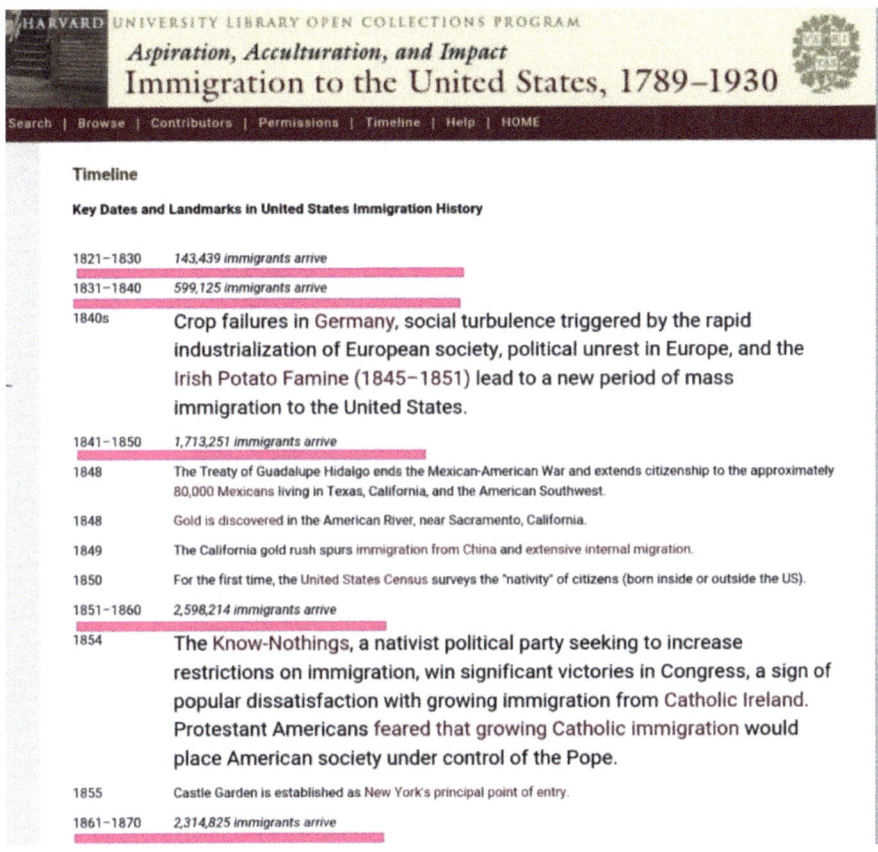

AFRICAN-AMERICANS ARE THE AMERICAN INDIANS

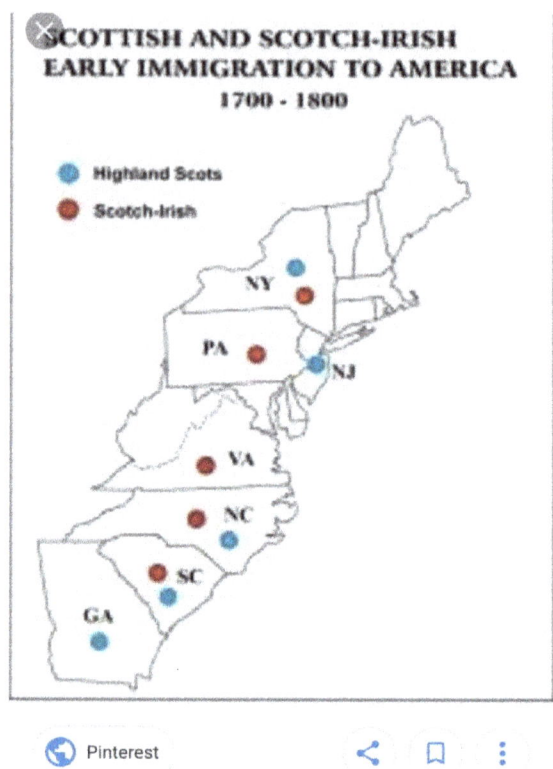

Scottish and Scots-Irish Early Immigration to America #genea...

We all heard the story of how Africa was named. The Romans had finally conquered Hannibal and eventually name that area Africa. There are disputes about how it got its name, but I'm not here to debate whether or not it's entirely true that it was named after Scipio. Before that time, Africa went through several different names. As far as we know, the Europeans from Rome became the **FIRST AFRICANS**. Also, Africa was a country, and it applied to white (European) Residents.

AFRICAN-AMERICANS ARE THE AMERICAN INDIANS

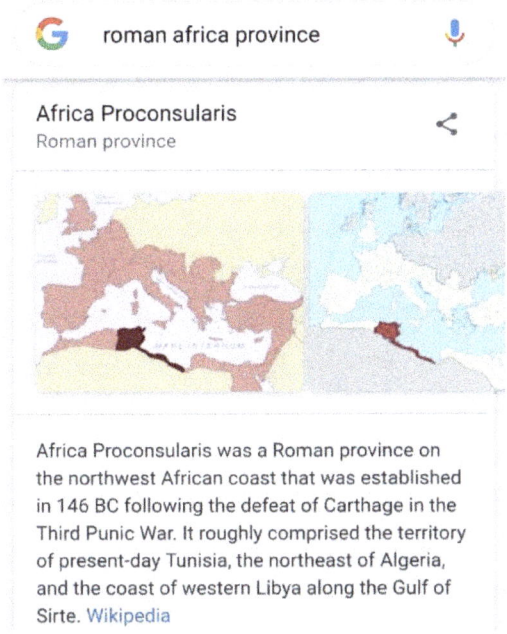

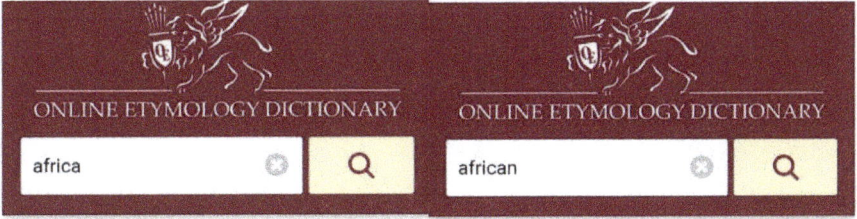

Africa (n.)

Latin *Africa (terra)* "African land, Libya, the Carthaginian territory, the province of Africa; Africa as a continent," fem. of adjective *Africus*, from *Afer* "an African," a word of uncertain origin. The Latin word originally was used only in reference to the region around modern Tunisia; it gradually was extended to the whole continent. Derivation from a Phoenician cognate of Arabic *afar* "dust, earth" is tempting. The Middle English word was *Affrike*.

African (n.)

Old English *Africanas* (plural) "native or inhabitant of Africa," from Latin *Africanus* (adj.) "of Africa, African," from *Africa* (see **Africa**). Used of white residents of Africa from 1815. Used of black residents of the U.S. from 18c., when it especially meant "one brought from Africa" and sometimes was contrasted to native-born **Negro**. As an adjective by 1560s, "pertaining to Africa or Africans" (Old English had *Africanisc*); from 1722 as "of or pertaining to black Americans."

Page | 45

The map shows that Africa is a country that is ruled by the same Europeans that conquered and name that area long ago. This map is from 1554. You can also see other countries as well.

Münster, Sebastian, 1489-1552. "Totius Africæ tabula, & descriptio uniuersalis, etiam ultra Ptolemæi limites extensa." Woodcut map, with added color, 26 x 35 cm. From Münster's Cosmographia uniuersalis (Basel, 1554)

https://rosebankkillarneygazette.co.za/206200/mother-africa-crowned/amp

AFRICAN-AMERICANS ARE THE AMERICAN INDIANS

DICTIONARY

Search for a word

Af·ri·kaans
/ˌafrəˈkänz/ 🔊

noun

1. a language of southern Africa, derived from the form of Dutch brought to the Cape by Protestant settlers in the 17th century, and an official language of South Africa.

adjective

1. relating to the Afrikaner people, their way of life, or their language.

Friendly Borders
Afrikaners Of South Africa

Wikipedia
Afrikaners - Wikipedia

Page | 48

AFRICAN-AMERICANS ARE THE AMERICAN INDIANS

Not only did the term African apply to the Europeans, but Africa was also a country first and ruled by the Europeans. Europeans were the first slaves to be sent to the Americas in the 1600s up until a little after slavery ended in large amounts that shared a similar story as the Africans. Some of the Europeans were even called **NEGROES**.

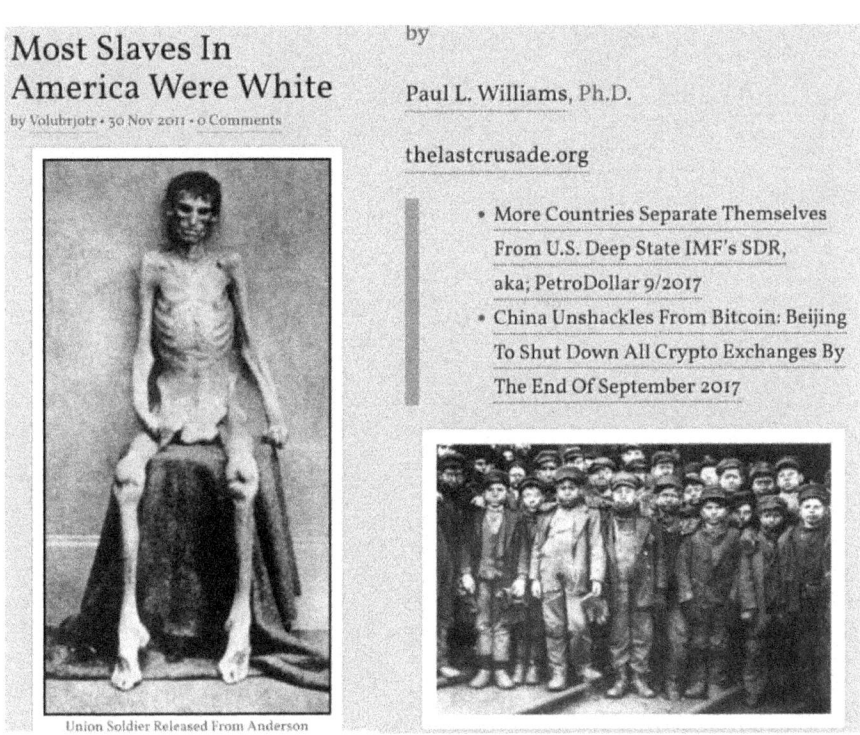

Union Soldier Released From Anderson

The first black slaves arrived in America in the early years of the 17th Century.

At the time of the ratification of the Constitution in 1788, there were less than 50,000 slaves in America - - and the vast majority of them were white.

> Sorry, Barack, but white slavery pre-dates black slavery in America. This fact has been verified by forensic evidence from archaeological digs and historical documents uncovered by contemporary scholars, including Don Jordan and Michael Walsh in White Cargo (**New York University Press**: 2009).

The white slaves not indentured, who began to arrive here in 1618, included hundreds of children - - waifs and strays - - who had been rounded up from streets of London to serve wealthy farmers in Virginia.

Other slaves came from the ranks of the homeless and the poor, whom **King James I** held responsible for spreading the plague, and from England's swelling prison population.

The scheme was supported by James I, who believed the homeless and itinerant of London were spreading plague.

Of the first 300 white slaves to land in Virginia, only 12 managed to survive four years. The others died of ill treatment, disease, attack by native Americans or overwork.

Contemporary records show that one child victim, Elizabeth Abbott, was beaten to death when her master ordered her to be given 500 lashes for running away.

At least 70,000 white men, women, and children from England and Ireland were shipped to the colonies to be sold as slaves on the auction block during the 170 years of British rule.

Independent investigator A.B. Ellis in the Argosy writes concerning the transport of white slaves, "The human cargo, many of whom were still tormented by unhealed wounds, could not all lie down at once without lying on each other. They were never suffered to go on deck. The hatchway was constantly watched by sentinels armed with hangers and blunder busses. In the dungeons below all was darkness, stench, lamentation, disease and death."

In the past, white slavery was acknowledged as having existed in America only as "indentured servitude."

Such indentured servants were, for the most part, convicts, who served a term of four to seven years laboring on the farms, plantations, and estates in Virginia, Georgia, Maryland, and the Carolinas in exchange for their freedom. But they represented only a small fraction of the hundreds of thousands of whites who remained slaves for life. Such slavery was hereditary: children of the white slaves also became chattel without hope of freedom.

AFRICAN-AMERICANS ARE THE AMERICAN INDIANS

In George Sandy's laws for Virginia, Whites were enslaved "forever." The service of Whites bound to Berkeley's Hundred was deemed "perpetual."

Throughout the colonial period, white slaves remained the main labour force on the Virginia and Maryland plantations, outnumbering Africans by as many as four to one.

Benjamin Franklin suggested the American authorities should send rattlesnakes back to England in return for such unwelcome imports.

Whites remained slaves until the Emancipation Proclamation. In 1855, Frederic Law Olmsted, the landscape architect who designed New York's Central Park, was in Alabama on a pleasure trip and saw bales of cotton being thrown from a considerable height into a cargo ship's hold. The men tossing the bales somewhat recklessly into the hold were Negroes; the men in the hold were Irish.

Olmsted inquired about this to a ship worker. "Oh," said the worker, "the niggers are worth too much to be risked here; if the Paddies are knocked overboard or get their backs broke, nobody loses anything."

https://politicalvelcraft.org/2011/11/30/most-slaves-in-america-were-white/

They Were White and They Were Slaves

The Untold History of the Enslavement of Whites in Early America

Michael A. Hoffman II

(Michael Hoffman, They Were White and They Were Slaves *and Ulrich B. Phillips,* Life and Labor in the Old South, *pp. 25, 26)*

Irish Slave Facts

The Irish slave trade began when **James II sold 30,000 Irish prisoners as slaves to the New World**. His Proclamation of **1625** required Irish political prisoners be sent overseas and sold to English settlers in the West Indies.

By the mid **1600s**, the **Irish were the main slaves** sold to Antigua and Montserrat (70% of the total population of Montserrat were Irish slaves at this time).

From **1641 to 1652**, over 500,000 Irish were killed by the English and **over 300,000 were sold as slaves**.

Ireland's population fell from about 1,500,000 to 600,000 in one single decade.

During the **1650s**, over **100,000 Irish children** between the ages of 10 and 14 were forcibly taken from their parents and sold as slaves in the West Indies, Virginia and New England. Another **52,000 Irish (mostly women and children)** were sold to Barbados and Virginia while **30,000 Irish men** were sold to the highest bidder.

In **1656**, Oliver Cromwell ordered that **2000 Irish children** be taken to Jamaica and sold as slaves to English settlers.

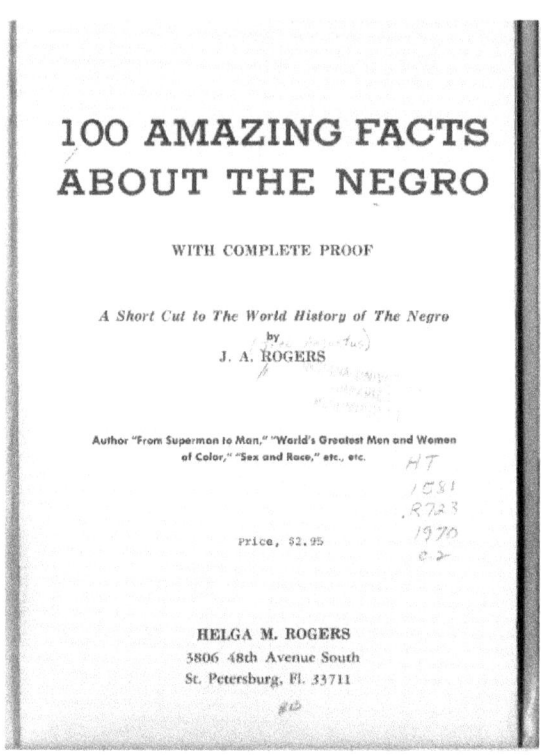

64. The first slaves held in the United States were not black, but white. They were Europeans, mostly British, who died like flies on the slave-ships across. On one voyage 1,100 perished out of 1,500. At another time 350 out of 400. In Virginia, white servitude was for a limited period, but was sometimes extended to life. In the West Indies, particularly in the case of the Irish, it was for life. White people were sold in the United States up to 1826, fifty years after the signing of the Declaration of Independence. Andrew Johnson, President of the United States, was a runaway, and was advertised for in the newspapers.

67. White children were kidnapped in the British Isles at the rate of several thousands yearly in the 17th and 18th Centuries and sold into slavery in America and the West Indies. Sometimes they were bootlegged and sold as Negroes. White Americans, North and South, were also kidnapped or seduced and sold as Negroes as late as 1859. One of the most celebrated cases of a white person sold as a Negro was Sally Muller, who was held in servitude in Louisiana for twenty-six years. Court after court ruled against her. Finally her birth certificate was dug up in Germany and she was freed by the Supreme Court in 1818.

AFRICAN-AMERICANS ARE THE AMERICAN INDIANS

docsouth.unc.edu
Richard Hildreth, 1807-1865. The White Slave; or, Memoirs of a ...

thegeneralreport.wordpress.com
White Slavery in America | The General Report

AFRICAN-AMERICANS ARE THE AMERICAN INDIANS

A Childhood in the Factory

savethetruearabs.proboards.com
White Slaves in America | SAVE THE

Redeemed in Virginia

By Catharine S. Lawrence. Baptized in Brooklyn, at Plymouth Church, by Henry Ward Beecher, May, 1863. Fannie Virginia Casseopia Lawrence, a Redeemed SLAVE CHILD, 5 years of age.

Entered according to Act of Congress, in the year 1863, by C. S. Lawrence, in the Clerk's Office of the district Court of the United States, for the Southern District of New York.

Photograph by Renowden, 65 Fulton Av. Brooklyn.

RUN AWAY from the Subscriber, living at Warwick furnace, Minehole, on the 23d ult. an Irish servant man, named DENNIS M'CALLIN, about five feet eight inches high, nineteen years of age, has a freckled face, light coloured curly hair. Had on when he went away, an old felt hat, white and yellow striped jacket, a new blue cloth coat, and buckskin breeches; also, he took with him a bundle of shirts and stockings, and a pocket pistol; likewise, a box containing gold rings, &c. Whoever takes up said servant and secures him in any goal, so as his master may get him again, shall have the above reward and reasonable charges paid by   JAMES TODD.

N. B. All masters of vessels, and others, are forbid from harbouring or carrying him off, at their peril.

FIVE SHILLINGS REWARD.

RUN AWAY from the subscriber living in Fourth-street, a little above Race-street, the 25th ult. a girl named Christiana Lower, 13 years of age: Had on a blue calimancoe cap, blue and white checked handkerchief, a short red gown, blue and white striped linsey petticoat, an old pair of black stockings and new shoes. Whoever takes up said girl and brings her home, shall have the above reward and reasonable charges.

CHRISTIAN LOWER.

REPUBLICAN BULLETIN, No. 9.

THE ISSUE.

WHITE SLAVERY.

THE EXTENSION OF SLAVERY IS THE QUESTION NOT ONLY OVER **FREE SOIL**, BUT OVER **FREE MEN**. DO YOU DOUBT IT? READ THE WORDS OF THE HIGHEST AUTHORITIES IN THE SOUTH.

The *Richmond* (*Va.*) *Enquirer*, the oldest Democratic paper in the Old Dominion, a most able supporter of Buchanan for the Presidency, and of the Cincinnati Platform, speaks thus on this question. We take its own forcible words.

"Until recently, the defence of Slavery has labored under great difficulties, because its apologists, (for they were mere apologists,) took half way ground. They confined the defence of slavery to mere *negro* slavery; thereby giving up the slavery *principle*, admitting *other forms* of slavery to be *wrong*.

that SLAVERY IS RIGHT, NATURAL, AND NECESSARY, AND DOES NOT DEPEND UPON DIFFERENCE OF COMPLEXION. THE LAWS OF THE SLAVE STATES JUSTIFY THE HOLDING OF WHITE MEN IN BONDAGE."

Another leading press of the Democratic party, and a worthy organ of Mr. Buchanan, published in South Carolina, sustains the views we have quoted from the Enquirer. It uses this plain, straightforward language on the subject:—

"*Slavery is the natural and normal condition of the laboring man, whether white or black.* The great evil of Northern *free* society is, that it is burthened with a SERVILE CLASS OF MECHANICS AND LABORERS, UNFIT FOR SELF-GOVERNMENT, and yet clothed with the attributes and powers of citizens. Master and slave is a relation in society as necessary as that of parent and child; and the Northern States will yet have to introduce it. Their *theory of a free government* is a delusion."

But there is still broader ground on the subject of society, taken by the *Richmond Enquirer*. It says, in a recent number:—

"Repeatedly have we asked the North, 'Has not the experiment of universal liberty FAILED? Are not the evils of **FREE SOCIETY INSUFFERABLE**? And do not most thinking men among you propose to subvert and reconstruct it?' Still no answer. This gloomy silence is another conclusive proof, added to many other conclusive evidences we have furnished, THAT FREE SOCIETY, IN THE LONG RUN, IS AN IMPRACTICABLE FORM OF SOCIETY."

Another paper, published in Virginia, the *South Side Democrat*, a journal distinguished for its faithful support of Mr. Buchanan, says:

BY THE PRESIDENT OF THE UNITED STATES OF AMERICA.

A Proclamation.

Whereas, on the twenty-second day of September, in the year of our Lord one thousand eight hundred and sixty-two, a proclamation was issued by the President of the United States, containing, among other things, the following, to wit:

"That on the first day of January, in the year of our Lord one thousand eight hundred and sixty-three, all persons held as slaves within any State or designated part of a State, the people whereof shall then be in rebellion against the United States, shall be then, thenceforward, and forever, free; and the Executive government of the United States, including the military and naval authority thereof, will recognize and maintain the freedom of such persons, and will do no act or acts to repress such persons, or any of them, in any efforts they may make for their actual freedom.

and sixty-three, all persons held as slaves within any State or designated part of a State, the people whereof shall then be in rebellion against the United States, shall be then, thenceforward, and forever, free; and the Executive government of the United States, including the

all persons held as slaves with

We read that the original term African was used and applied to the Europeans; Africa was a country in 1554 occupied by those same European powers. They were shipped over to the Americas as slaves before the first supposed African in 1619 (who were natives from the Caribbean) they suffered the same struggles and deaths across the middle passage but without the imaginary slave ships having them stacked like sardines. Lastly, sources reveal that many of them were sold into slavery as Negroes. That's why Abraham Lincoln didn't abolish slavery for only Negroes. He removed it for **"All Persons"** because he knew that many of the slaves in America were Europeans. Are the millions of Africans that came over, really the Europeans? Hmm.

Chapter 4
THE TRANSATLANTIC SLAVE TRADE HAPPENED IN REVERSE

Many people labeled as African Americans are so focused on the African transatlantic slave trade that it never crossed their mind that it might have happened in reverse. Massive amount of American Indians was shipped from North America to the Caribbean and back. Indians were sent from the Caribbean to Africa, Europe, and from the Caribbean to South America and back. The colonizers had no reason to kidnap or buy Africans because they had all of the slaves they needed in the Americas.

⌃ Native Americans

Main article: Slavery among Native Americans in the United States

During the 16th, 17th and 18th centuries, Indian slavery, the enslavement of Native Americans by European colonists, was common. Many of these Native slaves were exported to the Northern colonies and to off-shore colonies, especially the "sugar islands" of the Caribbean.[14] Historian Alan Gallay estimates that from 1670–1715, British slave traders sold between 24,000 and 51,000 Native Americans from what is now the southern part of the U.S.[167]

https://en.m.wikipedia.org/wiki/Slavery_among_Native_Americans_in_the_United_States

> 🔒 Colonists shipped Nativ...
> https://www.futurity.org

While natives had been forced into slavery and servitude as early as 1636, it was not until King Philip's War that natives were enslaved in large numbers, Fisher writes in the study. The 1675 to 1676 war pitted Native American leader King Philip, also known as Metacom, and his allies against the English colonial settlers.

During the war, New England colonies routinely shipped Native Americans as slaves to Barbados, Bermuda, Jamaica, the Azores, Spain, and Tangier in North Africa, Fisher says.

Native Americans sold overseas occasionally made it back to the United States, Fisher writes. Others died or disappeared into a wider slave market and labor force, or became established in the locations where they were sent, like the modern-day community of individuals in Bermuda who claim New England Indian descent.

Source: *Brown University*

Original Study   DOI: 10.1215/00141801-3688391

https://www.futurity.org/native-americans-slavery-1361262-2/

AFRICAN-AMERICANS ARE THE AMERICAN INDIANS

For Early Colonists, Indians Were A Bloody Enemy And The Spoils Of War
Rick Green
September 29, 2002
The Hartford Courant

Out of a swampy thicket, near the blue waters of Long Island Sound, 200 old men, women and children stepped into the bright sunshine and entered a new world.

Hundreds of edgy soldiers, mustered from villages and farms across Connecticut, had finally surrounded the Pequots and their leader, Sassacus.

It was July 13, 1637, a critical day in the Pequot War that had consumed Puritan Connecticut for several years. Six weeks before, in a key victory for the colonists, Capt. John Mason had led a massacre at the Pequot fort in Mystic, killing as many as 700 Indians in a single hour.

This summer afternoon was a jubilant one for the Puritans and their Mohegan scouts who had cornered these "most terrible" Pequots. A new chapter in American history was about to begin: Indian enslavement in Colonial America.

Captured Indian warriors were frequently executed – or shipped to slave markets around the world. By the time King Philip's War began, Indian slaves, often women and children, were a common sight across southern New England.

From Newport, R.I., to Portsmouth, N.H., Indians came to public auction, "tied neck to neck," and sold for half of what an African might bring.

A 7-year-old girl was toted to Connecticut from a battle in Massachusetts, a spoil of war who was handy around the house. At times, there were so many captured Indians available that a few bushels of corn or 100 pounds of wool sufficed for payment. A New London man left "an Indian maidservant" as part of his estate. Another, a farmer and businessman from the New London area, kept a careful diary noting how common Indian slaves were on the farms and in the homes of southeastern Connecticut.

And on sailing ships, bound for the slave markets in Europe, Africa, the Caribbean and the Azores, Indians were packed away tightly by the profiteers, who kidnapped or bought them wholesale from Colonial authorities eager to finance an increasingly costly war against the Indians.

Among the Pequots caught in the bog in what's now part of Fairfield, a group of perhaps 17, mostly children, were thought to have been exported as slaves. Others were handed out to soldiers as wartime booty. Historians believe these 17 Pequots later ended up on an island off Nicaragua. Like many of the Indian slaves sent from America over the next century, there is little record of what happened to them.

Barely five years after their first recorded contact with Europeans, this final battle of the bloody Pequot War conclusively finished a doomed experiment by Indians and Puritans to live side by side. By the time the Treaty of Hartford was signed the following September, formally ending the war, the English had killed or enslaved more than 1,500 Pequot men, women and children, scholars believe.

During the uneasy decades that followed, as the Puritans pushed deeper into Indian country and their numbers swelled, it was difficult to travel through Connecticut, Massachusetts or Rhode Island and not encounter an Indian slave, working in a field, orchard or boatyard.

Indians who surrendered were treated only slightly more gently in the colony, with the Connecticut General Court ordering children sold as indentured servants for 10-year terms, though some would be slaves far longer if they got into legal trouble in Puritan courts.

A note left by attacking Nipmuck Indians after the plundering of Medfield, Mass., in February 1676 reveals much about the time: "We have nothing but our lives to loose but thou has many fair houses and cattell & much good things."

The rewards of war

In the fall of 1676 the sailing ship Seaflower departed Boston Harbor for the Caribbean, its cargo hold filled with nearly 200 "heathen Malefactors men, women and children" sentenced to "Perpetuall Servitude & slavery."

As Lepore recounts in her book – one of the few published scholarly examinations of Indian slavery – the sale and lucrative export of Indians had become by 1676 one of "the rewards of war" that replenished "coffers emptied by wartime expenses." Despite government efforts to regulate it, much of the trade was conducted illegally and ruthlessly.

"Slavery really did have a devastating impact on the Native American population. Men were more likely to be exported. You had some tribes and populations where the ratio of women to men is completely out of whack," said Newell.

In the 20th century this would lead to tribes, such as the Narragansetts and Pequots, with members who, to an outsider, look distinctly African American – but who nevertheless descend from historic New England tribes.

For many modern Indians in southern New England, slavery remains an essential and too-little-discussed element of their being, a chapter that must be acknowledged to understand the dynamics of today's often fragile relationship between Indians and non-Indians.

Back to the past

This year, on the 365th anniversary of the Fairfield "swamp fight" of 1637, "Tall Oak" Weeden and a delegation of Wampanoag Indians and Mashantucket Pequots went hunting for remnants of this forgotten slavery era.

Searching for clues, they traveled to St. David's Island in Bermuda. There they met with a small clan claiming to be descendants of New England Indian slaves shipped there centuries ago. Those who went came away convinced they had struck gold when they saw the faces, the dances and rituals of the St. David's Indians.

"I was struck by how much they looked like us," said Michael J. Thomas, a Mashantucket tribal leader who went on the Bermuda trip this past summer.

https://pequotwar.org/2012/02/did-you-know-after-the-pequot-war-pequot-women-children-were-sold-into-slavery-isle-of-nevis-bermuda-providence-isle/

AFRICAN-AMERICANS ARE THE AMERICAN INDIANS

as documented in his own journals. Every European nation that colonized North America utilized Indian slaves for construction, plantations, and mining on the North American continent but more frequently in their outposts in the Caribbean and in the metropoles of Europe.

As the pieces of the puzzle come together in the scholarship, historians note that nowhere is there more documentation than in South Carolina, what was the original English colony of Carolina, established in 1670. It is estimated that between 1650 and 1730 at least 50,000 Indians (and likely more due to transactions hidden to avoid paying government tariffs and taxes) were exported by the English alone to their Caribbean outposts. Between 1670 and 1717 far more Indians were exported than Africans were imported.

Major slaving ports included Boston, Salem, Mobile and New Orleans. From those ports Indians were shipped to Barbados by the English, Martinique and Guadalupe by the French and the Antilles by the Dutch. Indian slaves were also sent to the Bahamas as the "breaking grounds" where they might've been transported back to New York or Antigua.

The historical record indicates a perception that Indians did not make good slaves. When they weren't shipped far from their home territories they too easily escaped and were given refuge by other Indians if not in their own communities. They died in high numbers on the transatlantic journeys and succumbed easily to European diseases. By 1676 Barbados had banned Indian slavery citing "too bloody and dangerous an inclination to remain here."

https://www.thoughtco.com/untold-history-of-american-indian-slavery-2477982

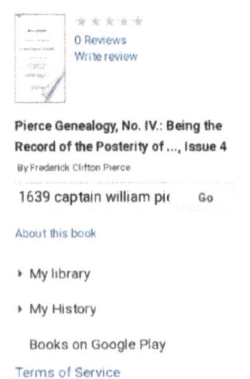

Pierce Genealogy. 13

ice, rescuing refugees from the Connecticut Valley and returning them to Boston. In 1636, with the fine new ship "Desire," one hundred and twenty tons, built for him at Marblehead, he went with Endicott's force to Block Island. In 1637, he carried supplies from Boston for the soldiers of the Pequod War and acted as tender. In 1638, he sailed between Boston and the West Indies; and it is sad to relate that according to the usage of the times, he took out several Pequod prisoners as bondmen, and returned with a few negro slaves, though even then some leading citizens condemned this traffic. At this time he seems to have presented Winthrop with what the latter calls an *aligarto*—an animal which much interested the grave Bostonians. In 1638, he cleared the "Desire" from London with passengers for Boston; the English officers writing his name "Piers." From Boston he kept on to the West Indies. In 1639, he sailed the "Desire"* from Boston to the Thames in twenty-three days — a passage which would even now reflect much credit on such a craft and its captain.

AFRICAN-AMERICANS ARE THE AMERICAN INDIANS

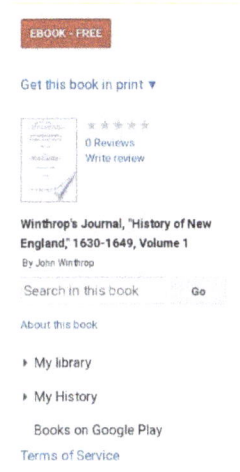

wounds. Here our men gat some booty of kettles, trays, wampom, etc., and the women and children were divided, and sent some to Connecticut, and some to the Massachusetts. The sachem of the place, having yielded, had his life, and his wife and children, etc. The women, which were brought home, reported that we had slain in all thirteen sachems, and that there were thirteen more left. We had now slain and taken, in all, about seven hundred. We sent fifteen of the boys and two women to Bermuda, by Mr. Peirce; but he, missing it, carried them to Providence Isle.[1]

Mo. 6 (*August*).] Mr. Stoughton sailed, with some of his company, from Pequod to Block Island. They came thither in the night, yet were discovered, and our men having killed one or two of them, and burnt some of their wigwams, etc., they came to parley, and, submitting themselves to become tributaries in one hundred fathom wampompeague, and to deliver any that should be found to have any hand in Mr. Oldham's death, they were all received, and no more harm done them.

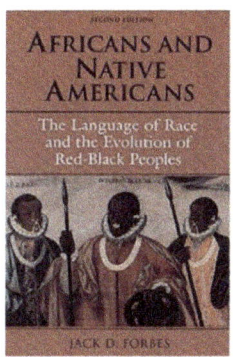

TAKING THE CARIBBEAN TO EUROPE AND AFRICA: COLUMBUS AND THE SLAVE TRADE

In any case, by the 1490s Americans were appearing once again in European cities. Although Terranova (Newfoundland) and Greenland continued to be a source of captives from 1501 on, it is best at this point to turn away from northern waters to examine the activities of Columbus and the catastrophic slave trade in American flesh which he initiated in the Caribbean region.

Columbus seems not to have been the first bearded white navigator to have reached the Caribbean region, but his immediate predecessor's name is unknown and no record of any return voyage to European or North African waters exists.⁶¹ Moreover, Columbus' impact was singular in that he was, from the first, a dedicated slaver and exploiter with an extremely callous and indifferent attitude towards culturally different human beings.

Columbus on his first voyage kidnapped at least 27 Americans, two of whom escaped, leaving a total of 25 in his hands. His attitude is expressed as follows, when, after abducting seven males, he says: 'when your highnesses so command, they can all be carried off to Castille or held captive in the island itself, since with fifty men they would be all kept in subjection and forced to do whatever may be wished.' Thus, at the very first island reached (Guananí), Columbus already was able to express his willingness to depopulate the entire island in order that the Americans might be sold as slaves in Europe, or held as captives in their own land. This, it should be noted, is long prior to any disappointment about the failure to find gold or other riches in quantity.

A month later, after capturing five boys, Columbus says:

afterwards I sent to a house which is near . . . and they brought seven head of women, small and large, and three boys. I did this, in order that the men might conduct themselves better in Spain, having women of their own land . . . because *already it has many times been my business to bring men from Guinea*, in order that they might learn the language of Portugal, and afterwards when they had returned and they thought that use might be made of them in their own land . . . when they reached their own land this result never appeared . . . So that, having their women, they will be willing to do that which is laid upon them, and also these women will do much to teach our people their language, which is one and the same throughout these islands of India. (Italics added)

After two boys escaped, Columbus stated: 'and I have no great confidence in them, because many times they have attempted to escape.' His philosophy of conquest and colonialism was extremely well developed: 'And they are fitted to be ruled and to be set to work, to cultivate the land and to do all else that may be necessary, and you may build towns and teach them to go clothed and to adopt our customs.' Also: 'They would make good and industrious servants.'⁶²

After learning of the existence of so-called 'Cannibal' (Carib) groups in the Indies, Columbus began to emphasize the enslavement of the latter. While still at sea, on his first return voyage, Columbus advocated the capture of Caribs: 'very fierce people and well proportioned and of very good understanding, who, after being removed from their inhumanity, we believe will be better than any other slaves whatsoever.' On January 30, 1494 he addressed to the Spanish monarchs a plan for sending men, women, and children to Spain to learn the Castillian language and to be trained in service, with more care 'than other slaves' receive, saying that this plan would save a great number of souls while at the same time providing the colonizing Spaniards with the profit needed to supply themselves with goods. In other words, Columbus proposed (after his first voyage) that American slavery be used to finance the conquest.⁶³

Subsequently, Columbus began to enslave Taino (Arawak) people who were definitely not cannibalistic and it would appear that the idea of punishing Caribs (for being allegedly so) was simply an expedient financial strategy. The logic of his activities was well expressed by Las Casas who noted that

> el acabará en muy poco tiempo de consumir toda la gente desta isla [Haiti], porque tenía determinado de cargar los navios que viniesen de Castilla de esclavos y enviarlos a vender a las islas de Canarias, y de los Azores y a las de Cabo Verde y adonde quiera que bien se vendiesen; y sobre esta mercadería fundaba principalmente los aprovechamientos para suplir los dichos gastos y excusar a los reyes de costa, como en principal granjería.

Thus Columbus, according to las Casas, was determined to 'consume' the entire population of Haiti by filling every ship with slaves to be sold in the Canary, Azores and Cabo Verde islands or wherever, and planned that these slaves would finance the conquest.

As Las Casas points out, for Columbus the lives of Americans were obviously 'nothing' and the continuous wars to obtain slaves were simply necessary to fill the ships.[64] Columbus wrote to the monarchs that from Haiti

> it is possible, in the name of the Holy Trinity, to send all the slaves which it is possible to sell ... of whom, if the information which I have is correct, they tell me that one can sell 4,000. ... And certainly, the information seems authentic, because in Castille and Portugal and Aragon and Italy and Sicily and the islands of Portugal and Aragon and the Canaries they utilize many slaves, and I believe that those from Guinea are not now enough. ... In any case there are these slaves and brazilwood, which seem a live thing [profitable], and still gold.

Thus, even as Columbus was loading five ships with slaves, he was proposing to sell 4,000 in various parts of the Mediterranean and along the coast of Africa.

Columbus was also unconcerned that many Americans would die in the slave trade because, as he said, the blacks and the native Canary Islanders when first enslaved also had died in great numbers. For Columbus the Americans were *piezas* (pieces) or *cabezas de cabras* (heads of goats), and it did not matter if only ten per cent lived to reach a market, according to Las Casas (who, incidentally, possessed Columbus' diaries, letters and notes).[65]

The shipment of Americans to Europe and Africa by Columbus (and by other Spaniards) was, then, not an accident, nor was it a result of armed resistance or alleged cannibalism. It was a direct extension of the style of commercial slavery long practiced by the Genoese and Venetians in the Mediterranean and used by the Portuguese along the west coast of Africa. Columbus' voyages, in a very real sense, were mere extensions of the old galley routes from Italy to North Africa and the Black Sea or of Portuguese routes along the African coast.

What was the result? First, many thousands of Americans were shipped to Spain during Columbus' period of dominance in the Caribbean. It is difficult to calculate the exact number because many ships departed from Haiti without leaving any record of their cargo, but we may be sure that they did not leave empty. On the very first voyage, although Columbus only carried 25, it is

In any case, at least 3,000 Americans are known to have been shipped to Europe between 1493 and 1501, with the likely total being possibly double that. Most were sent to the Seville area, where they seem to show up in the slave markets as *negros* without a place of origin being mentioned. Others were probably sold in the Azores and other islands, partly to avoid the wrath of Queen Isabel (who, on occasion, expressed hostility towards the dividing up of 'her' vassals without her prior permission).[66]

Columbus reached Lisbon in early March 1493. Many people came to see the captive Americans and it is very likely that some of the latter were taken nine leagues into the interior to see the king of Portugal. There it was that two Americans drew maps which showed the Lucayos (Bahamas), Cuba, Haiti, and other islands. It may be also that Columbus left some Americans with the Portuguese, as discussed earlier.[67]

Shortly thereafter some of the Americans were taken to Seville, perhaps seven to ten being still alive and together. Some were left in that area, while about six or seven were taken overland across Spain to Barcelona where they were displayed before the monarchs in mid-April. In the fall of 1493 some Americans were taken on Columbus' second westward voyage, but only two of these reportedly arrived alive. One was able to run away immediately upon landing in Haiti.[68]

African–American Contacts, to 1500

world population is approximately 400 million, of whom 80 million inhabit the Americas. By the middle of the sixteenth century, out of these 80 million, there remain ten.

If the word genocide has ever been applied to a situation with some accuracy, this is here the case.[70]

But the tens of millions of Americans who disappeared after 1492 did not all die in the 'holocaust' inflicted within the Americas. Many thousands were sent to Europe and Africa where their descendants still live.

I hope that the people in the Caribbean read this with understanding. What you think were Africans that came to your islands were more than likely American Indians from North Central and South America. They were also the Indians that were sold to Africa, Europe, and brought back to the Caribbean. That is why some of the west Africans look like some of the "African American" people. It's not because we come from the African. It's because those Africans are descendants of the American Indians that were shipped over into Africa up until the slave trade ended. These Indians learned the languages of wherever they were sent and served as translators when they returned. Understandably, many of the Caribbean people have this belief that their ancestors are African, and that may be true for some. However, many of them don't know that many of the people

AFRICAN-AMERICANS ARE THE AMERICAN INDIANS

they thought were Africans were the descendants of American Indians. Those American Indians have been living in Africa since 1492. Africa declined the Haitians from joining the African Union because they know they didn't send a massive amount of Africans to the Caribbean during the Transatlantic Slave Trade era.

A Haitian flag is used as an ornament by a spectator attending a ceremony marking the anniversary of the Battle of Vertire. Haiti maintains a close connection to its ancestral homeland in Africa. Photo by Swoan Parker/Reuters.

Despite reports, Haiti not joining the African Union

By - Kenya Downs

World May 20, 2016 06:02 PM EDT

The African Union is denying that Haiti will become the organization's first non-African member, stating that "only African States can join the African Union."

https://www.pbs.org/newshour/world/despite-reports-haiti-not-joining-the-african-union

CONCLUSION

We have come to the closing of this section of the book dealing with the slave trade. We covered how Columbus knew where he was going because he met some Indians years before setting sail and How he was an informant exposing the Americas. He understood that he wasn't in India because the country of India didn't exist at that time. We went over how the transportation of large amounts of Africans stacked like sardines in the belly of a ship was impossible and several factors to support the claim. We also showcased that maybe the millions of Africans/negroes were Europeans and how the actual transatlantic slave trade was American Indians being transported to the Caribbean, Africa, and Europe. The transatlantic slave trade story is a severe exaggeration and was used to enslave the people's minds in the U.S.A to keep them away from claiming their birthright as American Indians.

It's time for African Americans to wake up to the deception of the slave trade. There isn't any archaeological evidence of giant slave ships, just old slave trinkets that proves one slave was in shackles. They have never found 40 chains at the bottom of an ocean all connected. There are many plot holes with the transatlantic slave trade. It is time to get into the heart of the book about why I say, **"THE AFRICAN AMERICANS ARE THE AMERICAN INDIANS"** Let's get started.

Section 2: Indian Descriptions Match African Americans

Chapter 5

THE AMERICAN AND THEIR COMPLEXIONS

When most people hear the term American, they think of European people. The reality is the Americans are the aboriginal people found in the Americas by the Europeans. The Europeans identified today as Americans were called colonists or pale faces. In this chapter, we will go over how the explorers and others describe the American Indian people's complexion, which is one of many reasons why the people labeled as African Americans are the American Indians.

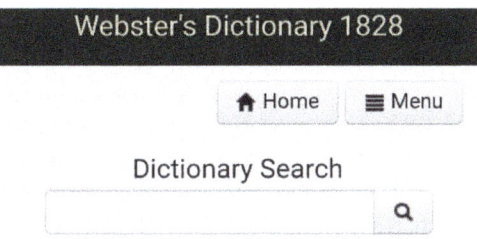

American

AMER'ICAN, *adjective* Pertaining to America.

AMER'ICAN, *noun* A native of America; originally applied to the aboriginals, or copper-colored races, found here by the Europeans; but now applied to the descendants of Europeans born in America.

http://webstersdictionary1828.com/Dictionary/american

AFRICAN-AMERICANS ARE THE AMERICAN INDIANS

The Spruce Crafts

What Color is Your Copper Coin?

The Primitive Black Nations of America.

By Professor C. S. Rafinesque.

The Society of Geography having offered a reward for the best Memoir on the Origin of the Asiatic Negroes, I sent them last year two Memoirs; one on those Asiatic Negroes, wherein I demonstrated the affinities of their languages with the African and Polynesian Negroes, as well as with the Hindus and Chinese, and renders it probable that all the Negroes originated in the Southern Slopes of the Imalaya Mountains, as they did once exist all over India, South China, Japan, Persia and Arabia. My second Memoir was on the Negroe or Black Nations, found in America before Columbus, wherein I proved their existence and connection by

2. The *Califurnams* of the Carib Islands, called Black Caribs or Guanini by others, are a black branch of Caribs. See Rochefort, Herrera, &c.

3. The *Arguahos* of Cutara mentioned by Garcias in the West Indies, quite black.

Pinterest

Carib Woman Stann Creek 1878 | Belize Vintage in 2019 | Black ...

Carib Woman Stann Creek 1878 Native American History, American Indians, Vintage Black Glamour,

Page | 76

3. The *Arguahos* of Cutara mentioned by Garcias in the West Indies, quite black.

4. The black *Aroras* of Raleigh, or *Yaruras* of the Spaniards, ugly black or brown Negroes, yet existing near the Oronoco, and language known, called Monkeys by their neighbours.

brown skin

5. *Chaymas* of Guyana, brown Negroes like Hottentots, see Humboldt.

6. The *Mangipas* and *Porcigis* of Nienhof, the *Motayas* of Knivet, &c., all of Brazil, brown Negroes with curly hair. See also Vespucius and Pigafetta.

brown skin men

7. The *Nigritas* of Martyr in Darien, yet existing in Choco under the name of *Chuanas* or *Gaunas* or *Chinos*. See Mollièn. Ugly black or red Negroes.

8. Those of Popayan called *Manabi*, blackish with negro features and hair. See Stevenson.

9. The *Guabas* and *Jaras* of Taguzgalpa near the Honduras. See Juaros, &c., now called Zambos.

10. The *Enslen* or *Esteros* of New California, ugly blackish Negroes. See Vanegas, Langsdorf, &c.

AFRICAN-AMERICANS ARE THE AMERICAN INDIANS

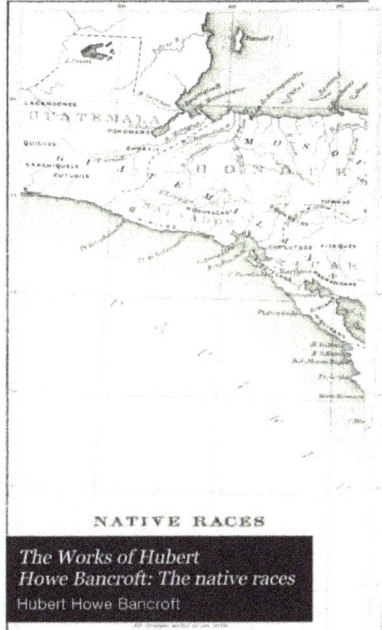

The Works of Hubert Howe Bancroft: The native races
Hubert Howe Bancroft

...Their complexion is a dark mahogany, or often nearly black, their faces round or square, with features approximating nearer to the African than the Indian. Wide, enormous mouth, noses nearly flat, and hair straight, black, and coarse.... Small, gleaming eyes.' *Johnson's Cal. and Ogn.*, pp. 142-3. Of good stature, strong and muscular. *Bryant's Cal.*, p. 266. 'Rather below the middle stature, but strong, well-knit fellows......Good-looking, and well limbed.' *Kelly's Excursion to Cal.*, vol. ii., pp. 81, 111. 'They were in general fine stout men.' A great diversity of physiognomy was noticeable. *Pickering's Races*, in *U. S. Ex. Ex.*, vol. ix., pp. 105, 107. On the Sacramento 'were fine robust men, of low stature, and badly formed.' *Wilkes' Nar.*, in *U. S. Ex. Ex.*, vol. v., p. 198. 'The mouth is very large, and the nose broad and depressed.' 'Chiefly distinguished by their dark color.... broad faces, a low forehead.' *Hale's Ethnog.*, in *U. S. Ex. Ex.*, vol. vi., p. 222. 'Their features are coarse, broad, and of a dark chocolate color.' *Taylor*.

At Bodega Bay 'they are an ugly and brutish race, many with negro profiles.' *Id.*, p. 103. 'They are physically an inferior race, and have flat, unmeaning features, long, coarse, straight black hair, big mouths, and very dark skins.' *Revere's Tour*, p. 120. 'Large and strong, their colour being the same as that of the whole territory.' *Maurelle's Jour.*, p. 47. It is said of the natives of the Sacramento valley, that 'their growth is short and stunted; they have short thick necks, and clumsy heads; the forehead is low, the nose flat with broad nostrils, the eyes very narrow and showing no intelligence, the cheek-bones prominent, and the mouth large. The teeth are white, but they do not stand in even rows; and their heads are covered by short, thick, rough hair....Their color is a dirty yellowish-brown.' *Pfeiffer's Second Journ.*, p. 307. 'This race of Indians is probably inferior to all others on the continent. Many of them are diminutive in stature, but they do not lack muscular strength, and we saw some who were tall and well-formed.

 yellow brown skin

https://books.google.com/books?id=1TETAAAAYAAJ&pg=PA365&lpg=PA365&dq=their+complexion+is+a+dark+mahogany+or+often+black&source=bl&ots=bMd0MQUrvx&sig=ACfU3U1hw9mAGCs-E3iAMtI6IYebDqKwCw&hl=en&sa=X&ved=2ahUKEwiGwPCvr9nhAhVKnKwKHXnIDHYQ6AEwCnoECAQQAQ#v=onepage&q=their%20complexion%20is%20a%20dark%20mahogany%20or%20often%20black&f=false

AFRICAN-AMERICANS ARE THE AMERICAN INDIANS

RED MAN. A name first applied to the Beothuk Indians of Newfoundland because they colored their bodies, utensils, and weapons with red ocher. Sebastian Cabot, the English navigator, on discovering Newfoundland, mentioned "people painted with red ocher." Other writers later commented on this and soon the name Beothuk was translated by the white man as "Red Indian," or "Red Man." The Beothuk actually were light brown in color. See INDIAN, PAINT.

 light brown skin

Document # 1

The Written Record of the Voyage of 1524 of Giovanni da Verrazano as recorded in a letter to Francis I, King of France, July 8th, 1524

1524 Voyage Route
- Verrazano sailed west from France to Cape Fear, North Carolina
- While exploring the coastline he found Pamlico Sound.
- Travelling further north he discovered New York Harbour, Block Island, and Narragansett Bay.
- He sailed even further north to Maine and Newfoundland before returning to France.

[Adapted from a translation by Susan Tarrow of the Cellere Codex, in Lawrence C. Wroth, ed., <u>The Voyages of Giovanni da Verrazzano, 1524-1528</u> (Yale, 1970), pp. 133-143]

They go completely naked except that around their loins they wear skins of small animals like martens, with a narrow belt of grass around the body, to which they tie various tails of other animals which hang down to the knees; the rest of the body is bare, and so is the head. Some of them wear garlands of birds' feathers. **They are dark in color, not unlike the Ethiopians,**

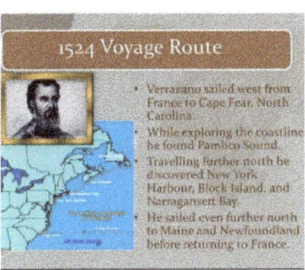 ethiopian men

http://www.columbia.edu/~lmg21/ash3002y/earlyac99/documents/verrazan.htm

AFRICAN-AMERICANS ARE THE AMERICAN INDIANS

CHAPTER II

FRENCH NAVIGATOR DESCRIBES NATIVES

IN OCTOBER, 1523, five years before the Spanish adventurer, Narvaez landed at Tampa Bay, the King of France outfitted an expedition to America under the command of the Florentine, Verrazano. In March of the following year Verrazano landed not far from what later was named Cape Fear, on the south Atlantic coast. Here were found natives whom the explorer described as black-skinned, naked excepting a girdle of grass from which depended a marten skin, their thick, black hair worn tied back on the head. The natives displayed no hostility, but rather gave many evidences of friendliness. Somewhat farther north Verrazano encountered natives of fairer complexion, their bodies covered with light draperies made of what was perhaps Spanish moss, woven with threads of wild hemp, living in huts constructed of small trees and shrubbery. For transport along the rivers these natives used dug-out log canoes.

Here again seeds were sown for lasting enmity against the whites. A native boy was captured to be taken back to France as a specimen. All up the Atlantic coast Verrazano encountered numerous tribes. On Narragansett Bay he found what he reported as a superior tribe, well-formed, stately, friendly, and dressed in tanned skins, many of whom wore necklaces of precious or semi-precious stones. This country then, as

https://archive.org/details/amerindiansfroma0000mcni/page/20

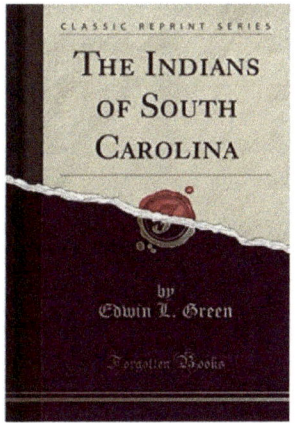

10 THE INDIANS OF SOUTH CAROLINA.

Waxhaws, Edistos, Pedees, Saraws (Cheraws), Seewees, Wandos, Winyaws and Saludas.

The Indians of South Carolina were of a reddish brown or copper color. The men were tall and straight, with well shaped limbs and an almost perfect figure: the Cherokees were the tallest of all. They were never deformed or humpbacked, and were very dexterous in the use of their limbs. An old traveler, who has left us the story of his journey through South Carolina not many years after it was first settled, says that he never saw a left-handed Indian. They were hardy and possessed wonderful powers of endurance, but they could not perform the labor of the white man. The features of the Cherokees are described as regular: the cheekbone was high; the nose was inclined to be aquiline or hooked; the eyes were small, black and full of fire. No hair grew upon the face; if any did appear it was plucked out by the roots. The head, which was covered with long, coarse hair, black as a raven, never became bald.

The women were tall, slender and

https://books.google.com/books?id=QP8SAAAAYAAJ&printsec=frontcover#v=onepage&q&f=false

History of the Indians of Connecticut from the earliest ...
John William De Forest, Felix Octavius Carr Darley

The forests were filled with animals; some of them beasts of prey, others suitable for food, others valuable on account of their furs. Flocks of wild turkeys roamed through the woods; herons fished in the marshes or along the banks of the rivers; quails, partridges, and singing birds abounded, both in the forests and open country; and, at certain times of the year, the pigeons collected in such numbers that their flight seemed to obscure the light of the sun. The ponds, creeks and rivers swarmed with water-fowl, and various kinds of shell-fish were found in profusion along the shores of the sound. The waters seemed everywhere alive with fish; and, every spring, great numbers of shad and lamprey eels ascended the rivers, furnishing a seasonable supply to the natives when their provisions were exhausted by the long and severe winter. Such was the appearance and condition of Connecticut when it first became known to Europeans; and such were its capacities for supporting a people who depended almost wholly for subsistence upon fishing and the chase.*

THE PEOPLE.

In complexion, our uncivilized predecessors were of that tawny color, inclining to red, which, differing from the complexion of every other portion of the human family, seems peculiar to most, if not all of the aboriginal American race. Their cheek bones were high and prominent; their eyes widely separated; their noses usually

* See New England's Plantation. Mass. Hist. Coll., Vol. I, pp. 117—122; and Roger Williams' Key. Mass. Hist. Coll., Vol. III, pp. 219—225.

https://books.google.com/books?id=4OwNAAAAIAAJ&printsec=frontcover#v=onepage&q&f=false

AFRICAN-AMERICANS ARE THE AMERICAN INDIANS

THE DISCOVERY OF AMERICA

I

ANCIENT AMERICA

WHEN the civilized people of Europe first became acquainted with the continents of North and South America, they found them inhabited by a race of men quite unlike any of the races with which they were familiar in the Old World. Between the various tribes of this aboriginal American race, except in the sub-arctic region, there is now seen to be a general physical likeness, such as to constitute an American type of mankind as clearly recognizable as those types which we call Mongolian and Malay, though far less pronounced than such types as the Australian or the negro. The most obvious characteristics possessed in common by the American aborigines are the copper-coloured or rather the cinnamon-coloured complexion, along with the high cheek-bones and small deepset eyes, the straight black hair and absence or scantiness of

The discovery of America, with some account of ancient America and the Spanish conquest
John Fiske

The American aborigines

1

https://books.google.com/books?id=XBQQAAAAYAAJ&pg=PA1&lpg=PA1&dq=the+most+obvious+characteristic+possessed+in+common+by+the+american+aborigines&source=bl&ots=Lg4LOwQi04&sig=ACfU3U2i3M8TzUCR5eJk6oV5i9uL-qAckQ&hl=en&sa=X&ved=2ahUKEwiC472emNnhAhUPCKwKHRgJCFYQ6AEwAHoECAEQAQ#v=onepage&q=the%20most%20obvious%20characteristic%20possessed%20in%20common%20by%20the%20american%20aborigines&f=false

Page | 85

49th Event. A black people came to Hayti from the south or south-east, who had darts of Guanin metal, and were called the Black Guaninis.

This tradition preserved by Herrera, Garcia and Charlevoix, indicates a colony of *Negroes* or men painting black, from South America. They might be the black Negroes of Quarequa mentioned by Dangleria, or some other American Negro nation, of which there are many.—See my account of ancient Black Nations of America. Dangleria mentions two wild tribes [pg 194] of savages in Hayti towards 1500, one speechless! (which means they

102

https://books.google.com/books?id=JehaDwAAQBAJ&pg=PA102&lpg=PA102&dq=a+black+people+came+hayti+from+the+south+or+south+east+who+had+darts+of+guanin+metal&source=bl&ots=Bs7S7-wbKC&sig=ACfU3U0vqr2ljJLDZn-1SQieIStVVmfYVQ&hl=en&sa=X&ved=2ahUKEwiO-PrMmtnhAhUGC6wKHVO6BNcQ6AEwAHoECAAQAQ#v=onepage&q=a%20black%20people%20came%20hayti%20from%20the%20south%20or%20south%20east%20who%20had%20darts%20of%20guanin%20metal&f=false

CHAPTER IX.

Up to the time of barbarism fixed wealth consisted in houses, clothing, ornaments, the tools for obtaining and preparing food, boats, weapons and household articles of the simplest kind. A new supply of food must be obtained practically each day. This is the condition in which we found, and will leave, the North American Indians, while we turn our attention to the peoples which, having had the same institutions that obtained among the copper colored races of North America when discovered by Europeans, have advanced through barbarism to civilization.

In the Old World with the passing of the upper stage of savagery the new social forces became active. Hunting and fishing had ceased to be the normal occupation of the men. The domestication of animals and the breeding of flocks had developed a hitherto unknown source of wealth and created entirely new social conditions. The increase in numbers and the yield of livestock required that the energies of the people should be devoted to the care of the herds, for these had come to furnish the means of sustenance instead of game, as formerly. Hence, all the former means and methods of obtaining the necessaries of life were forced

48

https://books.google.com/books?id=v0uIQrRLnIYC&pg=PR1&lpg=PR1&dq=the+evolution+of+society+from+primitive+savagery+word+h+mills&source=bl&ots=36IZmr0zrg&sig=ACfU3U21Y0xQYvq5gOLy36VdFGpOjLNGkg&hl=en&sa=X&ved=2ahUKEwiimsCJotnhAhUHRK0KHc7LBvIQ6AEwBHoECAQQAQ#v=onepage&q=the%20evolution%20of%20society%20from%20primitive%20savagery%20word%20h%20mills&f=false

AFRICAN-AMERICANS ARE THE AMERICAN INDIANS

78 CRUEL CONDUCT EXERCISED

"In the summer of the year 1763, some friendly Indians from a distant place, came to Bethlehem to dispose of their peltry for manufactured goods and necessary implements of husbandry. Returning home well satisfied, they put up the first night at a tavern, eight miles distant. *The landlord not being at home, his wife took the liberty of encouraging the people who frequented her house for the sake of drinking, to abuse those Indians, adding, that she would freely give a gallon of rum to any one of them that should kill one of those black devils. Other white

https://books.google.com/books?id=POg_AQAAMAAJ&pg=PA164&lpg=PA164&dq=in+the+summer+of+1763+some+friendly+indians+came+to+bethlehem&source=bl&ots=65hI7Spjol&sig=ACfU3U0aziuUl5bWed6_r2kMIYw0p9PwZg&hl=en&sa=X&ved=2ahUKEwjEwrbQzdnhAhVMXKwKHRTcBLwQ6AEwAXoECAcQAQ#v=onepage&q=in%20the%20summer%20of%201763%20some%20friendly%20indians%20came%20to%20bethlehem&f=false

Chapter 6
AMERICAN INDIAN FACIAL FEATURES

In this chapter, we will share some descriptions of the American Indian facial features and how African Americans share them. Of course, there are many more, but these are a few descriptions.

black hair, the brown or cinnamon-coloured skin, the heavy brow, the dull and sleepy eye, the full and compressed lips, and the salient but dilated nose. These traits, moreover, are

Heavy Brow

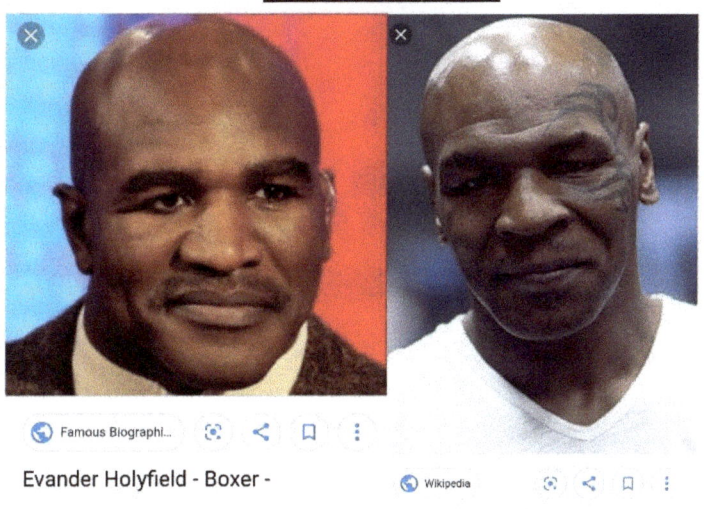

Evander Holyfield - Boxer -

Mike Tyson - Wikipedia

Full & Compressed Lips

Brandy Norwood 1998 - #traffic-

amertribes.proboards.com
Goes to War? | www.American-Tribes.com

Salient But Dilated Nose

Coming to America' Cast Then

Sleepy Eyes

Ronald Slim Williams

https://books.google.com/books?id=0hwAAAAAMAAJ&pg=PA143&lpg=PA143&dq=the+heavy+brow,+the+dull+and+sleepy+eye&source=bl&ots=nAO5giUEcq&sig=ACfU3U0emvV9EHyUPjDijQIJKj4QXnvvnw&hl=en&sa=X&ved=2ahUKEwipq-3W6t_hAhWqi1QKHX7WB9QQ6AEwCnoECAMQAQ#v=onepage&q=the%20heavy%20brow%2C%20the%20dull%20and%20sleepy%20eye&f=false

AFRICAN-AMERICANS ARE THE AMERICAN INDIANS

The discovery of America, with some account of ancient America and the Spanish conquest
John Fiske

high cheek-bones and small deepset eyes, the straight black hair and absence or scantiness of

AFRICAN-AMERICANS ARE THE AMERICAN INDIANS

man. The features of the Cherokees are described as regular: the cheekbone was high; the nose was inclined to be aquiline or hooked; the eyes were small, black and

Aquiline Or "roman" Noses In Black Americans | Lipstick Alley

1969 Press Photo Max Julien

History of the Indians of Connecticut from the earliest ... John William De Forest, Felix Octavius Carr Darley

American race. Their cheek bones were high and prominent; their eyes widely separated; their noses usually

* See New England's Plantation. Mass. Hist. Coll., Vol. I, pp. 117—122; and Roger Williams' Key. Mass. Hist. Coll., Vol. III, pp. 219—225.

Page | 93

AFRICAN-AMERICANS ARE THE AMERICAN INDIANS

History of the Indians of Connecticut from the earliest ...
John William De Forest, Felix Octavius Carr Darley

nent; their eyes widely separated; <u>their noses usually</u>

* See New England's Plantation. Mass. Hist. Coll., Vol. I, pp. 117—129; and Roger Williams' Key. Mass. Hist. Coll., Vol. III, pp. 219—225.

4   HISTORY OF THE INDIANS

<u>broad, even when curved in outline</u>; and the ordinary

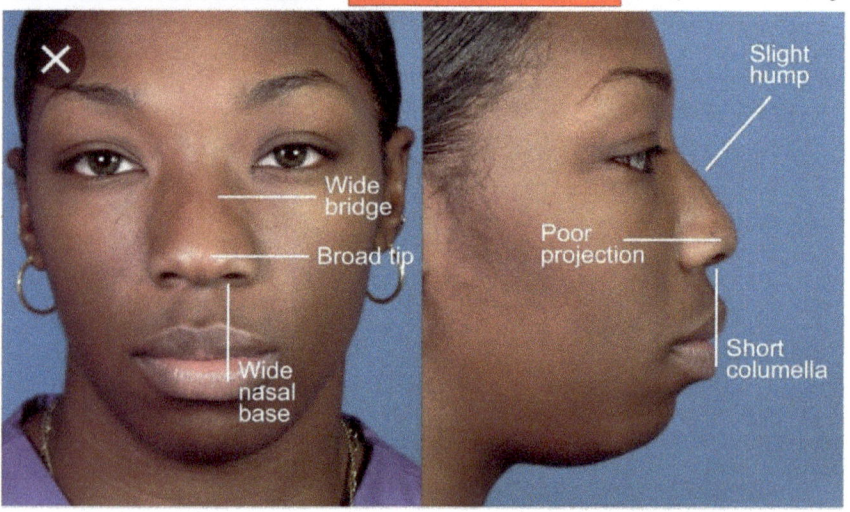

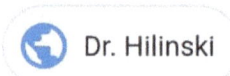

African American Rhinoplasty

Chapter 7
AMERICAN INDIAN HAIR

In this chapter, we will go over several types of American Indian hair. Most people only think of American Indians having bone straight hair. Many people don't know that American Indians had curly, wavy hair, afros, and dreadlocks. For many years, African Americans wore hairstyles such as afros and dreadlocks, thinking it was African. In reality, they were only repeating their American Indian ancestors' hairstyles.

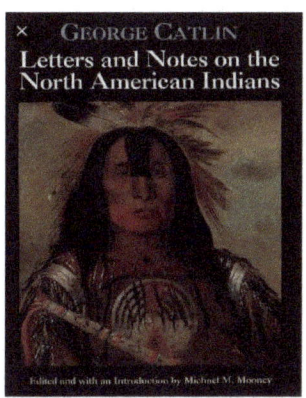

BOOKS LETTERS AND NOTES ON THE NORTH AMERICAN INDEGINOUS PEOPLE OF AMERICA, by George Catlin 1841
All primitive tribes known in America are dark, coppered color with jet black hair, while most possess curls in the extreme, and every level of wavy hair in between. The texture of the hair is generally fine, soft or silk or course or harsh. The hair of the men, falling down to their hams and sometimes to the ground, is divided into plaits or slabs two inches wide and filled with a profusion of glue and earth, which become very hard and remains unchanged from year to year. Today this form of hair is called locks.

AFRICAN-AMERICANS ARE THE AMERICAN INDIANS

Curls & Afro Curls

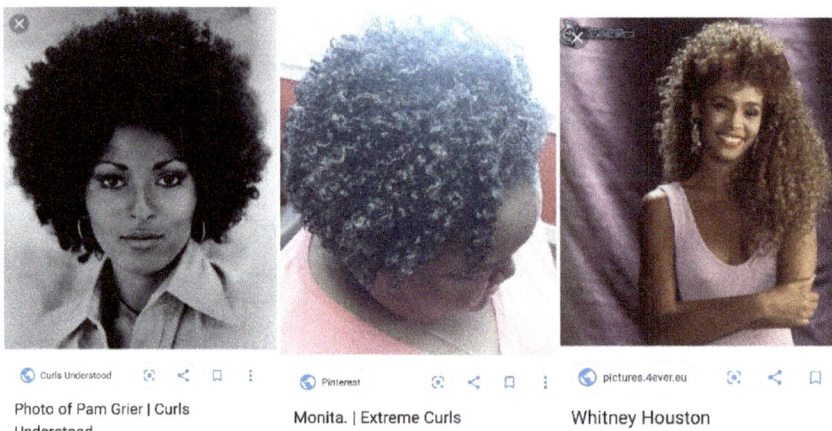

Photo of Pam Grier | Curls Understood

Monita. | Extreme Curls

Whitney Houston

terapeak.com
Pair Lrg Antique 19thc South American Indian Farmers Oil

"A Female Savage of Tierra del Fuego" engraving from a drawing by Johann Ihle from Ebenezer Sibly's "Universal System of Natural History" 1794. (Tierra del Fuego is an archipelago off the southernmost tip of the South American mainland, across the Strait of Magellan. The archipelago is divided between Chile and Argentina).

AFRICAN-AMERICANS ARE THE AMERICAN INDIANS

rulideas
rulideas: natives of south amrica
Native South Americans (1816 - 1831)

AFRICAN-AMERICANS ARE THE AMERICAN INDIANS

moonwishesstore.ecrater.com
Butterick Sewing Pattern 4783 Native North South American Indian ...

AFRICAN-AMERICANS ARE THE AMERICAN INDIANS

18/26 "Choctaw Girl", 2007, oil, paint marker on Masonite wood panel, 14 x 11 inches

NATIVE INHABITANTS: THE OHLONE TRIBE

Figure 1: An illustrated depiction of the Ohlone people
(http://www.missionscalifornia.com/sites/default/files/snjose-05-Ohlone-indians-dancing.jpg)

The coastal region of central and northern California, which includes Oakland, has a history recording back to 2000 B.C.E. The inhabitants at the time were the Ohlone people- a Native American tribe formally known as the "Costanoans." Up until the 1770's when Spanish explorers first discovered the area, the Ohlone people occupied the land and utilized its resources. They were mainly recorded as

pinterest.com

The descendants, Descendants of and The state on Pinterest

Native Races of the Pacific States of North America" Hubert Howe Bancroft, 1874 Descriptions of the California Indians.. "thick lips, broad flat negro-like ...

AFRICAN-AMERICANS ARE THE AMERICAN INDIANS

Deputation of Indians from the Chippawa Tribes to the President of Upper Canada, Sir Francis Bond Head, K.C.B., Major General &c. &c. 1815

http://www.davidrumsey.com/amica/amico889446-107678.html

AFRICAN-AMERICANS ARE THE AMERICAN INDIANS

Deputation of Indians from the Missisipi Tribes to the Governor General of British North America, Sir George Prevost Bart. Lieut. General &c. in 1814

https://www.museedelaguerre.ca/guerre-de-1812/content_assets/contacts-with-native-americans/

AFRICAN-AMERICANS ARE THE AMERICAN INDIANS

Douglas Stewart F...

[ADVERTISING] Amérique

AUD $30.00* · Brand: Douglas Stewart Fine Books

[Nantes, France : Lefèvre-Utile, circa 1901]. Trade card, 110 x 80 mm, recto with superb chromolithographic illustration depicting a Native American, ...

Wavy Hair

Pinterest

chilli | chilli in 2019 | Black hair 90s, Chilli tlc, Black girl ...

Pinterest

Aaliyah - wavy hair | hair idea |

Page | 105

AFRICAN-AMERICANS ARE THE AMERICAN INDIANS

1800 Black Cherokee Princess | native american | Pinterest ...

AFRICAN-AMERICANS ARE THE AMERICAN INDIANS

Locks

59 Best Locs - Long! Long! images | Dreadlocks, Dreads, H

Heir apparent: Bob Marley's son Damian shows off dreadlocks t...

Damian Marley's dreads... I can't

Lantern Press

Hudson Bay Brand - Native American - Vintage Cigar Inner ...

$7.99* · In stock · Brand: retail.lanternpress.com

... Quality Poster Prints Printed in the USA on heavy stock paper Crisp vibrant color image that is resistant to fading Standard size print, ready for ...

Page | 107

AFRICAN-AMERICANS ARE THE AMERICAN INDIANS

www.pinterest.com
Antonitto, an Apache man, with his hair in hair rolls or dreadlocks wrap...

www.pinterest.com
Native American Men with dreadlocks and twists. 1800'S | Ado...

www.pinterest.com
Shoshone Native Americans were called The Snake People. Dreadlock...

AFRICAN-AMERICANS ARE THE AMERICAN INDIANS

www.pinterest.com
All things dread on Pinterest | Dread Beads, Dreads and Dreadlocks

www.pinterest.com
Native American Man with dreadlocks. 1800'S | Adornment ...

www.pinterest.com
Cree Chief Poundmaker - 1885 by Oliver Buell - Cree Chief ...

AFRICAN-AMERICANS ARE THE AMERICAN INDIANS

The hair of the women is also worn as long as they can possibly cultivate it, oiled very often, which preserves on it a beautiful gloss and shows its natural color. They often braid it in two large plaits, one falling down just back of the ear, on each side of the head; and on any

Photo of Indigenous Americans – black native Americans

Pinterest
637 best AMERICAN INDIAN WOMEN images on Pinterest
Native American Black woman - Apache

https://books.google.com/books/about/Letters_and_Notes_on_the_Manners_Customs.html?id=ofMNAAAAIAAJ&printsec=frontcover&source=kp_read_button

SECTION 3: They Tried Telling You That You're Indian

Chapter 8
THEY'VE BEEN TELLING YOU

From the time the Europeans arrived in the Americas, they have documented the people they have encountered. They have always known that the people today that call themselves African American are the descendants of the American Indians. In modern times, everything is confusing with the stories of the African slave trade and that we are the descendants of those people. However, if you pay attention closely, you will see the truth. They have been trying to tell the masses in various ways. They show you in old paintings, maps, postcards, movies, books, magazines, and multiple other works. In this chapter, you will see the numerous ways of how they have been telling the African Americans that they are the American Indians.

1. EMBLEMS OF AMERICA

https://www.britishmuseum.org/research/collection_online/collection_object_details/collection_image_gallery.aspx?assetId=949400001&objectId=3338907&partId=1

AFRICAN-AMERICANS ARE THE AMERICAN INDIANS

An EMBLEM of AMERICA.

https://www.americanantiquarian.org/Inventories/Europeanprints/b4f1.htm#9243a

AFRICAN-AMERICANS ARE THE AMERICAN INDIANS

https://www.raremaps.com/gallery/detail/25975/title-page-america-ogilby

AFRICAN-AMERICANS ARE THE AMERICAN INDIANS

Original in the John Carter Brown Library at Brown University

AFRICAN-AMERICANS ARE THE AMERICAN INDIANS

AFRICAN-AMERICANS ARE THE AMERICAN INDIANS

https://jcb.lunaimaging.com/luna/servlet/s/6nz0we

AFRICAN-AMERICANS ARE THE AMERICAN INDIANS

2. MAPS AND STATES

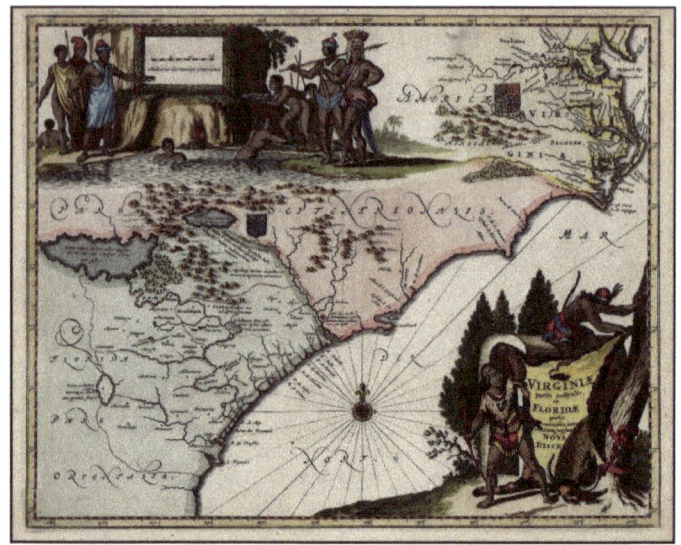

https://images.app.goo.gl/u14TNDoQBnummg9e7

AFRICAN-AMERICANS ARE THE AMERICAN INDIANS

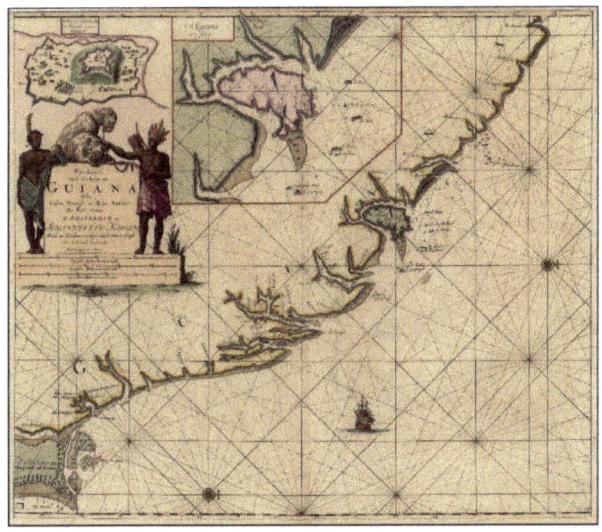

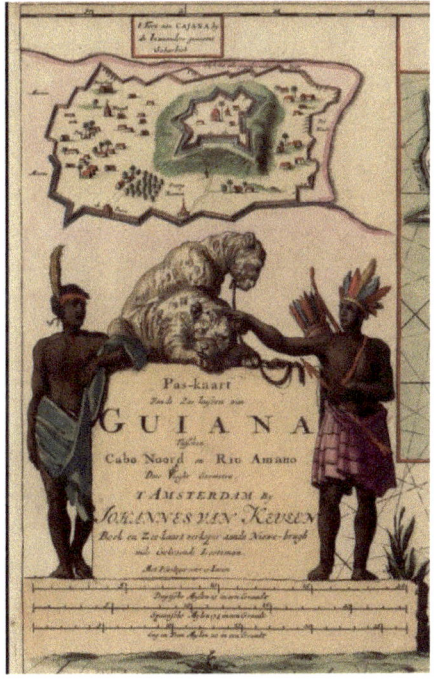

https://www.raremaps.com/gallery/detail/55190/pas-kaart-van-de-zee-kusten-van-guiana-tusschen-cabo-noord-e-van-keulen

http://www.swaen.com/item.php?id=19617

https://www.raremaps.com/gallery/detail/39647/novus-orbis-sive-america-meridionalis-et-septentrionalis-seutter-probst

AFRICAN-AMERICANS ARE THE AMERICAN INDIANS

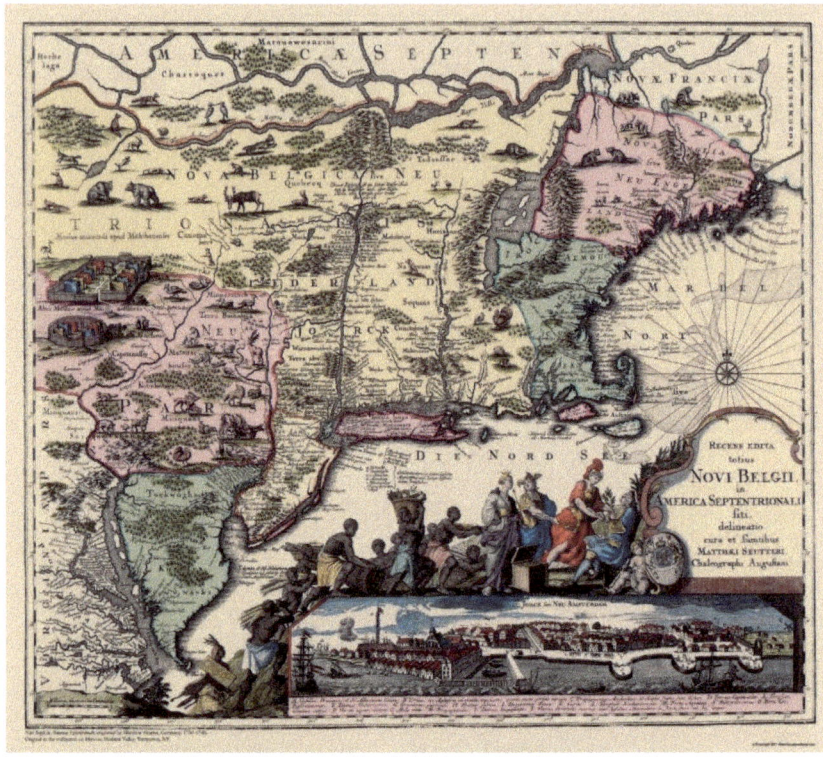

https://www.christies.com/lotfinder/Lot/seutter-matthaeus-recens-edita-totius-novi-1746269-details.aspx

N. Amsterdam, ou N Iork in Ameriq

New Amsterdam, or New York in America, New York, 1700. Native Americans in foreground with Dutch settlement of New Amsterdam beyond, and many ships in the harbor. Colored engraving by Pieter Mortier. (Photo by The New York Historical Society/Getty Images)

https://www.gettyimages.com/detail/news-photo/new-amsterdam-or-new-york-in-america-new-york-1700-native-news-photo/529332695

AFRICAN-AMERICANS ARE THE AMERICAN INDIANS

https://cepuckett.com/inventory/index.php?no_cache=20190421215152&main_page=product_info&products_id=1231

3. AMERICAN INDIAN DOLLS

antique indian doll – Etsy

Shop Vintage Native American Dolls on Wanelo

Vintage Native American Indian Dolls Boy and Girl Pair Beads Felt .

Set 2 Duck House/golden Keepsakes Native American Indian ...

Popular items for native american doll on Etsy

Native American Women Clothing Authentic | Allpix.Club

AFRICAN-AMERICANS ARE THE AMERICAN INDIANS

Carlson Native American Indian Doll Mohawk Brave from rarefinds on ...
www.rubylane.com

eBay
Cherokee Doll | eBay
Vtg Cherokee Native American Indian Doll 6201

PicClick UK
Vintage American Indian Doll With Baby • £1.99 - PicClick UK
Vintage Black Cloth Doll With Baby In Brightly Coloured Costume 11 Inches High

Vintage American Indian Doll Set Buckskin and by VandyleeVintage

Ruby Lane
12 inch Vintage American Indian Wood Doll w/ Beaded Leather Dress

Price* $123.00

This is an unusual 12 inch tall vintage American Indian carved wood doll with fringed and beaded leather dress. She has long braids of coarse human ...

Page | 126

4. BOOKS

AFRICAN-AMERICANS ARE THE AMERICAN INDIANS

Wampanoag Life

If you were a Wampanoag child in the 1620s, you would probably sleep under a cozy fur blanket on a cold night.

You and your family would live in a home called a **wetu** (WEE-too). The wetu would have rounded walls made of bark and reeds.

You would dress in clothes made of deerskin. You might also wear jewelry made of shells or beads.

You would have chores too! If you were a girl, you might help your mother farm. If you were a boy, you might help your father hunt and fish.

Chores prepared Pilgrim children and Wampanoag children for the jobs they would do as adults. People had to work hard in the 1620s!

—Blah Reinsford

AFRICAN-AMERICANS ARE THE AMERICAN INDIANS

AFRICAN-AMERICANS ARE THE AMERICAN INDIANS

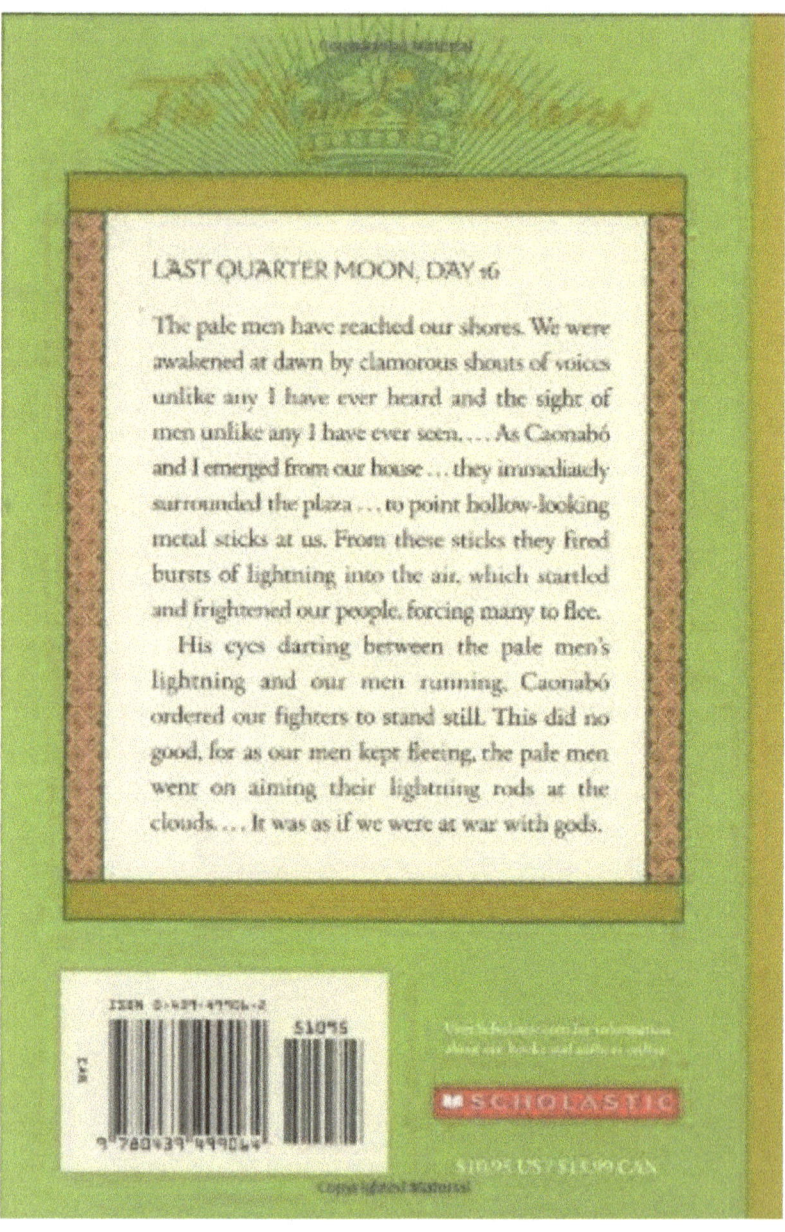

https://books.google.com/books/about/Anacaona_Golden_Flower.html?id=3nf5GwAACAAJ&source=kp_cover

AFRICAN-AMERICANS ARE THE AMERICAN INDIANS

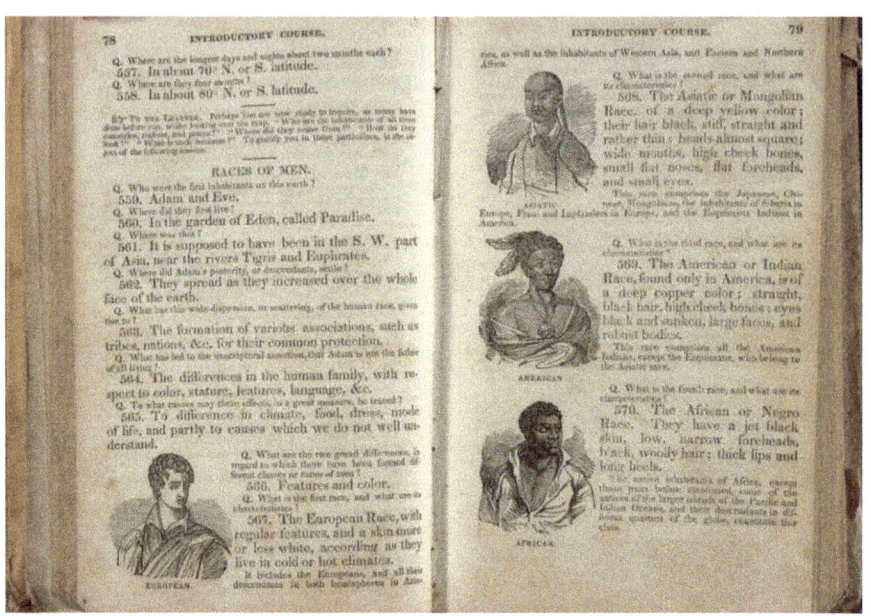

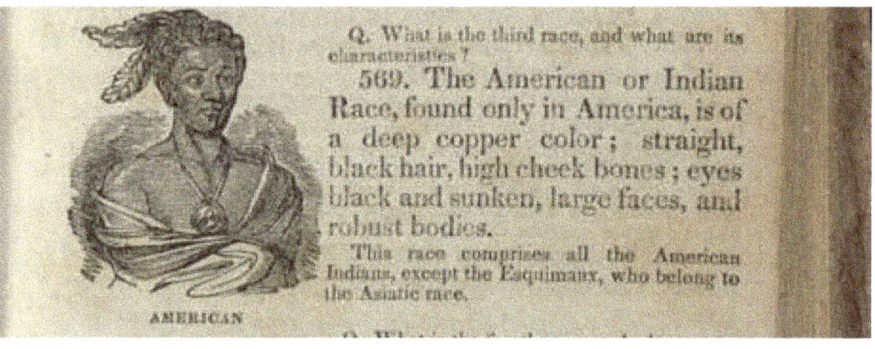

https://books.google.com/books?id=VpMZAAAAYAAJ&pg=PA79&lpg=PA79&dq=what+is+the+third+race+and+what+are+its+characteristics&source=bl&ots=8Dr3hwIv8u&sig=ACfU3U0by5E25EOKpWq356-SZoVN3NELzA&hl=en&sa=X&ved=2ahUKEwjkzbLcxeThAhUMpJ4KHU7mDUQQ6AEwBXoECAcQAQ#v=onepage&q=what%20is%20the%20third%20race%20and%20what%20are%20its%20characteristics&f=false

5. MAGAZINES

American

AMER'ICAN, *adjective* Pertaining to America

AMER'ICAN, *noun* A native of America; originally applied to the aboriginals, or copper-colored races, found here by the Europeans; but now applied to the descendants of Europeans born in America.

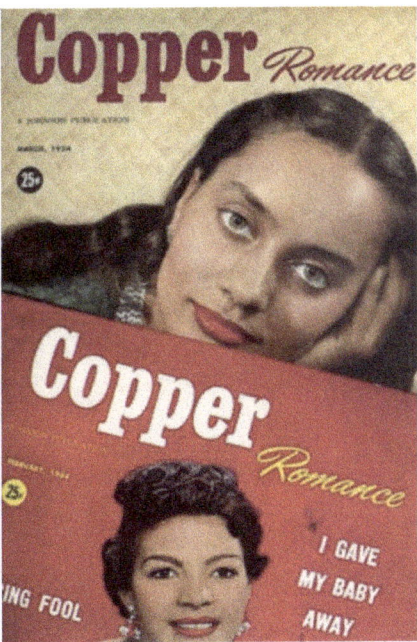

6. SONGS

9 September 1936. New York.

Fats Waller and His Rhythm (piano/vocal)

0339-1 S'posin' (RCA 730 572)
0340-1 Copper Colored Gal (RCA FPM1 7025)

Stride: The Music of Fats Waller
By Paul S Machlin

https://books.google.com/books?id=QqGuCwAAQBAJ&pg=PA141&lpg=PA141&dq=copper+colored+gal+of+mine+fats+waller&source=bl&ots=zj_x5TIICW&sig=ACfU3U07rCVmZ7Gi7bg1FLN9vCBP55hR6g&hl=en&sa=X&ved=2ahUKEwi6vp-p0-ThAhWLup4KHVjNDbk4ChDoATADegQIBRAB#v=onepage&q=copper%20colored%20gal%20of%20mine%20fats%20waller&f=false

https://youtu.be/xWieF1lphsY

7. POSTCARDS

Digital Commonwealth

A Cherokee Indian Basket
Maker on Cherokee Indian Re...

A cotton field near Houston, Texas

AFRICAN-AMERICANS ARE THE AMERICAN INDIANS

567—Indian Basket Makers, Cherokee, N. C.

AFRICAN-AMERICANS ARE THE AMERICAN INDIANS

https://www.cardcow.com/187780/indian-bay-his-bear-cub-pets-ethnic-native-americana/

AFRICAN-AMERICANS ARE THE AMERICAN INDIANS

https://www.cardcow.com/191239/happy-south-ethnic-native-americana/

8. LOGOS AND MASCOTS

AFRICAN-AMERICANS ARE THE AMERICAN INDIANS

Pinterest

cleveland indians logo history - Google Search | ...

Cleveland Indians Retro Primary Team Logo Chief Wahoo Patch (1946-1950)

eBay

Boxing Vintage Bobble Heads | eBay

An emblem of the US Negro league baseball.

Negro superseded *colored* as the most polite word for African Americans at a time when *black* was considered more offensive.[7] In Colonial America during the 1600s the term Negro was, according to one historian, also used to describe Native Americans[8] The American Negro Academy was founded in 1897, to support liberal arts education. Marcus Garvey used the word in the names of black nationalist and pan-Africanist organizations such as the Universal Negro Improvement Association (founded 1914), the *Negro World*

9. CRAYON

CHESTNUT REPLACES A COLOR CRAYOLA CALLED INDIAN RED

CHICAGO TRIBUNE

JULY 27, 1999

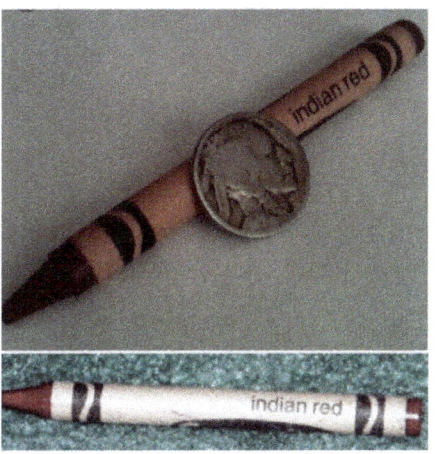

After sifting through more than 250,000 suggested names, Crayola has renamed its reddish-brown crayon to avoid misunderstandings over the color's origin.

The color indian red, which Crayola said was based on a reddish-brown pigment commonly found near India, was dropped because teachers complained students thought it described the skin color of American Indians.

https://www.chicagotribune.com/news/ct-xpm-1999-07-27-9907280062-story.html

10. POLITICAL ACTIVIST

Frederick Douglass

"All this native land talk, however, is nonsense. The native land of the American Negro is America. His bones, his muscles, his sinews, are all American."

https://teachingamericanhistory.org/library/document/the-folly-of-colonization/

swing from almost paternal affection to the most savage anger. Douglass, whom the master occasionally called "my little Indian boy" (there was something of American Indian in his appearance), remarked of him that he was "a man at war with his own soul, and with all the world around him."

https://books.google.com/books?id=4Lx8nXxmAlcC&printsec=frontcover#v=onepage&q&f=false

Malcolm X

"Our forefathers weren't the Pilgrims. We didn't land on Plymouth Rock; the rock was landed on us."

https://youtu.be/fKEzkJJReJI

https://youtu.be/lIRQmkg8ovA

http://www.vlib.us/amdocs/texts/malcolmx0364.html

"Aborigine which means what? Black folks! Yet You'll never find a white aborigine! Aborigines are called natives or they're always dark skin people, you and I are Aborigines but you don't like to be called an aborigine."

https://youtu.be/IQpl3Qvimo0

https://youtu.be/IB9NiMaeigM

James Baldwin

"In the case of the American Negro, from the moment you are born every stick and stone, every face, is white. Since you have not yet seen a mirror, you suppose you are, too. It comes as a great shock around the age of 5, 6, or 7 to discover that the flag to which you have pledged allegiance, along with everybody else, has not pledged allegiance to you. It comes as a great shock to see Gary Cooper killing off the Indians, and although you are rooting for Gary Cooper, that the Indians are you."

http://movies2.nytimes.com/books/98/03/29/specials/baldwin-dream.html

https://youtu.be/O-S2o_wX5cw

https://youtu.be/oFeoS41xe7w

Martin Luther King Jr.

"One hundred years later, the Negro is still languished in the corners of American society and finds himself in exile in his own land."

https://kinginstitute.stanford.edu/king-papers/documents/i-have-dream-address-delivered-march-washington-jobs-and-freedom

https://youtu.be/smEqnnklfYs

https://youtu.be/I47Y6VHc3Ms

"Our destiny is tied up in the destiny of America. Before the Pilgrims landed at Plymouth, we were here. Before the pen of Jefferson etched across the pages of history the majestic words of the Declaration of Independence, we were here."

https://youtu.be/TyCiENQquuA

https://youtu.be/yaOYmPEG-y0

AFRICAN-AMERICANS ARE THE AMERICAN INDIANS

11. HOLLYWOOD

(Soundbite of movie "Cadillac Records")

Unidentified Actor #1: He says he's Chuck Berry.

Unidentified Actor #2: Let me see some ID.

Mr. MOS DEF: (As Chuck Berry) All right then, ID.

Unidentified Actor #1: This license says you're Indian. That pinup make you look like a white man. What the hell are you?

Mr. DEF: (As Chuck Berry) Well, I'm a musician, and my name is Chuck Berry. And I can be whatever you need me to be to play in your fine establishment this evening.

https://youtu.be/hpZ4PX7rYM0

AFRICAN-AMERICANS ARE THE AMERICAN INDIANS

is his name?

- Ghost Dog.

- What?

- Ghost Dog.

- Ghost Dog?

- He said Ghost Dog!

- He calls himself Ghost Dog.

A lot of these black guys, gangster type guys,

they all got names like that.

- (Mr Vargo) Is that true?

- He means like the rappers.

(Sonny) The rappers got names like that - Snoop Doggy Dogg,

Ice Cube, Q-Tip, Method Man.

My favourite was always

Flavor Flav from Public Enemy.

(Sonny) He got the funky

fresh fly flava.

"Live lyrics

from the bank of reality.

"I kick da flyest dope manoeuvre

Ghost Dog Script - 百度...
https://wk.baidu.com

百度文库

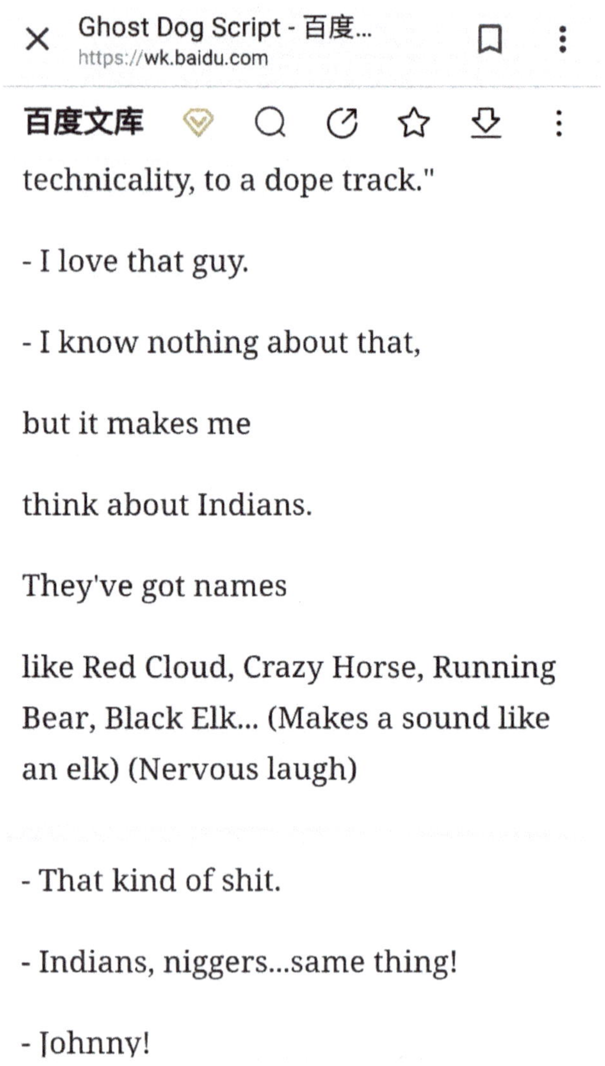

technicality, to a dope track."

- I love that guy.

- I know nothing about that,

but it makes me

think about Indians.

They've got names

like Red Cloud, Crazy Horse, Running Bear, Black Elk... (Makes a sound like an elk) (Nervous laugh)

- That kind of shit.

- Indians, niggers...same thing!

- Johnny!

https://wk.baidu.com/view/75166b27a5e9856a5612602c?pcf=2

https://youtu.be/qzQacZB0NRw

https://youtu.be/929NqFZm63c

AFRICAN-AMERICANS ARE THE AMERICAN INDIANS

Woody Strode in Two Rode Together (1961)

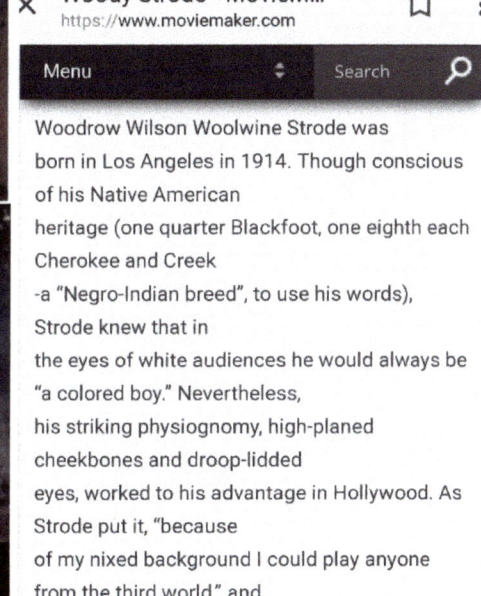

Woodrow Wilson Woolwine Strode was born in Los Angeles in 1914. Though conscious of his Native American heritage (one quarter Blackfoot, one eighth each Cherokee and Creek -a "Negro-Indian breed", to use his words), Strode knew that in the eyes of white audiences he would always be "a colored boy." Nevertheless, his striking physiognomy, high-planed cheekbones and droop-lidded eyes, worked to his advantage in Hollywood. As Strode put it, "because of my nixed background I could play anyone from the third world," and he did (a Comanche in *Two Rode Together*, an

https://www.moviemaker.com/archives/moviemaking/directing/articles-directing/woody-strode-3134/

AFRICAN-AMERICANS ARE THE AMERICAN INDIANS

https://familyguy.fandom.com/wiki/Native_American_What%27s_Happening!!

https://youtu.be/L5hSjAmOKp8

https://youtu.be/-38WxNtSgHc

Page | 150

Section 4: African Americans Look Like Past Indians

Chapter 9

DOPPELGANGER

Many people suggest that you look like the people from the place that you may have originated, and that is one way you can identify a particular group of people. You can recognize an Ethiopian, Irish, Chinese, and various ethnic groups of people when you see them. Some people say that African Americans are African. However, Most African Americans don't look like the majority of West Africans. I say West Africans because, supposedly, this is where the slaves derived. On the contrary, when you research old American Indian photos, you see how much African Americans look like American Indian Ancestors. In this section, I will show my relatives, associates, and celebrities that look like the American Indians of the past.

doppelgänger

noun | dop·pel·gäng·er | \'dä-pəl-ˌgaŋ-ər, -ˌgeŋ-, ˌdä-pəl-'\

Simple Definition of
DOPPELGÄNGER

: someone who looks like someone else

AFRICAN-AMERICANS ARE THE AMERICAN INDIANS

MY FAMILY

Pinterest
Mojave family - no date | Mojave | Pinterest | Dates and Families
Mojave Jim - Mojave Apache - 1886 https://scor lhr3-1

AFRICAN-AMERICANS ARE THE AMERICAN INDIANS

RED CROW, HEAD CHIEF OF THE BLACKFEET NATION, 1895

AFRICAN-AMERICANS ARE THE AMERICAN INDIANS

AFRICAN-AMERICANS ARE THE AMERICAN INDIANS

AFRICAN-AMERICANS ARE THE AMERICAN INDIANS

Florida Memory - View of a young Seminole girl at th...

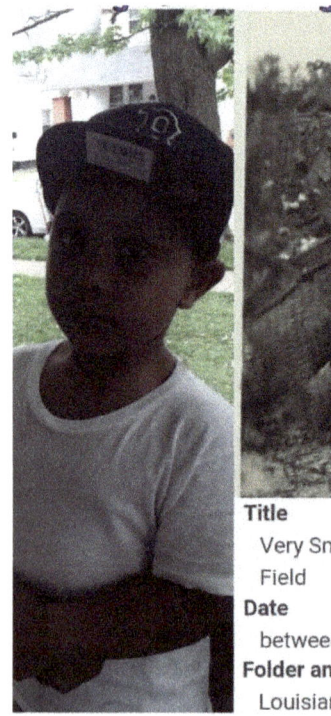

Title
Very Small American Indian Boy and Girl in a Cotton Field
Date
between 1912 and 1953
Folder and Group Title
Louisiana: Quasadis Indians; Louisiana

AFRICAN-AMERICANS ARE THE AMERICAN INDIANS

AMP · Red Shaman Intergalactic Ascens...
The Truth About Hair and why Native/Indians would keep th...

A Kiowa Girl, 1892

brownskinpopped

AFRICAN-AMERICANS ARE THE AMERICAN INDIANS

. O-o-be, The Kiowas, 1894

Samuel G Cross.....1872
Wampanoag
Indigenous Amerindian
#westernhemisphereindians #coppercolored
#a4truth #amerindians #westillhere #paperge

AFRICAN-AMERICANS ARE THE AMERICAN INDIANS

James F. Mye - Wampanaog circa

AFRICAN-AMERICANS ARE THE AMERICAN INDIANS

Florida Memory - Young Seminole woman wearing a decorated ...

African Americans Are The American Indians

Pinterest

Red Plume - Blackfeet / Sioux (Lakota) | indigeno...

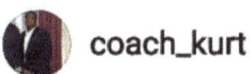 coach_kurt

AFRICAN-AMERICANS ARE THE AMERICAN INDIANS

FRIENDS

Pinterest
163 best Cherokee images on Pinterest | Cherokee indians, N...

AFRICAN-AMERICANS ARE THE AMERICAN INDIANS

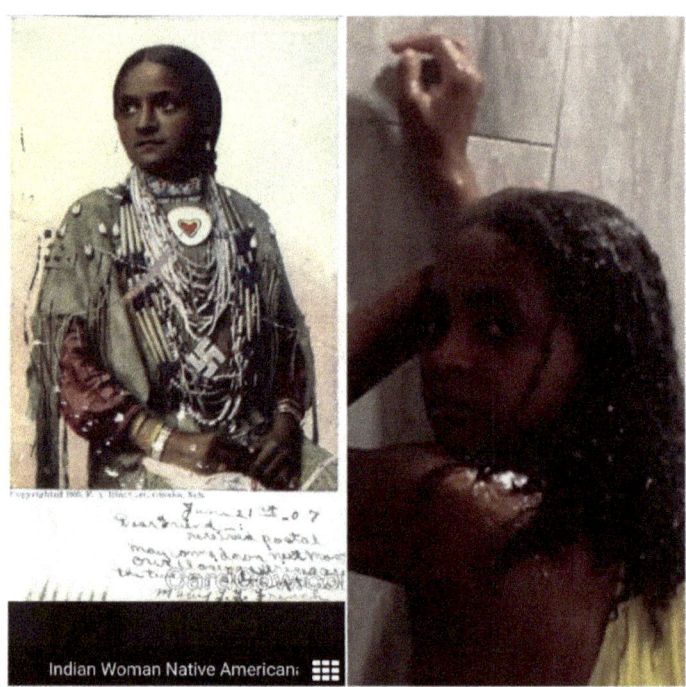

Indian Woman Native American

Pinterest

Alabama | Crazy horse, Native americans and Ind

AFRICAN-AMERICANS ARE THE AMERICAN INDIANS

American-Tribes.com - ProBoards
Photos - Cherokee |

Native American Girl, 1870-1900 msnobootysadface

AFRICAN-AMERICANS ARE THE AMERICAN INDIANS

pinterest.com
Beautiful Cherokee black indin goddess | Beautiful Cherokee

Musée McCord
M930.50.2.54 | Human races | Engraving | John Henry Walker ...

CELEBRITIES

Master P

French Creole | Choctaw Indians
www.frenchcreoles.com

AFRICAN-AMERICANS ARE THE AMERICAN INDIANS

African Americans Are The AMERICAN INDIANS

Valentino D. Harrison
(Bobby - Boyz in da Hood)

Pinterest

Grand L. Bush (remember him from Colors?) was in...

Grand L. Bush (remember him from Colors?) w
Roots.

AFRICAN-AMERICANS ARE THE AMERICAN INDIANS

Pinterest
296 best Native American - Blackfoot images on Pinterest ...

Three Bulls (the brother of Crowfoot) - Blackfoot (Siksika

Michael Coylar

Chris Brown
chrisbrown

Following

Just found out I'm from the Pamunkey Indian Tribe! Wow, thats awesome!

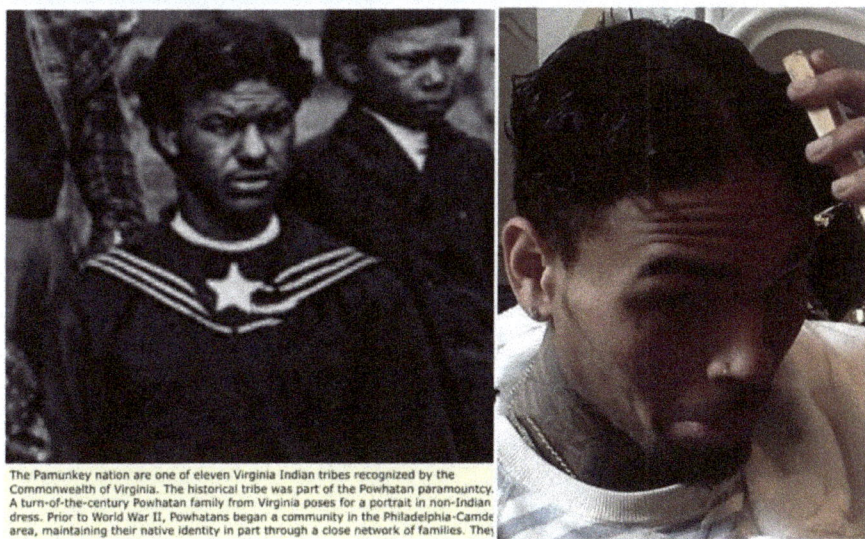

The Pamunkey nation are one of eleven Virginia Indian tribes recognized by the Commonwealth of Virginia. The historical tribe was part of the Powhatan paramountcy. A turn-of-the-century Powhatan family from Virginia poses for a portrait in non-Indian dress. Prior to World War II, Powhatans began a community in the Philadelphia-Camden area, maintaining their native identity in part through a close network of families. They

AFRICAN-AMERICANS ARE THE AMERICAN INDIANS

312 best Cherokee Nation images on Pinterest | Cheroke...
Huckleberry Downing - Cherokee - circa 1868

Waka Flocka

Three Young Blackfoot Men

Image No: NA-3981-6 Title: Three young Blackfoot men. Date: [ca. 1887] Photographer/Illustrator: Ross, Alexander

AFRICAN-AMERICANS ARE THE AMERICAN INDIANS

PicClick
Native American Crow Indian Man "Which Way" - Historic P...
Native American Assinaboine "Cloud Man" - 1898 - Historic Photo Print
Images may be subject to copyright.

Bill Duke

AMP · Pinterest
Comanche Indians | coming

Shannon Sharpe

AFRICAN-AMERICANS ARE THE AMERICAN INDIANS

Quora
Is it true that Native Americans don't grow beards? - Quora

Dick Gregory

Floyd Mayweather Sr.

AFRICAN-AMERICANS ARE THE AMERICAN INDIANS

Pinterest
California, Facials and Culture on Pinterest
Edward S. Curtis's The North American Indian - volume 14 facing: page 134 A Chukchansi Yoku

UPI.com
Whoopi Goldberg News | Quotes Wiki - UPI.com

AFRICAN-AMERICANS ARE THE AMERICAN INDIANS

www.pinterest.com
Antonitto, an Apache man, with his hair in hair rolls or dreadlocks wrap...

Cam Newton
Carolina Panthers QB

www.camerontradingpost.com
LMP098 - BLACK AND WHITE SOUTHWESTERN & NATIVE AMERI..

Ray Allen

AFRICAN-AMERICANS ARE THE AMERICAN INDIANS

www.pinterest.com
1000+ images about American Indians on Pinterest | Edward Curtis..

Faizon love

American Indian Chief **Flava Flav**

AFRICAN-AMERICANS ARE THE AMERICAN INDIANS

www.pinterest.com
A Crow husband and wife. Old Crow and Pretty Medicine Pipe. Photo ...

Young Joc

www.old-picture.com
Crow Indian

Monica Calhoun

www.pinterest.com
1000+ ideas about Cherokee Indian Women on Pinterest | Cherokee ...

Manny Fresh

www.afterimagegallery.com
Edward Curtis, A Cree Girl

Queen Latifah

AFRICAN-AMERICANS ARE THE AMERICAN INDIANS

Iroquois Indigenous....circa 1913
#westernhemisphereindians #copperc
#a4truth #amerindians #westillhere #p

Lady Of Rage (Baby D)

Mikasuki Indian Elizabeth Osceola

Erykah Badu

AFRICAN-AMERICANS ARE THE AMERICAN INDIANS

Mike Epps

Legends of Kansas
The Potawatomi Indians of

Pinterest
Pin by Armando on Native Americans - Portraits | Pi...
Historical pictures

Scottie Pippen

AFRICAN-AMERICANS ARE THE AMERICAN INDIANS

Jasmine Guy

Indian Chief's Daughter Visits

Rainbow Sistesso, Sioux Indian girl and grand-daughter of Chief Yellow Cloud, who died in 1927 at the age of 116 years, is in Los Angeles after having hiked from Chicago.

Sistesso does her walking at night, often traveling from thirty-five to forty miles at one time. Coming via Death Valley last week she was forced to go without food and water two days when her baggage was lost. She was saved by the arrival of a stagecoach.

While here she will be the guest of Little Chief White Eagle.

RAINBOW SISTESSO

SECTION 5: Paper Genocide Of The American Indian

Chapter 10
FROM INDIAN TO AFRICAN THROUGH RECLASSIFICATION

Most people believe that European diseases decimated the American Indians. However, it was reclassification that destroyed the American Indians. When the Europeans arrived in the Americas, they considered it to be paradise, and they wanted to stay. They understood that they would have to eliminate the indigenous population for this to take place.

They knew that they could not kill off the American Indian population, so they figured out another way. They changed the identity of the Indians several times throughout the centuries so that the new generations would believe that they came from another land. The constant reclassification allowed more Europeans to immigrate and occupy more land in the Americas. In this section, I will show how they kept changing their identity through laws, enslavement, census records, etc. I will utilize various sources and examples of my family.

reclassification
noun
re·clas·si·fi·ca·tion | \ (ˌ)rē-ˌkla-sə-fə-ˈkā-shən 🔊 \
plural **reclassifications**

Definition of *reclassification*
: the act or process of classifying something again or anew

AFRICAN-AMERICANS ARE THE AMERICAN INDIANS

In attempting to lay before the Public a sketch of the History of the Red Indians of North America, with a view to excite a general sympathy in behalf of an oppressed and suffering people, I am aware of the great importance of my undertaking, and sensibly feel my inability to stand forward as an advocate, in any degree equal to the task I have thus imposed on myself.

With but few exceptions, the American Indians have been abandoned by the Christian world, as a cruel, blood-thirsty, and treacherous race, incapable of civilization, and therefore, unworthy of that attention which the inhabitants of other barbarous climes have received from the zeal and devotion of many learned and pious members of society.—Thousands have raised their voices against the wrongs of our black brethren of Africa. From one end of Europe to the other, the humane have been aroused to a sense of their injuries, and are now actively engaged in the prosecution of every measure calculated to alleviate their sufferings; while but few have been stimulated to similar exertions in behalf of the Red American Indians, from whose native soil the wealth of a great portion of the civilized world has been derived. The African is submissive; his patient endurance of labour renders his servile and debased state important to us; he is therefore, preserved. The North American Indian, on the contrary, prefers banishment, and even death, to slavery; but *his* lands are serviceable to us, therefore his extinction

b 2

viii   PREFACE.

seems to be desired. The one submits to the yoke,—we oppress and pity him: the other disdains to become the servant of man—and his whole race is devoted to gradual extermination; for such must be the inevitable consequence of all those measures which have been, and still are in operation against him, though their infliction is marked by different shades of guilt. In a few ages, perhaps a few years, these sons of Edom will be so far removed from the reach or eye of any but those engaged in the work of destruction, that no trace will be left to posterity of the wrongs which have been perpetrated upon the Aborigines of the great American Continent.

https://books.google.com/books?id=ivJOAAAAcAAJ&pg=PR7&lpg=PR7&dq=the+north+american+indian+on+the+contrary,+prefer+banishment&source=bl&ots=_ksEAJNs-x&sig=ACfU3U1WrQLDgAA73IFoHNSxS_KtdxuJYw&hl=en&sa=X&ved=2ahUKEwjWuKT3lvzhAhVFhq0KHTjfCksQ6AEwCXoECAQQAQ#v=onepage&q=the%20north%20american%20indian%20on%20the%20contrary%2C%20prefer%20banishment&f=false

FROM INDIAN TO NEGRO

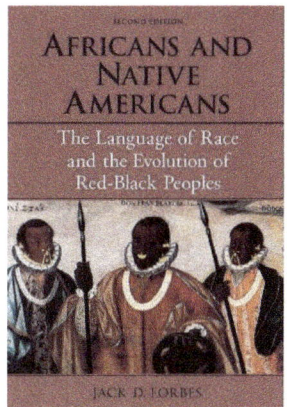

In July 1559 Nóbrega wrote to Portugal that the Christians (Portuguese) were, for the most part, 'living in the interior areas with their *negras* as mistresses' and that their slaves were also living together without proper marriage. Nóbrega also wrote, in a letter to the governor, that 'eight *negros* of Guiné' were killed by a party of 'sixty valiant *negros*'. By using '*negros* of Guiné' for Africans and *negros* for native Americans, Nóbrega is able to refer to both in the same sentence.

In September 1561 Father Leonard Do Vale wrote to Rome that another Jesuit was *muy suave* to 'whites as to *negros*' in his work in Brazil. The next year, June 1562, Do Vale also wrote to Rome using *os negros* for Americans while in June 1565 he wrote to the Jesuits of Portugal about *hum negro bautizado* and he also uses *o negro* for a Tamóio. In a footnote the editor states:

"Negro" por "Indio" (não negro de África); o que é evidente na sequência deste mesmo parágrafo, aplicado ao Indio Tamóio. ... Donde se segue que a intromissão aqui de negro por indio parece da responsabilidade de quem no momento superintendia na Europa as trabalho destas cópias.

Thus *Negro* is used for 'Indian', not for someone from Africa. The editor suggests that a European copyist might have been responsible for this usage, but as we have seen it is too consistent over the years to require such an explanation. In any case, it is clear that many Iberians and Italians, whether in Europe or America, were comfortable in using *negro*, *negri*, etc., for Americans.[24]

https://books.google.com/books?id=5D17DwAAQBAJ&pg=PT86&lpg=PT86&dq=%22negro%22+por+%22indio%22+(+nao+negro+de+africa)&source=bl&ots=reSPCxCJgK&sig=ACfU3U3mIgEInd5wKfJt_Woc8CRdL5LDvA&hl=en&sa=X&ved=2ahUKEwjui-rV-fvhAhVImK0KHYLKBV44ChDoATABegQIBRAB#v=onepage&q=%22negro%22%20por%20%22indio%22%20(%20nao%20negro%20de%20africa)&f=false

AFRICAN-AMERICANS ARE THE AMERICAN INDIANS

INDIAN SLAVERY IN COLONIAL TIMES WITHIN THE PRESENT LIMITS OF THE UNITED STATES

BY

ALMON WHEELER LAUBER, Ph.M.

SUBMITTED IN PARTIAL FULFILMENT OF THE REQUIREMENTS
FOR THE DEGREE OF DOCTOR OF PHILOSOPHY
IN THE
FACULTY OF POLITICAL SCIENCE
COLUMBIA UNIVERSITY

NEW YORK
1913

CHAPTER IV

THE NUMBER OF INDIAN SLAVES

To arrive at any knowledge of the exact number of Indian slaves in any of the English colonies is impossible. Census reports and other vital statistics are infrequent or lacking, especially in the early colonial period; and often in such statistics as are extant Indian slaves either receive no mention, or are classed with negro slaves without distinction. From existing records, however, one is able to obtain a knowledge of the comparative numbers in the different groups of colonies, and to some extent in the individual colonies, during the colonial period. New England and the southern colonies were the sections that employed Indian slave labor most extensively, the south taking precedence, for climatic conditions there were more favorable, and economic conditions made necessary a larger quantity of servile labor than was required in the north.[1] Yet New England made use of the natives as slaves as long as they lasted,[2] and drew further supplies from Maine,[3] the Carolinas,[4] and other districts.[5]

Among the English colonies, the Carolinas stood first

---

[1] Doyle, *English Colonies in America, The Puritan Colonies*, ii, p. 506.
[2] *I. e.*, until after the Pequot and King Philip Wars.
[3] Freeman, *The History of Cape Cod*, p. 72.
[4] *Connecticut Colonial Records*, 1715, p. 516.
[5] Coffin, *A Sketch of the History of Newbury*, etc., p. 337; *Essex Institute Historical Collections*, vii, p. 73; *Connecticut Colonial Records*, 1711, p. 233.

357]

https://books.google.com/books?id=OtFMAQAAMAAJ&pg=PA357&lpg=PA357&dq=to+arrive+at+any+knowledge+of+the+exact+number+of+indian+slaves+in+english+colonies+is+impossible.+census+reports&source=bl&ots=g5whbFicEQ&sig=ACfU3U2CgcvzlQieb9qZDnjTEgjqbfm8YA&hl=en&sa=X&ved=2ahUKEwiYsd6V_fvhAhUR0awKHYIfDTEQ6AEwC3oECAgQAQ#v=onepage&q=to%20arrive%20at%20any%20knowledge%20of%20the%20exact%20number%20of%20indian%20slaves%20in%20english%20colonies%20is%20impossible.%20census%20reports&f=false

AFRICAN-AMERICANS ARE THE AMERICAN INDIANS

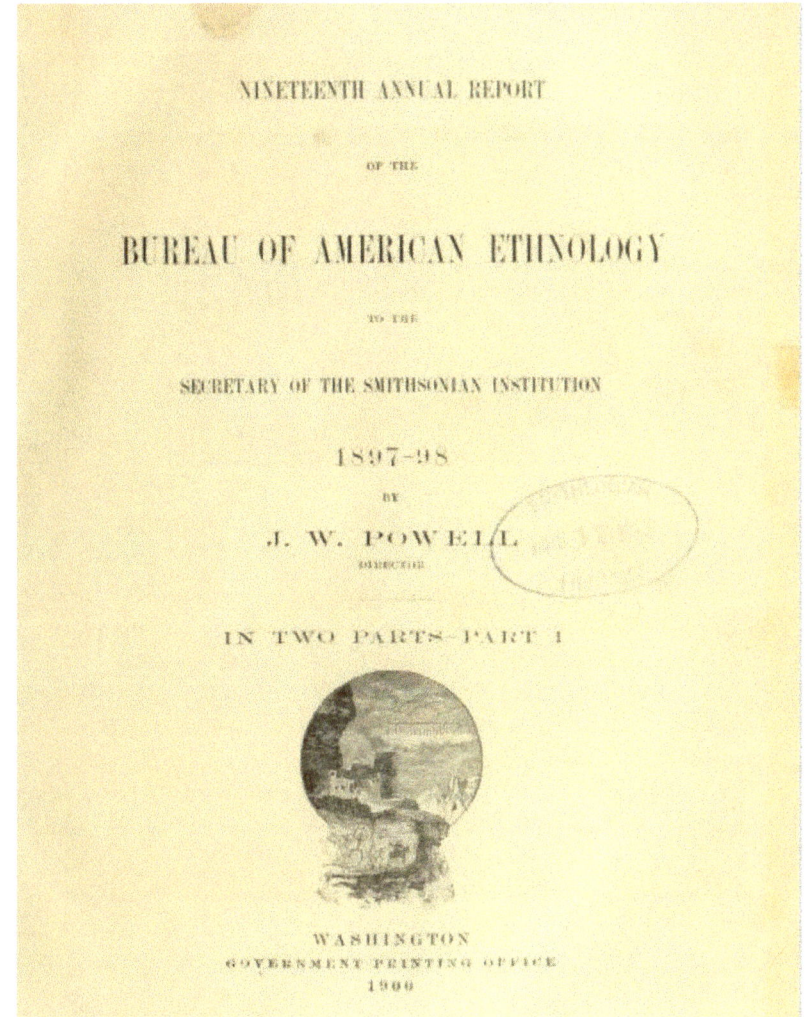

by his encouragement of slave hunts. Furthermore, as the coast tribes dwindled they were compelled to associate and intermarry with the negroes until they finally lost their identity and were classed with that race, so that a considerable proportion of the blood of the southern negroes is unquestionably Indian.

https://library.si.edu/digital-library/book/annualreportofbu191smit

AFRICAN-AMERICANS ARE THE AMERICAN INDIANS

TAKE THE JOURNEY

it comes" courses through my body. For the next four hours the three of us carefully go through the files in each box, looking for documents we could use to create our lesson. We religiously cross-reference what we had indicated that might be of interest. Priya and I go through the boxes of Plecker's correspondence while Amy looks through the box loaded with newspaper articles and opinion pieces of the time period. It is both heartening and sickening at the same time.

Much of what Priya and I encounter are letters of Plecker's that supported the proposed passing of similar legislation in states such as North Carolina, Ohio, Massachusetts, Arkansas, Texas, Oklahoma, Georgia, Tennessee, and Mississippi, and the District of Columbia. Many of the letters were responses to families making inquiries about birth and marriage record status. In most of them Plecker denied anyone who requested an identity change. He was a cagey old fox, too, obsessively researching family names long before people had written to him. If they had surnames that he had researched and deemed "Indian," requestors never had a chance to get the identity change to the "white" status they desired. To Plecker all Virginia Indians were black; he called them "Negros in feathers." Plecker pursued deep research into family names just to make certain no

https://books.google.com/books?id=lpaqDgAAQBAJ&pg=PA18&lpg=PA18&dq=plecker+who+called+indians+negroes+in+feathers&source=bl&ots=YrjumkCFeY&sig=ACfU3U3BB_GS5hmkxOrUKxoldGdr1Jlxvg&hl=en&sa=X&ved=2ahUKEwjGvdHxg_zhAhVph-AKHROkBs0Q6AEwCXoECAkQAQ#v=onepage&q=plecker%20who%20called%20indians%20negroes%20in%20feathers&f=false

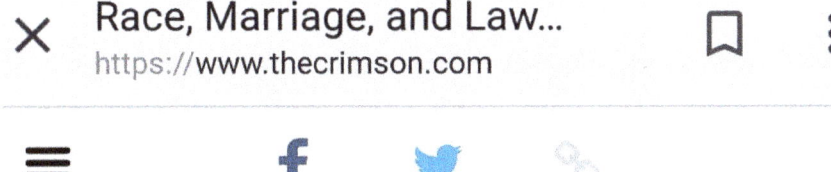

Furthermore, if a man is an inhabitant of an Indian tribal reservation and has at least one Indian grandparent *and* less than one-sixteenth "Negro blood," then despite the state's definition of a Negro he may be regarded as an Indian on the reservation. Once he leaves the reservation, however, he undergoes a legal metamorphosis and becomes a Negro. Of course he can then move to

https://www.thecrimson.com/article/1963/12/17/race-marriage-and-law-pamerican-racism/

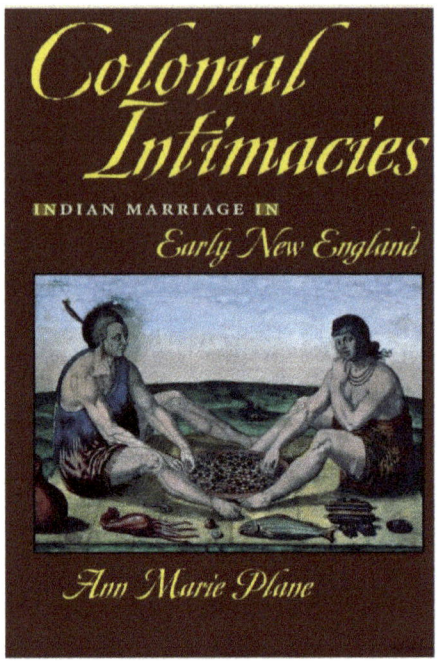

232   *Notes to Pages 146–49*

82. On intermarriage, see Mandell, "Shifting Boundaries of Race and Ethnicity," pp. 466–501. In the second half of the eighteenth century, designations shifted away from "Indian" or "mustee" and toward "mulatto" and "Negro" or "black" as Indian identity succumbed to the increasingly biracial preoccupations of Euro-American officials; see Ruth Wallis Herndon and Ella Wilcox Seketau, "The Right to a Name: The Narragansett People and Rhode Island Officials in the Revolutionary Era," *Ethnohistory* 44, no. 3 (1997): 444–47.

https://books.google.com/books?id=8FhuDwAAQBAJ&pg=PA232&lpg=PA232&dq=in+the+second+half+of+the+eighteenth+century,+designation+shifted+away+from+indian+or+mustee&source=bl&ots=t7RVrzaKHp&sig=ACfU3U3a1MMQ2tPsQUkl37ZpbrT2HwykBA&hl=en&sa=X&ved=2ahUKEwiajun6mPzhAhUMUa0KHaaRBu4Q6AEwAHoECAgQAQ#v=onepage&q=in%20the%20second%20half%20of%20the%20eighteenth%20century%2C%20designation%20shifted%20away%20from%20indian%20or%20mustee&f=false

WHO IS AN INDIAN? WHO IS A NEGRO?
Virginia Indians in the World War II Draft

by PAUL T. MURRAY[*]

WHO is an Indian? Who is a Negro? How does one decide a person's race? Few Americans have ever had the occasion to ponder deeply these questions. In most cases the answer is self-evident. A racial label is usually assigned by reference to obvious physical criteria, such as skin color, hair texture, and facial characteristics. But in any multiracial society there are some people who cannot be neatly placed into one of a limited number of categories. Further, in a society where one's social position depends heavily upon race, resolving questions of racial classification becomes a serious issue. People of mixed race may attempt to improve their position by changing their racial designation. Such an attempt forces government officials to confront directly the delicate issue of the determination of race. Their decisions have far-reaching consequences, not only for the people directly involved, but also for the entire society.

During the Second World War a small group of Virginia Indians challenged the prevailing system of racial classification. When called to register with the Selective Service System, they listed their race as Indian. Local draft boards, however, would not accept this claim. They recalled that in antebellum days some of the registrants' ancestors had married free Negroes. Based on this "evidence," the boards insisted that the proper classification for all alleged Indians was "Negro."[1] The Indians were adamant in refusing this designation. Draft board members were equally determined not to classify the men as Indians because such a classification would mean that they would be sent to military service together with whites. For five years the Indians appealed this decision through the channels of the state and federal Selective Service bureau-

---

[*] Paul T. Murray is an associate professor of sociology at Siena College in Loudonville, New York. The author appreciates the encouragement and careful criticism of Thomas Kelly, John Vallely, and the outside readers of the *Virginia Magazine*.

[1] When referring to Selective Service classifications and policies I shall use the terms "Negro" and "Indian," because these were the official designations being contested.

FROM INDIAN TO MUSTEE AND MULATTO

term "Mustee" as a first step in transforming "Indians" into "Negroes." In the latter half of the eighteenth century, town clerks used "Mustee" most frequently to describe children being bound out in indenture contracts. Where clerks record the parentage of these "Mustee" children, it is always the *mother* who is identified as Indian.[62] But what of the father? The use of "Mustee" indicates that officials considered the child to have a non-Indian father, even though no details about the father are provided. The implications of this designation are enormous. In the tribes of southern New England, a child was a member of the mother's clan and tribe, regardless of who the father was. But in the world of European Americans, inheritance came through the father. By denying "Mustee" children an "Indian" father, officials prepared the ground to deny these children any rights they might later claim as descendants of Narragansett or other native fathers.[63]

By such means, officials transformed Indians into "Mustees" and transformed both of these into "Negroes" and "blacks." The labels are applied with such a haphazard and casual hand in the record that the changes are easy to overlook. They would have passed undetected if we had assumed that a clerk used the same racial designation each time he referred to a particular individual. This is not so. The East Greenwich town clerk described Benjamin Austin as "Indian" in 1767, but as "a Malatoo Fellow" in 1768.[64] Sarah Hill was an "Indian or

https://books.google.com/books?id=LXrgK29zl2QC&pg=PT265&lpg=PT265&dq=term+mustee+as+a+first+step+in+transforming+indians+into+negroes&source=bl&ots=vlToD33cQi&sig=ACfU3U3EksmqiN-380CivMbtHvZ2vxEPTA&hl=en&sa=X&ved=2ahUKEwid6MTOh_zhAhXLsVQKHQxpCacQ6AEwAHoECAEQAQ#v=onepage&q=term%20mustee%20as%20a%20first%20step%20in%20transforming%20indians%20into%20negroes&f=false

Womack.

- ***Sybill a Mulatto*** V. Joseph Ashbrooke – dismissed.

(Sibell was most likely less than full blooded Indian...she was described as Indian up to the point it was determined that she was legally a slave, then she was described as mulatto...use of the term is influenced by the status of her servitude)

Dinwiddie County, VA

18 AUG 1794...registered free papers of "Nancy Coleman a dark brown, well made ***mulatto woman***..freed by judgement of the Gen'l Court of John Hrdaway ***being a descendant of an Indian.***"

10 FEB 1798...registered free papers of "Daniel Coleman a dark brown ***free Negro, or Indian...formerly*** held as a slave by Joseph Hardaway but obtained his freedom by a judgment of the Gen'l Court."

14 AUG 1800...registered free papers of "Hagar Jumper a dark brown ***Mulatto or Indian woman*** short bushy hair, obtained her freedom from Stephen Dance as ***being a descendant of an Indian.***"

27 MAY 1805...registered free papers of "Betty Coleman a dark brown ***Negro woman***...formerly held as a slave by John Hardaway...liberated by judgment of the Gen'l Court as ***descended of an Indian.***"

Goochland County, VA

7 MAR 1756...Elizabeth, daughter of Ruth Matthews, ***a free mulattoe***, baptized by the Rev. William Douglas of St. James Northam Parish.

26 SEP 1757....Cumberland County Court to bind out the children of Ruth Matthews, ***an Indian woman***, to William Fleming.

(Ruth is described as 'a free mulatto' at one time, 'an Indian' at another.)

Henrico County, VA

5 MAY 1712.....Thomas Chamberlayne brings before this Court his servant ***Mulatto man Robin*** and informed the Court that he hath several times run away. Ordered to serve one year from (release date).

- ***Robin Indian*** (filed) against Major Chamberlayne... next Court.

FEB 1712....***Robin Indian*** ordered free from Thomas Chamberlayne's service at end of year's service.

MARCH 1713....Thomas Chamberlayne against his servant ***Robin Mulatto*** hath unlawfully absented himself for 16 weeks.

(Robin is described as Mulatto until he is determined to be illegally held as a slave, then he is described as Indian...use of the term is influenced by his servitude...his former master tactfully uses the term Mulatto to influence the Court to return him to slavery)

APR 1722...***Peg an Indian*** woman servant belonging to Richard Ligon appeared...be adjudged free..he be summoned.

JUN 1722...***Peg a Mulatto*** servant born in this County whose ***mother was an Indian*** intitled to freedom at the age of thirty years, having petitioned for her freedom against her master Richard Ligon.

(Mulatto is used here to describe an Indian half-blood)

service at end of year's service.

MARCH 1713....Thomas Chamberlayne against his servant **Robin Mulatto** hath unlawfully absented himself for 16 weeks.
(Robin is described as Mulatto until he is determined to be illegally held as a slave, then he is described as Indian...use of the term is influenced by his servitude...his former master tactfully uses the term Mulatto to influence the Court to return him to slavery)

APR 1722...**Peg an Indian** woman servant belonging to Richard Ligon appeared...be adjudged free..he be summoned.

JUN 1722...**Peg a Mulatto** servant born in this County whose **mother was an Indian** intitled to freedom at the age of thirty years, having petitioned for her freedom against her master Richard Ligon.
(Mulatto is used here to describe an Indian half-blood)

JAN 1737....petition of **Tom a Mulatto or Mustee** setting forth that he is the grandson of a white free woman and hast a just right to freedom but that his master Alexander Trent contrary to law or equity detains him in slavery.
(the terms Mulatto and Mustee are used here interchangeably)

JUL 1739...On the petition of **Indian Jamey alias James Musttie** is exempted from paying County Levyes.

NOV 1740...petition of Thomas Baugh it is ordered that the Church Wardens of Dale Parish do bind out **Joe a Mulatto the son of Nan an Indian woman** according to law.
(Mulatto is used here to describe an Indian half-blood)

18 NOV 1747....will of Richard Randolph...to my son John the third part of my slaves, he taking **my two Negroes, Indian John and Essex** as a part of his third which two Negroes I propose he should have.
(an Indian is described here as a 'Negro'...the term is influenced by his servitude)

2 DEC 1754....Church wardens of Henrico Parish do bind out Ezekiel Scott and Sarah Scott, children of John Scott, Tommy son of **Indian Nan**, Henry Cockran son of John Cockran, and Isham Roughton **an Indian** according to Law.

5 MAR 1759....Ordered that the Church Wardens of Henrico Parish bind out Ben Scott and Roger **an Indian Boy** according to Law.

http://www.historical-melungeons.com/mixed_bloods.html

AFRICAN-AMERICANS ARE THE AMERICAN INDIANS

African descent." In Alabama, however, Indians are mulattoes, according to the courts, and therefore cannot marry whites. Filipinos in Louisiana must be

https://www.thecrimson.com/article/1963/12/17/race-marriage-and-law-pamerican-racism/

FROM INDIAN TO COLORED

records. In some cases such as in Virginia, even when people were designated as Indians on birth or death certificates or other public records, their records were changed to reflect "colored." Census takers, determining a person's race by their looks, often recorded mixed-race people as simply black, not Indian.

https://www.thoughtco.com/untold-history-of-american-indian-slavery-2477982

ACTS
AND
RESOLVES
PASSED BY THE
General Court of Massachusetts,
IN THE YEAR
1869,
TOGETHER WITH
THE MESSAGES OF THE GOVERNOR, A LIST OF THE CIVIL GOVERNMENT, CHANGES OF NAMES OF PERSONS, ETC., ETC., ETC.

PUBLISHED BY THE
SECRETARY OF THE COMMONWEALTH.

BOSTON:
WRIGHT & POTTER, STATE PRINTERS,
79 Milk Street, (corner of Federal.)
1869.

Approved June 23, 1869.

Chap. 463   AN ACT TO ENFRANCHISE THE INDIANS OF THE COMMONWEALTH.

Be it enacted, &c., as follows:

Indians, &c., made citizens.

SECTION 1. All Indians and people of color, heretofore known and called Indians, within this Commonwealth, are hereby made and declared to be citizens of the Commonwealth, and entitled to all the rights, privileges and immunities, and subject to all the duties and liabilities to which citizens of this Commonwealth are entitled or subject.

https://books.google.com/books?id=3UsSAAAAYAAJ&pg=PA780&lpg=PA780&dq=all+indians+and+people+of+color,+heretofore+known+and+called+people+of+color&source=bl&ots=6QLf81YR_n&sig=ACfU3U2GqqUeWi31L70gIYNdr2M17v6L2A&hl=en&sa=X&ved=2ahUKEwi9mYj3jPzhAhUon-AKHTNCCJcQ6AEwB3oECAcQAQ#v=onepage&q=all%20indians%20and%20people%20of%20color%2C%20heretofore%20known%20and%20called%20people%20of%20color&f=false

FROM INDIAN TO AFRICAN AMERICAN

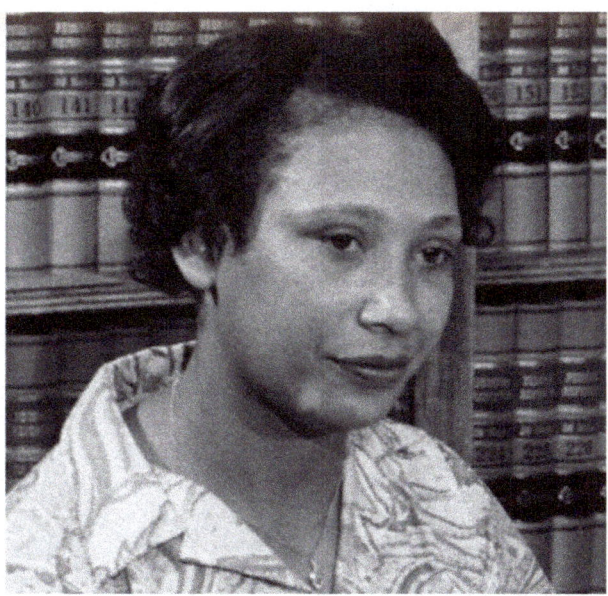

Mildred Loving

*Mildred Loving was born on this date in 1939. She was an African and Native American activist.

Born Mildred Delores Jeter, she was African American and Rappahannock Native American descent. She met Richard Loving a white man when she was 11 and he was 17. He was a family friend and years later they began dating. They lived in the

https://aaregistry.org/story/mildred-jeter-loving-love-will-find-a-way/

× 🔒 Loving v Virginia: What Y... 🔖 ⋮
tps://time-com.cdn.ampproject.org

myth than reality. While researching my book *That the Blood Stay Pure: African Americans, Native Americans and the Predicament of Race and Identity in Virginia*, I spoke to Mildred Loving, who died in 2008. "<u>I am not black</u>," she told me during a 2004 interview. "<u>I have no black ancestry. I am Indian-Rappahannock</u>. I told the people so when they came to arrest me."

At approximately 2 a.m. on July 11, 1958, Sheriff R. Garnett Brooks and his deputies barged into the couple's bedroom. "What are you doing in bed with this woman?" Brooks barked as he shined his flashlight on the startled couple. Mildred responded, "I'm his wife." She pointed to the framed marriage license displayed on the dresser. The document read: "Richard Perry Loving, white, Mildred Delores Jeter, <u>Indian</u>."

http://time.com/4362508/loving-v-virginia-personas/

Marriage Certificate

Page | 196

CENSUS RECORDS

In this section, I will show my family and how they were reclassified numerous times, almost a hundred years. In the early times of the census, American Indians were categorized differently. I will show two of my ancestors on my maternal side, **JASON BASS & OBA(E)DIAH BASS.** I am utilizing www.familysearch.org.

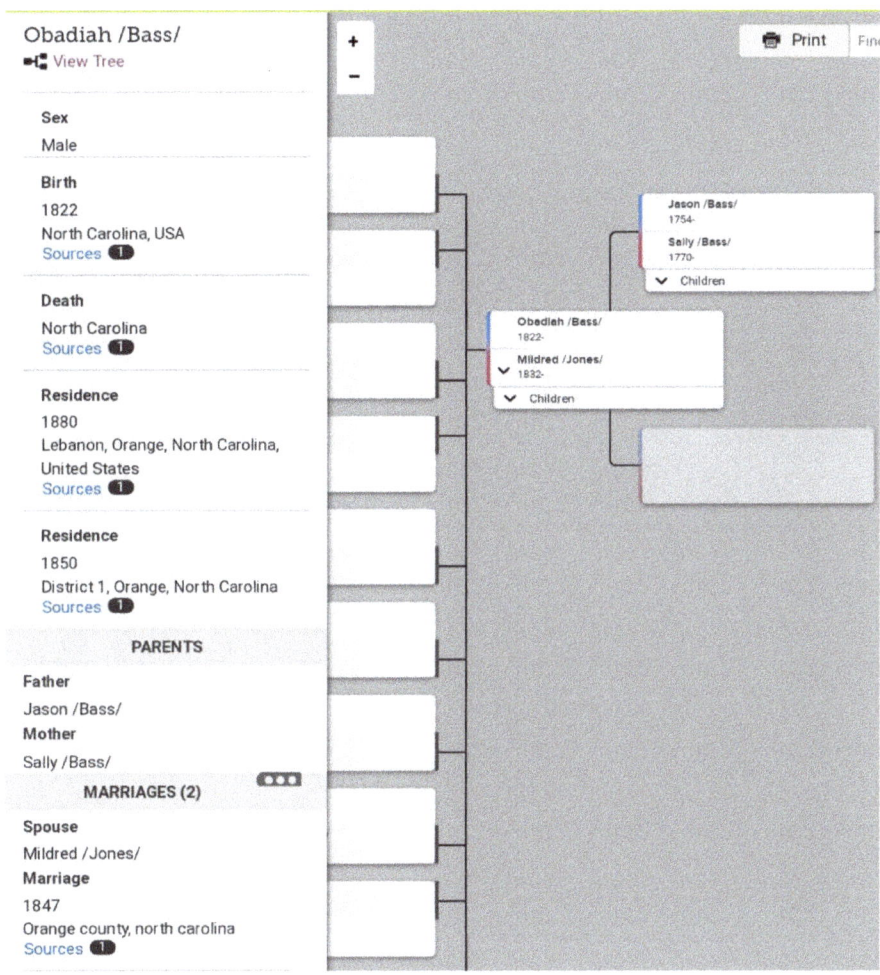

1820 – Indians living off of reservations would have been recorded in the "free colored persons" categories. Other options were free whites, slaves and "all others except Indians not taxed."

Jason Bass
United States Census, 1820

Name:	Jason Bass
Event Type:	Census
Event Date:	1820
Event Place:	Oxford, Granville, North Carolina, United States
Page:	3

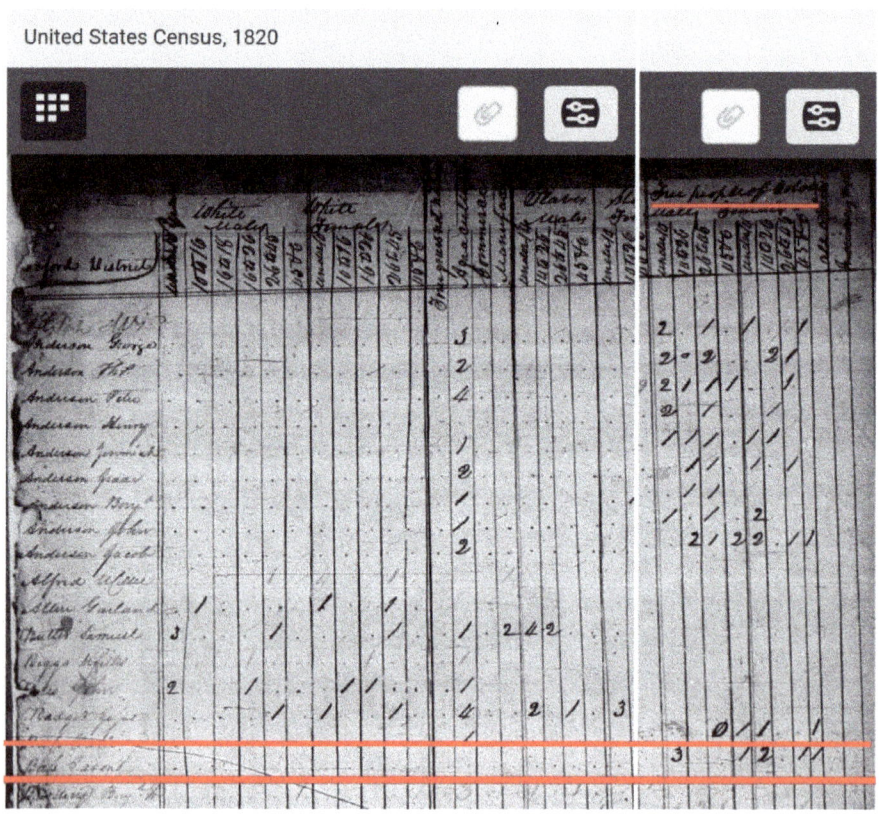

AFRICAN-AMERICANS ARE THE AMERICAN INDIANS

1830 – Indians living off of reservations and not "wild" would have been recorded in the "free colored persons" category. Other options were free whites and slaves.

1840 – Essentially the same as 1830 with the exception that an additional column labeled "pensioners for revolutionary or military services" with a blank for the pensioner's name to be included and applies to all individuals.

Jason Bass

United States Census, 1840

Name:	Jason Bass
Event Type:	Census
Event Date:	1840
Event Place:	Person, North Carolina, United States
Page:	299

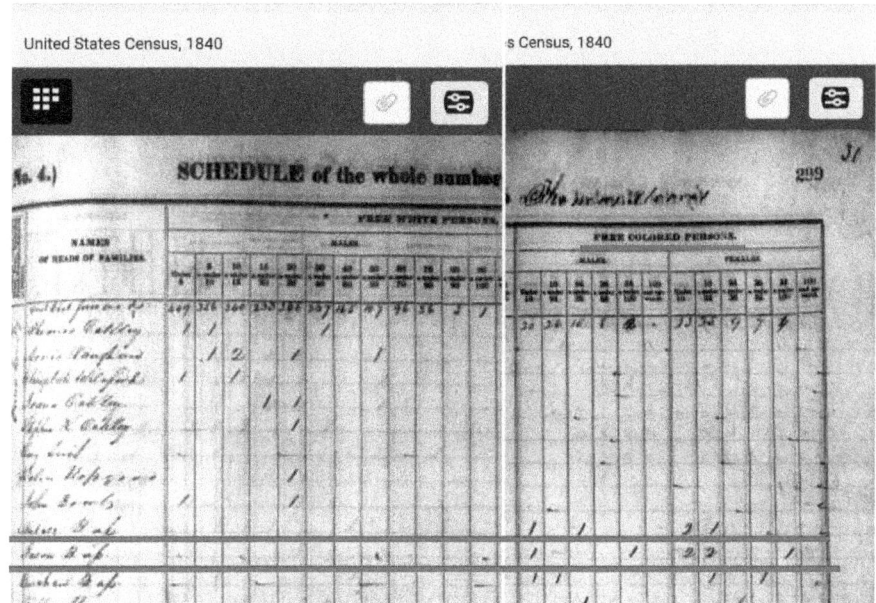

1850 – 1850 is the first census in which every individual in the household was enumerated. In prior years, only the name of the head of household was recorded and other household members were recorded by age grouping by category. In 1850, the instructions say that Indians not taxed (meaning on reservations) were not to be enumerated and the categories for race were white, black, mulatto. So if your ancestor looked "dark" and was an Indian, chances are they were recorded as M for mulatto. There was no "Indian" category until 1860.

https://nativeheritageproject.com/2013/05/14/indians-and-the-census-1790-2010/

Obadiah Bass
United States Census, 1850

Name	**Obadiah Bass**
Event Type	Census
Event Year	1850
Event Place	Orange county, Orange, North Carolina, United States
Gender	Male
Age	28
Race	Mulatto
Race (Original)	M

Obediah Bass
United States Census, 1880

Name:	Obediah Bass
Event Type:	Census
Event Date:	1880
Event Place:	Lebanon, Orange, North Carolina, United States
Gender:	Male
Age:	58
Marital Status:	Married
Race:	Black
Race:	B
Occupation:	Farmer
Relationship to Head of Household:	Self
Relationship to Head of Household:	Self
Birth Year (Estimated):	1822
Birthplace:	North Carolina, United States
Father's Birthplace:	North Carolina, United States

Attach to Family Tree

Obediah Bass
mentioned in the record of Garland Dick and Susan Bass

Name:	Obediah Bass
Sex:	Male
Wife:	Mildred Bass
Daughter:	Susan Bass

LAWS

In this section, we will discuss laws that made it illegal for Indians to claim Indian status, made Indians slaves extinct if they weren't in amity (friendly relationship) with the government, and combined Africans and Indians into one category as negroes and other slaves.

RACE - History - Colonial Authority
www.understandingrace.org

 Virginia passed two acts in 1682 that combined Native Americans and Africans into one category as "negroes and other slaves."

LAWS OF VIRGINIA

and purposes, any law, usage or custome to the contrary notwithstanding.

ACT II.

An act declaring Indian women servants tithables.

Edit. 1733 and 1752.
Purvis 294.

Indian women to be charged with levies or taxes the same as negroes.

WHEREAS it hath bin doubted whether Indian women servants sold to the English above the age of sixteene yeares be tythable, *Bee it enacted and declared, and it is hereby enacted and declared by the governour, councill and burgesses of this generall assembly and the authority thereof,* that all Indian women are and shall be tythables, and ought to pay levies in like manner as negroe women brought into this country doe, and ought to pay.

AT A GENERALL ASSEMBLY.

L'd Culpeper governor.

BEGUNN ATT JAMES CITTY NOVEM. THE TENTH ANNO DOM. 1682, AND IN THE 34TH YEARE OF THE REIGN OF OUR SOVERAINE LORD KING CHARLES THE SECOND, BY THE GRACE OF GOD OF ENGLAND, SCOTLAND, FRANCE AND IRELAND, KING, &c.

ACT I.

Edd. 1733 and 1752.

An act to repeale a former law makeing Indians and others ffree.

Purvis 262. (See an p.285.)

Preamble, reciting the act of 1670, where by serv'ts, not being Christian, imported by shipp'g are declared to be slaves, & those brought in by land, to serve, if boys or girls, till 30 years of age, & if men or women, 12 years.

WHEREAS by the 12 act of assembly held att James Citty the 3d day of October, Anno Domini 1670, entituled an act declareing who shall be slaves, it is enacted that all servants not being christians, being imported into this country by shipping shall be slaves, but what shall come by land shall serve if boyes and girls untill thirty yeares of age, if men or women, twelve yeares and noe longer; and for as much as many negroes, moores, mollatoes and others borne of and in heathenish, idollatrous, pagan and mahometan parentage and country have heretofore, and hereafter may be purchased, procured, or otherwise obteigned as slaves of, from or out of such their heathenish country by some well disposed christian, who after such their obteining and purchaseing such negroe, moor, or molatto as their slave out of a pious zeale, have wrought the conversion of such slave to the christian faith, which by the laws of this country doth not manumitt them or make them free, and afterwards

---

* The commencement, as well as the acts of this session, [t]aken from the Northb. MS. which substantially agrees with the other MSS. with Purvis, and the edi. 1733 & 1752. This is the first time that the term *General Assembly* is used in the Northb. MS. which appears from this place forward to be in a different hand writing

https://www.encyclopediavirginia.org/ An_act_to_repeale_a_former_law_makeing_Indians_and_others_ffree_1682

VIRGINIA
HEALTH BULLETIN

Vol. XVI.   MARCH, 1924.   Extra No. 2.

The New Virginia Law
To Preserve Racial Integrity

W. A. PLECKER, M. D., *State Registrar of Vital Statistics, Richmond, Va.*

Senate Bill 219, To preserve racial integrity, passed the House March 8, 1924, and is now a law of the State.

This bill aims at correcting a condition which only the more thoughtful people of Virginia know the existence of.

It is estimated that there are in the State from 10,000 to 20,000, possibly more, near white people, who are known to possess an intermixture of colored blood, in some cases to a slight extent it is true, but still enough to prevent them from being white.

In the past it has been possible for these people to declare themselves as white, or even to have the Court so declare them. Then they have demanded the admittance of their children into the white schools, and in not a few cases have intermarried with white people.

In many counties they exist as distinct colonies holding themselves aloof from negroes, but not being admitted by the white people as of their race.

In any large gathering or school of colored people, especially in the cities, many will be observed who are scarcely distinguishable as colored.

These persons, however, are not white in reality, nor by the new definition of this law, that a white person is one with no trace of the blood of another race, except that a person with one-sixteenth of the American Indian, if there is no other race mixture, may be classed as white.

Their children are likely to revert to the distinctly negro type even when all apparent evidence of mixture has disappeared.

The Virginia Bureau of Vital Statistics has been called upon within one month for evidence by two lawyers employed to assist people of this type to force their children into the white public schools, and by another employed by the school trustees of a district to prevent this action.

Entered as second class matter July 28, 1908, at the Postoffice at Richmond, Va., under the Act of July 16, 1894.

under fourteen years of age, over the signature of a parent, guardian, or other person standing in loco parentis. One of said certificates for each person thus registering in every district shall be forwarded to the State registrar for his files; the other shall be kept on file by the local registrar.

Every local registrar may, as soon as practicable, have such registration certification made by or for each person in his district who so desires, born before June fourteen, nineteen hundred and twelve, for whom he has not on file a registration certificate, or a birth certificate.

2. It shall be a felony for any person wilfully or knowingly to make a registration certificate false as to color or race. The wilful making of a false registration or birth certificate shall be punished by confinement in the penitentiary for one year.

3. For each registration certificate properly made and returned to the State registrar, the local registrar returning the same shall be entitled to a fee of twenty-five cents, to be paid by the registrant. Application for registration and for transcript may be made direct to the State Registrar, who may retain the fee for expenses of his office.

4. No marriage license shall be granted until the clerk or deputy clerk has reasonable assurance that the statements as to color of both man and woman are correct.

If there is reasonable cause to disbelieve that applicants are of pure white race, when that fact is stated, the clerk or deputy clerk shall withhold the granting of the license until satisfactory proof is produced that both applicants are "white persons" as provided for in this act.

The clerk or deputy clerk shall use the same care to assure himself that both applicants are colored, when that fact is claimed.

5. It shall hereafter be unlawful for any white person in this State to marry any save a white person, or a person with no other admixture of blood than white and American Indian. For the purpose of this act, the term "white person" shall apply only to the person who has no trace whatsoever of any blood other than Caucasian; but persons who have one-sixteenth or less of the blood of the American Indian and have no other non-Caucasic blood shall be deemed to be white persons. All laws heretofore passed and now in effect regarding the intermarriage of white and colored persons shall apply to marriages prohibited by this act.

6. For carrying out the purposes of this act and to provide the necessary clerical assistance, postage and other expenses of the State registrar of vital statistics, twenty per cent of the fees received by local registrars under this act shall be paid to the State Bureau of Vital Statistics, which may be expended by the said bureau for the purposes of this act.

7. All acts or parts of acts inconsistent with this act are, to the extent of such inconsistency, hereby repealed.

https://www.encyclopediavirginia.org/media_player?mets_filename=evm00001754mets.xml

NEGRO LAW OF SOUTH CAROLINA.

CHAPTER I.

The Status of the Negro, his Rights and Disabilities.

SECTION 1. The Act of 1740, sec. 1, declares all negroes and Indians, (free Indians in amity with this Government, negroes, mulattoes and mestizoes, who now are free, excepted) to be slaves:— the offspring to follow the condition of the mother: and that such slaves are chattels personal. P. L. 163. 7 Stat. 397.

SEC. 2. Under this provision it has been uniformly held, that color is prima facie evidence, that the party bearing the color of a negro, mulatto or mestizo, is a slave: but the same prima facie result does not follow from the Indian color. The State vs. Harden, (note,) 2 Speer's, 155. Nelson vs Whetmore, 1 Rich'n, 334.

SEC. 3. Indians, and descendants of Indians are regarded as free Indians, in amity with this government, until the contrary be shown. In the second proviso of sec. 1, of the Act of 1740, it is declared that "every negro, Indian, mulatto and mestizo is a slave unless the contrary can be made to appear"—yet, in the same it is immediately thereafter provided—"the Indians in amity with this government, excepted, in which case the burden of proof shall lie on the defendant," that is, on the person claiming the Indian plaintiff to be a slave. This latter clause of the proviso is now regarded as furnishing the rule. The race of slave Indians, or of Indians not in amity to this government, (the State,) is extinct, and hence the previous part of the proviso has no application. Miller vs. Dawson & Brown, Dudley's Rep. 174. State vs. Belmont, decided in Charleston, Jan, 1848. P. L. 164. 7 Stat. 398.

https://play.google.com/books/reader?id=r9lBAAAAIAAJ&hl=en&pg=GBS.PA5

ANCESTRY.COM

💬 American Indians of Blood Classified as Black Negro or Mulatto on Census Records

➕ Begin New Thread

Replies: 4

American Indians of Blood Classified as Black Negro or Mulatto on Census Records

NCTuscarora (View posts)

Posted: 17 Aug 2013 10:20AM

Classification: Census

Since the beginnings of the Africa slave trade in America many Native American persons have unfortunately, to the detriment of Indian Heritage, were listed as Black Mulatto or Negro In order for white slave owners to keep an am ample supply of slaves. Many blood Indians have lost a God given Heritage due to slavery in Southern state in which approximately 24,000 or more full blood American Indians of color, men women and children alike, were forced by white slave owner to take part in slavery, and with that travesty starting from the first census ever taken in America Indians were falsely listed on all census records as (Negro) Black or Mulatto, an error which was passed down from generation to generation to the present. If you generation to generation to the present. If you know your Indian and don't know why you can't find census records stating this, it is because of white census takers being instructed to ignore Indian heritage and paint mostly southern states in America with either Black or White populations. Go over you grandparents oral history and If you are a person of color and have a strong family history of Indian blood and census records that don't match, you are more that likely of Indian Heritage and have had your Heritage striped from you. Reclaim it.

_____

"Native Americans were alternately ignored and categorized down to tiny fractions of black and white "blood."[7]"
Read more here
http://scholar.harvard.edu/jlhochschild/publications/racial-...

_____

" Chesterfield County, VA (Orders 1767-71)
6 APR 1770...On motion of Sibbell, an Indian woman held in slavery by Joseph Ashbrooke, have leave to prosecute for her freedom in forma pauperis.
- Sibbell an Indian wench V. Joseph Ashbrooke, for pltf. To take deposition of Elizabeth Blankenship and Thomas Womack.

https://www.ancestry.com/boards/topics.ethnic.natam.intertribal.ga/1130/mb.ashx

CONCLUSION

From what we've read so far, The American Indians' identity was changed several times until what we know today as African Americans. This type of paper genocide was put in place to continue stealing the birthright of the people. The pen is indeed mightier than the sword. It's challenging to claim who you are if, for generations, your ancestors thought that they were a different ethnic group that came from another land and passing that identity on to their offspring.

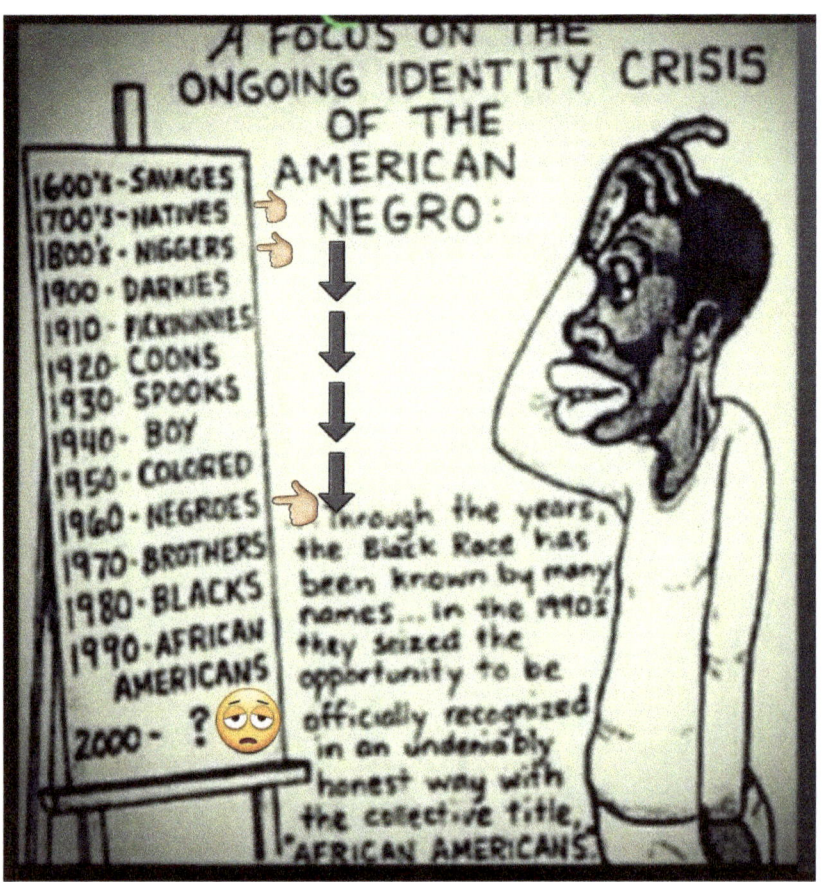

SECTION 6: OTHER MISCELLANEOUS FACTS

Chapter 11
AFRICAN AMERICAN SOUL FOOD IS AMERICAN INDIAN

The world knows about African Americans, "Soul Food." The southern U.S African Americans coined the name. Many people believe that soul food was slave food leftovers that were given to imported African slaves by their Caucasian masters. However, "Soul Food" is American Indian food. It was prepared and eaten before, during, and after slavery.

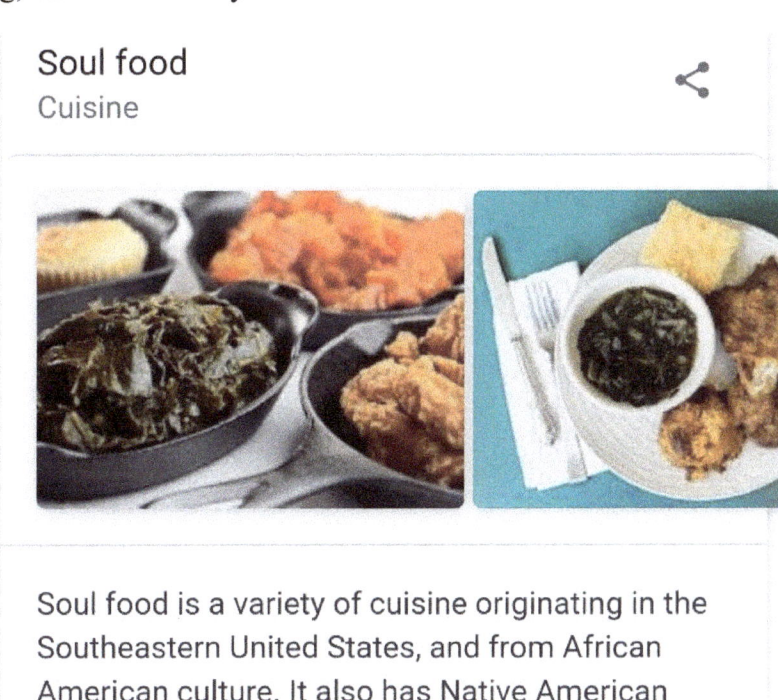

A traditional soul food dinner consisting of fried chicken with macaroni and cheese, collard greens, and fried okra

Soul food is a variety of cuisine originating in the Southeastern United States, and from African American culture. It also has Native American influences. It is common in areas with a historical presence of African Americans and has been a cultural staple among the African American and American Deep-South communities for centuries. The expression "soul food" originated in the mid-1960s, when "soul" was a common word used to describe African American culture.

∧ Native American influence

Southern Native American culture (Cherokee, Chickasaw, Choctaw, Creek, Seminole) is an important element of southern cuisine. From their cultures came one of the main staples of the Southern diet: corn (maize) – either ground into meal or limed with an alkaline salt to make hominy, in a Native American process known as nixtamalization.[10] Corn was used to make all kinds of dishes, from the familiar cornbread and grits, to liquors such as moonshine and whiskey (which is still important to the Southern economy[11]).

Many fruits are available in this region: blackberries, muscadines, raspberries, and many other wild berries were part of Southern Native Americans' diets, as well.

https://en.wikipedia.org/wiki/Soul_food

Chapter 12
AFRICAN AMERICAN HOLY GHOST DANCE IS AMERICAN INDIAN

The world knows that African Americans are famous for the Holy Ghost dance in the church. What if I told you that the dance is American Indian? The Europeans wanted to replace the American Indians' way of living with Christianity, so they outlawed their dances. The American Indians started practicing their dances in the Christian churches. That is why there are such similarities between the Ghost Dance and The African American Holy Ghost dance. The Holy Ghost dance is nothing more but the "Ghost Dance."

Ghost Dance

Ghost Dance of the Sioux, print from a wood engraving, 1891.

Library of Congress, Washington, D.C. (Digital file no. cph 3a51166)

Ghost Dance and Holy Ghost: The Echoes of Nineteenth-Century Christianization Policy in Twentieth-Century Native American Free Exercise Cases

Article *in* Stanford Law Review 49(4):773 · April 1997
with 50 Reads

DOI: 10.2307/1229337

 Cite this publication

Allison Dussias
5.22 · New England Law

Abstract

In the late nineteenth century, Native Americans were the subject of a United States government Christianization policy that attempted, with the help of Christian churches, to convert Native Americans to Christianity by assigning reservations to Christian groups for proselytization purposes and by suppressing Native American religious beliefs and practices. In this article, Professor Allison Dussias describes this Christianization policy, and the attitudes, conceptual difficulties, and tensions inherent in it.

otherwise supporting activities aimed at replacing Native American religious beliefs and practices with Christianity, the federal government took more direct steps to destroy Native American religions. As Secretary of the Interior Henry Teller remarked in 1883: "[I]f it is the purpose of the Government to civilize the Indians, they must be compelled to desist from the savage and barbarous practices that are calculated to continue them in savagery, no matter what exterior influences are brought to bear on them."[114] It was hoped that once their traditional gods and religious practices were destroyed, Native Americans would be driven to Christianity as the only available form of religious community.[115]

Ceremonial dances were the chief target of the government's suppression efforts. The government's ban on ceremonial dances in general, and its efforts to suppress the Sioux Ghost Dance and Pueblo dances in particular, are examined below. As Part II highlights, these incidents teach important lessons about the historical and continuing denial of religious freedom to Native Americans.

A. Suppressing "the Old Heathenish Dances": The 1883 Dance Ban

> [T]he great evils in the way of their ultimate civilization lie in these dances. The dark superstitions and unhallowed rites of a heathenism as gross as that of India or Central Africa still infects them with its insidious poison, which, unless replaced by Christian civilization, must sap their very life blood.[116]

In December 1882, Secretary of the Interior Henry Teller wrote a letter to the Commissioner of Indian Affairs expressing his belief that the "old heathenish dances" were a great hindrance to the civilization of the Indians, and ought to be discontinued.[117] If the Indians were not willing to discontinue the dances, Teller argued, then the agents should compel discontinuance.[118] Prompted by Teller's letter, the Commissioner of Indian Affairs in April 1883 distributed a set of "Rules for Indian Courts" that defined a number of "Indian Offenses," including participation in the sun dance, the scalp dance, and the war dance.[119] The rules also prohibited the practices of medicine men and the distribution or destruction of property which accompanied some ceremonial dances and

---

114. 1883 SECRETARY OF THE INTERIOR ANN. REP. at X [hereinafter 1883 SEC. OF INT. REPORT] (discussing Court of Indian Offenses).

115. *See* CLYDE HOLLER, BLACK ELK'S RELIGION: THE SUN DANCE AND LAKOTA CATHOLICISM 132 (1995).

116. 1882 COMM'R OF INDIAN AFFAIRS ANN. REP. 5 [hereinafter 1882 CIA REPORT] (report of J.H. Fleming, Moquis Pueblo Agency, Aug. 31, 1882). The agent noted that he had not yet attended any of the dances and could not speak from personal knowledge, but his judgment was based on "reliable authority." *Id.*

117. *See* 1883 SEC. OF INT. REPORT, *supra* note 114, at XI (letter from Henry Teller, Secretary of Interior, to the Commissioner of Indian Affairs (Dec. 2, 1882)).

118. *See id.*

119. *See* 1883 COMM'R OF INDIAN AFFAIRS ANN. REP. at XIV-XV [hereinafter 1883 CIA REPORT]; HOLLER, *supra* note 115, at 120; ROBERT M. UTLEY, THE LAST DAYS OF THE SIOUX NATION 31 (1963). An exception from the Rules was made for the Five Civilized Tribes. *See* 1883 CIA REPORT, *supra*, at XV.

AFRICAN-AMERICANS ARE THE AMERICAN INDIANS

Ghost Dance, either of two distinct cults in a complex of late 19th-century religious movements that represented an attempt of Indians in the western United States to rehabilitate their traditional cultures. Both cults arose from Northern Paiute prophet-dreamers in western Nevada who announced the imminent return of the dead (hence "ghost"), the ousting of the whites, and the restoration of Indian lands, food supplies, and way of life. These ends, it was believed, would be hastened by the dances and songs revealed to the prophets in their vision visits to the spirit world and also by strict observance of a moral code that resembled Christian teaching and forbade war against Indians or whites. Many dancers fell into trances and received new songs from the dead they met in visions or were healed by Ghost Dance rituals.

The first Ghost Dance developed in 1869 around the dreamer Wodziwob (d. c. 1872) and in 1871–73 spread to California and Oregon tribes; it soon died out or was transformed into other cults. The second derived from Wovoka (c. 1856–1932), whose father, Tavibo, had assisted Wodziwob. Wovoka had been influenced by Presbyterians on whose ranch he worked, by Mormons, and by the Indian Shaker Church. During a solar eclipse in January 1889, he had a vision of dying, speaking with God in heaven, and being commissioned to teach the new dance and millennial message. Indians from many tribes traveled to learn from Wovoka,

https://www.britannica.com/topic/Ghost-Dance

Indian Shaker Church, Christianized religious movement among Northwest American Indians. It is not connected with the Shaker communities developed from the teachings of Ann Lee.

In 1881 near Olympia, Washington, John Slocum, a Squaxon logger and a baptized Roman Catholic, reported that he had visited heaven while in a coma and was commissioned to preach a new way of life. The following year his wife, Mary, experienced a shaking paroxysm, which was interpreted as the Spirit of God curing John of a further illness. The Shaker church they founded effected reforms and replaced traditional Indian curing methods with spiritual healing through shaking and dancing rituals.

https://www.britannica.com/topic/Indian-Shaker-Church

AFRICAN-AMERICANS ARE THE AMERICAN INDIANS

The Holy Ghost continues to move Bishop Todd   Another joins in the Holy Ghost dance of joy.

Native American Indians practising the Ghost Dance, aka...

Chapter 13
NIGGER, JIGABOO, COON AND BUCK MEAN AMERICAN INDIAN

"Black" or African American people have been using these terms for a long time. What many African Americans do not know is that these terms applied to American Indians. These terms are used in the African American populations today because they are the American Indians.

1. NIGGER/A

AFRICAN-AMERICANS ARE THE AMERICAN INDIANS

a. A dark-skinned person of any origin. In early *U.S.* use usually with reference to American Indians. Usu. *offensive*.

1843 T. C. HALIBURTON *Attaché* (1846) 180 Heathen Indgean niggers.

2. JIGABOO

https://www.urbandictionary.com/author.php?author=jigaboo%20guy

3. COON

What is the origin of the slur "coon" (once commonly applied to African Americans)?

6 ANSWERS

Jonathon Green, worked at None.
Answered Oct 9, 2011 · Author has **298** answers and **1.7m** answer views

The earliest use of *coon* in any sense other than as an abbreviation for the animal, the racoon, was as a nickname for the American political party, the Whigs, in the 1840s. It was then used successively to mean a native American, and a sly rustic or peasant before the first recorded use for 'black' is recorded in 1848, in G.F. Ruxton's *Life in the Far West*.

https://www.quora.com/What-is-the-origin-of-the-slur-%E2%80%9Ccoon%E2%80%9D-once-commonly-applied-to-African-Americans

AFRICAN-AMERICANS ARE THE AMERICAN INDIANS

The raccoon, sometimes spelled racoon, also known as the common raccoon, North American raccoon, northern raccoon, or coon, is a medium-sized mammal native to North America. The

traditions and culture. The Wichita called themselves *Kitikiti'sh*, meaning "raccoon eyes," because the designs of tattoos around the men's eyes resembled the eyes of the raccoon. In central Kansas in 1541 the Coronado expedition visited Indians whom Coronado called *Quiviras* and who have been identified by archeological and historical studies as Wichitas. By 1719 these

AFRICAN-AMERICANS ARE THE AMERICAN INDIANS

About Famous Wichita Indians | native american ...
John Williams, Tonkawa Indian, (misspelled as Tongawa on the photo), ...

Chief Towonkonie Jim, Wichita

MY BLOOD RELATIVES

4. BUCK

List of ethnic slurs by et...
https://en.m.wikipedia.org

Buck

a black person or Native American.[14]

https://en.m.wikipedia.org/wiki/List_of_ethnic_slurs_by_ethnicity

Buck dictionary definitio...
https://www.yourdictionary.com

buck

noun

1. **a.** A male deer.
   b. The male of various other mammals, such as antelopes, kangaroos, mice, or rabbits.
   c. Antelope considered as a group: *a herd of buck.*
2. **a.** A robust or high-spirited young man.
   b. A fop.
3. *Offensive* A Native American or black man.

https://www.yourdictionary.com/buck

> 1. The aboriginal inhabitants of Guyana have for a considerable time been known by the appellation of "BUCKS," which term is probably derived from the Dutch word "*Bok.*" Dr. Hostmann in his work on the "*Civilisation of the Negro Race in America,*" says that the origin of the word "*Bok*" is to be found in the word "*Lokka,*" which in the Arrawaak language means "man." This Arrawaak term "*Lokka*" has an eastern origin, and is derived from the Sanskrit "*Lôka,*" (vernacularly "*Lôk,*" and vulgarly "*Lôg,*") signifying, in the ordinary use, man; mankind. The resort of men, a village, a town, is called "*Lôkâlaya.*" But the word "*Bok,*" or (as it is incorrectly written) "*Buck*" applied to the aborigines, though I confess, it is neither euphonious nor elegant, is a term suitable to them, as signifying the right of possession or enjoyment of any property, especially the Continent of America, for they were the lords of the soil for a considerable time, till it was by force taken from them by foreign nations—the Europeans. The word "*Bok*" itself is derived either from the Sanskrit

https://books.google.com/books?id=YfgDAAAAQAAJ&pg=PA452&lpg=PA452&dq=the+aboriginal+inhabitants+of+Guyana+have+for+a+considerable+time+been+known+by+the+appellation+of+bucks&source=bl&ots=XLazmTWP5_&sig=ACfU3U3YnCQLHegoNpzJ-mTTVQIzZpWw_g&hl=en&sa=X&ved=2ahUKEwippJiGy-DiAhWmq1kKHaPGDYMQ6AEwDHoECAMQAQ#v=onepage&q=the%20aboriginal%20inhabitants%20of%20Guyana%20have%20for%20a%20considerable%20time%20been%20known%20by%20the%20appellation%20of%20bucks&f=false

Chapter 14

THE " BLACK" PEOPLE OF BLACK WALL STREET WERE AMERICAN INDIAN

Origins of Black Wall Street

Black Wall Street

During the oil boom of the 1910s, the area of northeast Oklahoma around Tulsa flourished, including the Greenwood neighborhood, which came to be known as "the Negro Wall Street" (now commonly referred to as "the *Black* Wall Street").[3] The area was home to several prominent black businessmen. Greenwood boasted a variety of thriving businesses that were very successful up until the Tulsa Race Riot. Not only did black Americans want to contribute to the success of their own shops, but there were also racial segregation laws that prevented them from shopping anywhere

Many of the black Americans who traveled to Oklahoma had ancestors who could be traced back to Oklahoma. Many of the settlers were relatives of black Americans who had traveled on foot with the Five Civilized Tribes along the Trail of Tears. Others were the descendants of people who had fled to Indian Territory. Many Black residents were also from the various Muskogee speaking peoples, such as Creeks, Seminoles, and the Yuchi, while some had been adopted by the tribe after the Emancipation Proclamation. They were thus able to live freely in the Oklahoma Territory.[2]

https://en.m.wikipedia.org/wiki/Greenwood,_Tulsa

SECTION 7: Lets Clear Up Some Things

Chapter 15
ROOTS IS FICTION

The book Roots shocked the nation when the TV series aired. It gave an insight into what it was like for Africans during the transatlantic slave trade. It's about an African named Kunta Kinte that was brought to the Americas as a slave. Roots gave a visual depiction of this event, and African Americans took this depiction to be true. In reality, the book is fiction and never happened. Portions of Roots was copied from another book, "The African" by Harold Courlander. Alex Haley was sued for plagiarism. The book was used as propaganda to keep spreading the exaggeration of the transatlantic slave trade, promote a victim mentality, and strike fear in the hearts of the people labeled African American.

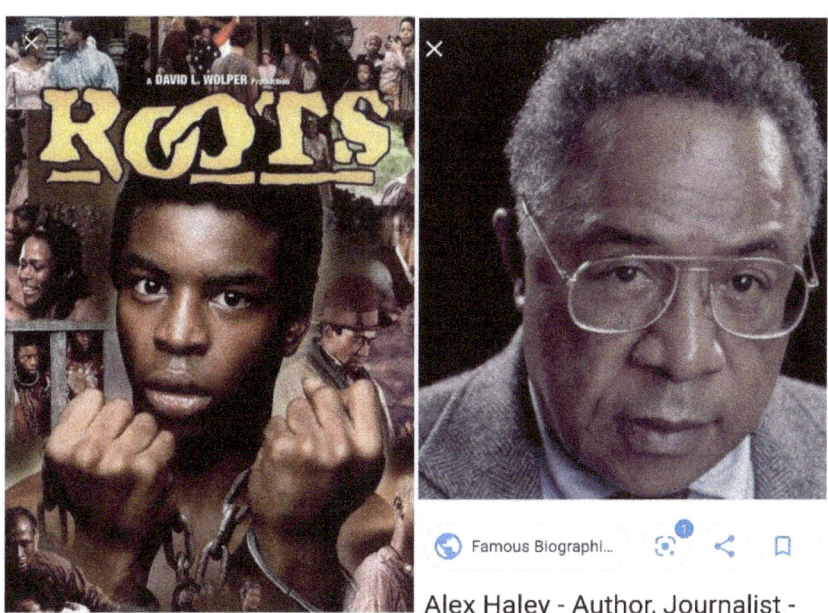

Alex Haley - Author, Journalist -

AFRICAN-AMERICANS ARE THE AMERICAN INDIANS

African American ...

Harold Courlander, Author Info,

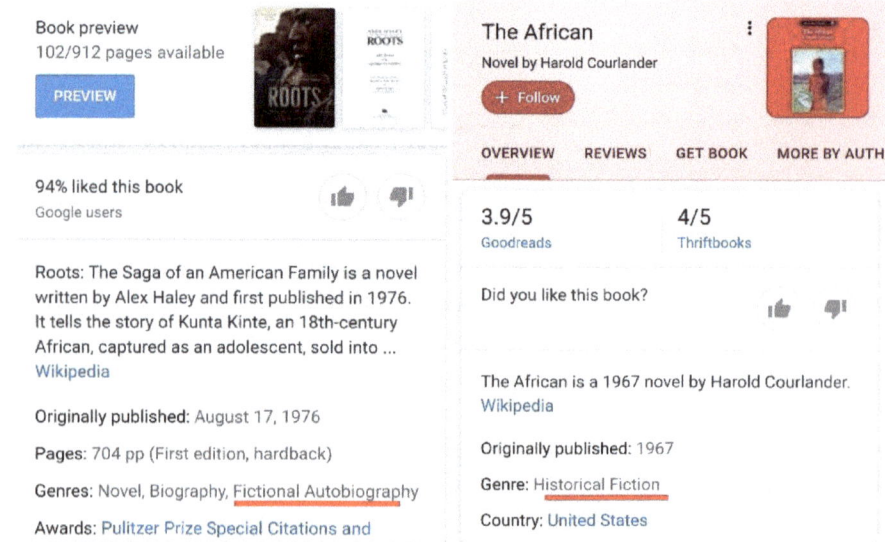

AFRICAN-AMERICANS ARE THE AMERICAN INDIANS

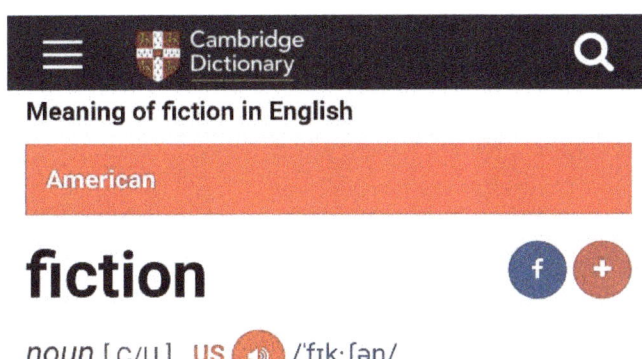

Meaning of fiction in English

American

fiction

noun [C/U] US /ˈfɪk·ʃən/

literature **the type of book or story that is written about imaginary characters and events and does not describe real people or deal with facts, or a false report or statement that you pretend is true:**

[U] *She wrote detective fiction and made a good living at it.*

[C usually sing] *It was a fiction, though widely believed, that he had once been rich.*

Margaret Walker
American poet

But **Haley**, who died in 1992, was famously accused of plagiarizing parts of the Pulitzer-winning "**Roots**" — and settled a very public **lawsuit** brought against him by another writer. Harold Courlander, who was white, wrote a novel called "The African" in 1967. ... Courlander **sued Haley** in 1977 for copyright infringement. May 19, 2016

New York Daily News › amazin...

Amazing 'Roots' returns after 40 years, dredging up Alex Haley ...

Meaning of plagiarism in English

English

plagiarism

noun [U] UK /ˈpleɪ.dʒ³r.ɪ.z³m/ US /ˈpleɪ.dʒɚ.ɪ.z³m/

the process or practice of using another person's ideas or work and pretending that it is your own:

She's been accused of plagiarism.

The techniques for detecting plagiarism are becoming increasingly advanced.

See
  plagiarize

BOOKS

Alex Haley Settles Suit Out Of Court: $500,000

Alex Haley

Pulitzer Prize winning author Alex Haley, of *Roots* fame, hammered out an out of court settlement with a White writer, who charged that Haley had "lifted" 81 different passages from his book.

In announcing the settlement before U. S. District Court Judge Robert Ward, Haley readily admitted that he was glad his latest legal ordeal was now behind him. Under terms of the agreement, Harold Courlander, who wrote *The African* in 1967, will be paid $500,000. "The suit has been amicably settled out of court. Alex Haley acknowledges and regrets that various materials from *The African* by Harold Courlander found their way into his book *Roots*," a statement said.

Throughout the two-week long trial Haley had maintained that he had never heard of *The African*, an assertion that prompted Judge Ward to remark, "That leaves me a little cold." Haley noted that often throughout his 12-year effort on *Roots* countless people gave him material.

To date, Haley's *Roots* has earned several million dollars and recently he received $1 million from ABC-TV for "*Roots*: The Next Generation." The 70-year-old Courlander pulled in $28,000 in royalties from his book. Haley, however, lamented that his legal jousts have cost him $100,000." Even when I won, I lost," he sighed.

Earlier last year Haley was successful in countering a suit brought by Margaret Walker Alexander, who charged he had copied large sections of her *Jubilee*.

ARMED FORCES

Black General Heads 48,000 Infantry Division Overseas

The first American Black general ever to control "the ground fire power of more than 48,000 infantrymen" recently took over his duties in Germany.

The man is 52-year-old Lt. Gen. Julius W. Becton Jr., who was sworn in as commanding general of headquarters, VLL Corps, in Frankfort. The command includes two infantry divisions and one German Panzer division.

The last Black to head a "ground fire unit" was Lt. Gen. Frederic Davison, who commanded a brigade of 5,000 men in Vietnam.

When he was sworn into his new post, Lt. Gen. Becton wore on his shoulder the patch of the long-disbanded all-Black division, in which he began his military service as a second lieutenant in the south Pacific during the Second World War. The general said, "Wearing that patch meant a great deal to me. Blacks proved that they could fight, and I have always been proud to talk about our accomplishments."

https://books.google.com/books?id=ZUIDAAAAMBAJ&pg=PA47&lpg=PA47&dq=pulitzer+prize+winner+alex+haley,+of+roots+fame,+hammered+out+an+out+of+court&source=bl&ots=vkwvhDhNlY&sig=ACfU3U2DN-qeL1O4gLIgITEpwuYnyo5TwQ&hl=en&sa=X&ved=2ahUKEwiEqbPG2u_iAhUPhOAKHcjJB0gQ6AEwAHoECAIQAQ#v=onepage&q=pulitzer%20prize%20winner%20alex%20haley%2C%20of%20roots%20fame%2C%20hammered%20out%20an%20out%20of%20court&f=false

Chapter 16

DNA TESTS FOR ANCESTRY ARE FRAUDULENT

DNA tests are a huge trend in society. African Americans are so confused about their identity and want to belong to an ethnic group that DNA companies use this to their advantage. These companies strip the American Indians of their heritage by giving them a place in Africa that they supposedly originated. What many African Americans do not know is that the DNA test in regards to ancestry is fraudulent and only for entertainment purposes. DNA can only tell you If you are directly related to a person such as; siblings, parents, grandparents, a child, other living relatives, or if you committed a crime. They sell your DNA to pharmaceutical companies to conduct experiments, and they give your DNA to law enforcement.

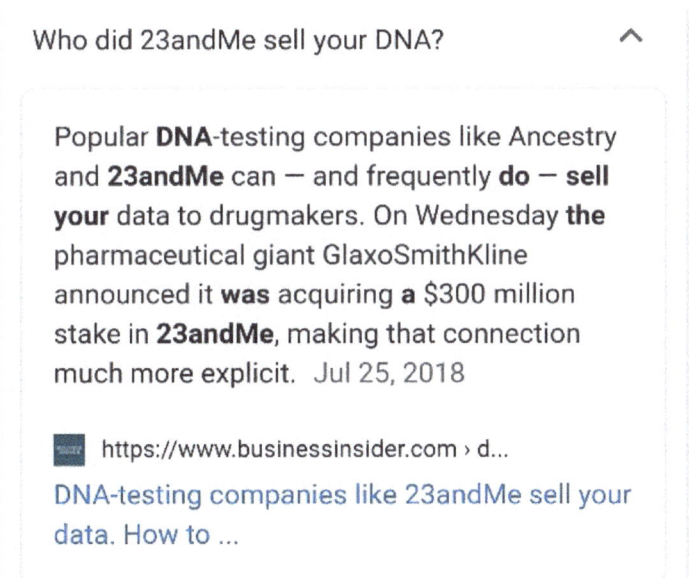

https://www.businessinsider.com/dna-testing-delete-your-data-23andme-ancestry-2018-7

AFRICAN-AMERICANS ARE THE AMERICAN INDIANS

gizmodo.com
Another DNA Testing Company Reportedly Gets Fooled by Dog DNA

The company in question, Viaguard Accu-Metrics, has been exclusively used to verify whether prospective members of the Confederation of Aboriginal People of Canada (CAPC) have any genetic ties to the indigenous populations of Canada. Those who were confirmed to have indigenous DNA via the lab's results are then given CAPC membership. The results would supposedly not only confirm someone's ancestry, but narrow down which tribes of the First Nations community they belonged to.

But Louis Côté, who worked with CAPC to collect DNA samples from hopeful members, became suspicious of the lab. So according to CBC News, Côté bought three kits from Viaguard himself last summer, then submitted two cheek swabs from himself and one from his girlfriend's good boy, Snoopy.

The results showed that both he and Snoopy seemingly had 20 percent Indigenous ancestry, 12 percent of which came from the Abenaki tribe and 8 percent from the Mohawk people.

"I thought it was a joke," Côté told CBC News. "The company is fooling people … the tests are no good."

https://gizmodo.com/another-dna-testing-company-reportedly-gets-fooled-by-d-1826842819

AFRICAN-AMERICANS ARE THE AMERICAN INDIANS

GENETICS

Report: A DNA Testing Company Could Not Tell the Difference Between Human and Dog DNA

Kristen V. Brown
5/02/18 1:30PM

GIZMODO SCIENCE

As part of an investigation into the accuracy of home testing kits, NBC Chicago sent in the DNA of Bailey, a Labrador retriever, to several companies. Most companies reported back that the DNA was unreadable. But one, Orig3n, "failed to note that Bailey was not human," the network said.

NBC Chicago decided to have Bailey try out the company's "Superhero" test, which looks at strength, intelligence, and speed.

The results:

> "...After we submitted the $29 test, the company sent a 7 page report, saying that her muscle force would probably be great for quick movements like boxing and basketball, and that she has the cardiac output for long endurance bike rides or runs."

This isn't the first time that Orig3n's test have been called into question. The good news is that most companies *did* detect that the doggie DNA was in fact not from a human. Still, it's a good reminder that every time you spit in a test tube and send your DNA away for analysis, it's good to take the results with a fairly large helping of salt.

[NBC Chicago]

https://gizmodo.com/report-a-dna-testing-company-could-not-tell-the-differ-1825715321

Inside The Shady World Of DNA Testing Companies

    +

By Evan V. Symon
December 04, 2017

Genetics experts from the University of Texas and the University of North Carolina have gone so far as to say that these companies are preying on people, because they don't truly have the information they need to pinpoint your origins on a map, and that it's not possible to trace unique ancestry that way. As they put it, "That's the beauty of this scam. The companies aren't scamming you. They're not giving you fraudulent information. They are giving you data, real data, and allowing you to scam yourself."

https://www.cracked.com/personal-experiences-2522-inside-shady-world-dna-testing-companies.html

Page | 235

Woman takes 2 ancestry tests, gets 2 wildly different results

The Grio
2017-11-03

A Chicago-area woman wanted to test the accuracy of the popular DNA tests that are supposed to find your family history, but when she mailed away her DNA, the results she got were vastly different from each other.

Jennifer Smith was interested in her family ancestry, so she tried out a DNA kit from Ancestry.com, but was shocked when her breakdown showed that she was 97 percent European and 2 percent Asian.

"I'm a Black girl; I am not a Jewish white lady," Smith told Fox32 Chicago, recalling her utter confusion at her results…

…William Gilliland, an associate biology professor at Depaul University, explained that "DNA tests for ethnicity are entertainment value only," noting that while DNA tests can connect you to family members, there is no solid DNA marker or "diagnostic nucleotide" for race…

http://www.mixedracestudies.org/?tag=william-gilliland

Chapter 17
"NATIVE AMERICAN" MEAN EUROPEAN NOT AMERICAN INDIAN

Many people believe that Native American and American Indian are interchangeable. European colonists did call the Indians, natives; however, Native means to be born in a place. Anyone born in America can be called a Native American. The Europeans came up with the term "Native American," and it applied to the descendants of the European Colonists. They started adding this label to the Real American Indians so that they could include themselves along with them.

DICTIONARY

AFRICAN-AMERICANS ARE THE AMERICAN INDIANS

Wikipedia

Lewis Charles Levin - Wikipedia

B orn in Charleston, SC in 1808, Lewis Charles Levin was a Philadelphia politician and one of the most brilliant orators of his day. He served in Congress from 1845 to 1851, and was the first Jewish U.S. Congressman. Levin was an outspoken foe of the Roman Catholic Church, and was a leader when riots erupted in Philadelphia during the summer of 1844 in which Catholic churches and institutions were burnt by a mob. Rather paradoxically for a Jew, he was one of the founders of the anti-immigrant Native American Party and movement (eventually known as the "Know Nothings"), and he published its newspaper, The Sun. In 1848 most in Levin's party supported the Whig ticket, and their support was important to Zachary Taylor's successful election bid. However, Taylor himself was personally disgusted by their Catholic-baiting and had no wish to encourage it. So in dealing with Lewis, the new President was involved in a delicate balancing act: setting his party's desire for Native American Party votes and its need to avoid antagonizing prominent Native American Party leaders, against the risk of being tainted by any association with demogagory and a genuine disinclination to promote anti-Catholic and anti-immigration activism.

1830-1860

The term "nativism" was first used by 1844: "Thousands were Naturalized expressly to oppose Nativism, and voted the Polk ticket mainly to that end."[30]

Nativism (politics)

Nativism is the political policy of promoting the interests of native inhabitants against those of immigrants.[1] However, this is currently more commonly described as an anti-immigrant position.[2] In scholarly studies *nativism* is a standard technical term. The term is typically not accepted by those who hold this political view, however. Dindar (2010 wrote "nativists... do not consider themselves as nativists. For them it is a negative term and they rather consider themselves as 'Patriots'".[3]

Nativism gained its name from the "Native American" parties of the 1840s and 1850s. In this context "Native" does not mean indigenous Americans or American Indians but rather those descended from the inhabitants of the original Thirteen Colonies. It impacted politics in the mid-19th century because of the large inflows of immigrants after 1845 from cultures that were different from the existing American culture. Nativists objected primarily to Irish Roman Catholics because of their loyalty to the Pope and also because of their supposed rejection of republicanism as an American ideal.[31]

NATIVE AMERICAN = EUROPEANS

https://en.m.wikipedia.org/wiki/Nativism_(politics)#1830-1860

Page | 238

AFRICAN-AMERICANS ARE THE AMERICAN INDIANS

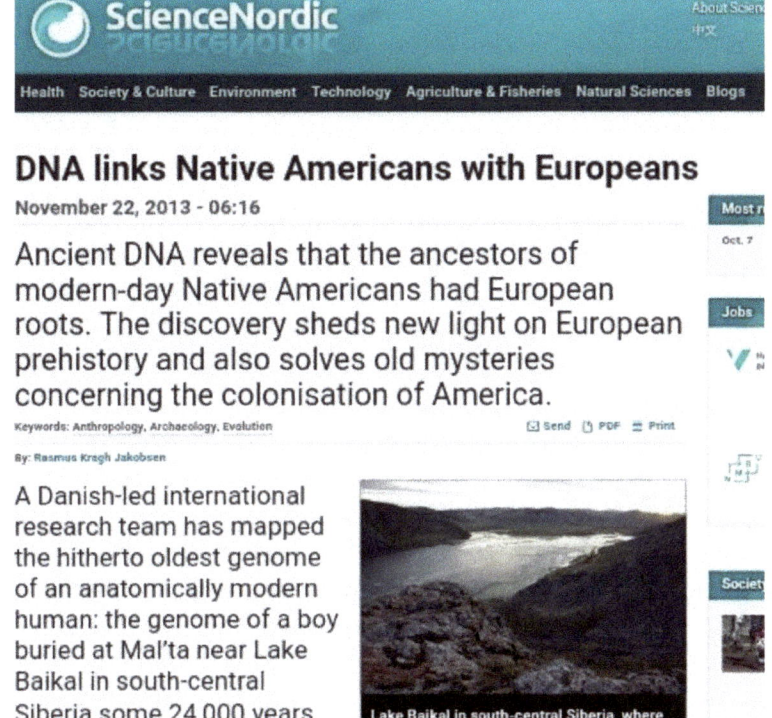

http://sciencenordic.com/dna-links-native-americans-europeans

https://www.latimes.com/nation/la-na-maryland-tribe-20180211-story.html

AFRICAN-AMERICANS ARE THE AMERICAN INDIANS

 Flickr

Two Rode Together Henry Brandon | Born In Germany Deceased | Flickr

Henry Brandon
American-German film actor

OVERVIEW   MOVIES   VIDEOS   PEOPLE ALSO SEAR

Henry Brandon was a German-American film and stage character actor with a career spanning almost 60 years, involving more than one hundred films; he specialized in playing a wide diversity of ethnic roles. Wikipedia

Chapter 18

AMERICAN INDIAN SLAVE MASTERS WERE THE "BLACK" SLAVE MASTERS

Indian and negro were synonymous in dealing with the identity of the American Indians. Do you think that the Europeans brought enslaved Africans to the Americas to free them so that they can own Europeans as slaves? NO!. That's how you know the Negro slave owners were American Indian slave owners. Please don't confuse it with Native American slave masters. Remember that "Native American" meant the European descendants of the 13 colonies. That's why Native American slave masters look European such as; John Ross.

https://images.app.goo.gl/VYvW6tUse9e8PBg19

AFRICAN-AMERICANS ARE THE AMERICAN INDIANS

CHAPTER V.

WHITE SERVITUDE.

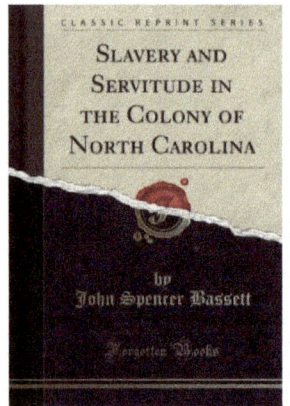

The first slaves that we hear of in North Carolina were white people, and their masters were Indians. Strachey, in his *Travayle into Virginia*,¹ speaks of a story that he had from the Indians of an Indian chief, Eyanoco, who lived at Ritanoe, somewhere in the region to the south of Virginia, and who had seven whites who escaped out of the massacre at Roanoke, and these he used to beat copper. It is not improbable that there is a shadow of truth in the statement, although the details must be fictitious. That the Indians of the colony later on did enslave the whites whom they could take in their waters, or who were shipwrecked off the coast, we know from the preamble of an act of the Assembly about 1707.¹ This form of white servitude left no trace in the life of the colony.

https://books.google.com/books/about/Slavery_and_Servitude_in_the_Colony_of_N.html?id=x5s4AQAAMAAJ&printsec=frontcover&source=kp_read_button

66. Act. V, Laws of Virginia, Oct. 1670 reads: "No Negro or Indian though baptised and enjoying their own freedom shall be capable of any such purchase of (white) Christians, but yet not debarred from buying any of their own kind." (Henings, Vol. II, p. 281.)

Act IX, Oct. 1748: "No Negro, mulatto, Indian, although a Christian or any Jew, Moor, Mohammedan....shall purchase any Christian white servants." (Hening's, Vol. V, p. 550.)

Statutes of Louisiana, Chap. 91, 13, Sec. 12, March 20, 1818, forbids the same. "It was not in fact until the year 1818 that the Legislature (of

43

Louisiana) found itself called upon to notice the frequency with which free persons of color bought the white stranger and in their tardy wisdom forbade any such further purchases on their part....they, however, permitted white persons of good fame and character to continue the traffic." (Quoted from Slavery Pamphlets, Vol. 23, No. 15, New York Public Library.)

69. In 1860 there were 487,000 free Negroes in the United States some of whom owned slaves. C. D. Wilson estimates that there were 6,230 Negro slave-holders. The tax returns of Charleston, S. C., for 1860 showed 132 Negro slave-holders with 390 slaves. The Negro slave-holders, like the white ones, fought to keep their chattels in the Civil War.

69. The U. S. Census of 1790 showed 195 Negro slaveholders, of whom 6 were in Connecticut, and 9 in New York. In 1830 there were about 4,500 Negro slave-holders. In 1836, slaves owned by Negroes in New Orleans numbered 640. On Negro slave-holders, see: Popular Science Monthly, Oct.

44

1912. C. G. Woodson: "Free Negro Owners of Slaves," gives the names of the slave-holders.

Chapter 19

MAROONS ARE ABORIGINES NOT AFRICANS

Some people say that maroons were Africans because they were runaways and that the slaves were African. However, if you made it this far in the book, then you understand that most of your runaway slaves were American Indians. That's why they kept shipping Indians to places like Jamaica and other parts of the west indies because they ran away and rebelled continuously. According to Europeans, Africans are subservient, and American Indians are not.

The Gleaner
AND
DE CORDOVA'S ADVERTISING SHEET
Published Daily.

1860s

Daily Gleaner, October 19, 1865

The Maroons.

This wonderful and loyal people [the aborigines of Jamaica,] have, under Col. A. G. Fyfe, who led them in the last rebellion, turned out for the government to clear the mountains of St. Thomas in the East of the rebels who seek shelter in the natural wildness of their strong holds.

The Maroons.

This wonderful and loyal people [the aborigines of Jamaica,] have, under Col. A. G. Fyfe, who led them in the last rebellion, turned out for the government to clear the mountains of St. Thomas in the East of the rebels who seek shelter in the natural wildness of their strong holds.

Their appearance, decorated with their well-known "war paint," covered with bushes and twigs of the Lignumvitæ, struck terror into the hearts of the rebels at Port[land] and St. Thomas in the East. Where they lay down nothing was discernable of their bodies,—nothing but the living bush that covered them. In this way they march without observation, and in this way they spring like tigers upon their prey, who, seeing nothing but a forrest of bush, imigine themselves secure.

The[y] are already scouring the country try for [reb]els dragging them from their conce[alm]ent and exterminating them where[ever th]ey may be[en] found. Over one h[undred] rebels are reported to have been shot by the Maroons in this mission already.

https://newspaperarchive.com/kingston-gleaner-oct-19-1865-p-2/

Chapter 20
(AFRO)-AMERICAN DOESN'T MEAN AFRICAN

The North Americans made the Afro famous in the 60s and 70s and began calling themselves Afro-Americans. Because of their influence, brown complexion people of various countries in the Americas started calling themselves AFRO-Brazilian, Mexican, Cuban. Some say that the AFRO part of the name denotes African, but this isn't true. The Afro wasn't the signature hairstyle of the West Africans at that time.

Musician Billy Preston with an afro in 1974

Afro, sometimes abbreviated to '**fro**, is a hairstyle worn naturally outward by people with lengthy or even medium length kinky hair texture (wherein it is known as a *natural*), or specifically styled in such a fashion by individuals with naturally curly or straight hair.[1][2] The hairstyle is created by combing the hair away from the scalp, allowing the hair to extend out from the head in a large, rounded shape, much like a cloud or ball.[1][2][3][4][5]

In people with naturally curly or straight hair, the hairstyle is instead typically created with the help of creams, gels or other solidifying liquids to hold the hair in place. Particularly popular in the African-American community of the late 1960s and early 1970s,[3][5] the hairstyle is often shaped and maintained with the assistance of a wide-toothed comb colloquially known as an Afro pick.[2][3][4]

∧ Etymology ✏

"Afro" is derived from the term "Afro-American".[2] The hairstyle is also referred to by some as "natural"—particularly the shorter, less elaborate versions of the Afro—since in most cases the hair is left untreated by relaxers or straightening chemicals and is instead allowed to express its natural curl or kinkiness.[3][5]

To some black African-Americans, the Afro also represented a reconstitutive link to West Africa and Central Africa.[3] However, some critics have suggested that the Afro hairstyle is not particularly African:[3][12] In his book *Welcome to the Jungle: New Positions in Black Cultural Studies*, cultural critic Kobena Mercer argued that the contemporary African society of the mid-20th century did not consider either hairstyle to denote any particular "Africanness"; conversely, some Africans felt that these styles signified "First-worldness".[3]

Similarly, Brackette F. Williams stated in her book *Stains on My Name, War in My Veins: Guyana and the Politics of Cultural Struggle* that African nationalists were irritated by the Afro's adoption by African Americans as a symbol of their African heritage; they saw this trend as an example of Western arrogance.[13]

https://en.m.wikipedia.org/wiki/Afro

AFRICAN-AMERICANS ARE THE AMERICAN INDIANS

Af·ro
/ˈafrō/
noun

a thick hairstyle with very tight curls that sticks out all around the head, like the natural hair of some black people.

American

AMER'ICAN, *adjective* Pertaining to America.

AMER'ICAN, *noun* A native of America; originally applied to the aboriginals, or copper-colored races, found here by the Europeans; but now applied to the

Chapter 21

AMERICAN INDIANS ARE NOT MOORS

A religious organization in the United States called the Moorish Science Temple of America teaches that "black" people in America are moors. I am here to tell you that American Indians are not moors. We will discuss whom the moors are as an ethnicity, where they are from, reasons why American Indians were called Moors, what American Indians had to say about mistakenly being called a moor, and that Queen Isabella knew the difference between moors and American Indians.

1. Moor As An Ethnicity

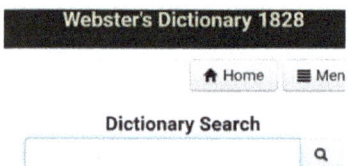

Moor

MOOR, *noun*

1. A tract of land overrun with heath.

2. A marsh; a fen; a tract of wet low ground, or ground covered with stagnant water.

MOOR, *noun* [Gr. dark, obscure.] A native of the northern coast of Africa, called by the Romans from the color of the people, Mauritania, the country of dark-complexioned people. The same country is now called Morocco, Tunis, Algiers, etc.

o. moonnt. 4. like moonlight. 5. mooning; listless.
Moor (moor), *n.* [ME. *More*; OFr. *More, Maure*; L. *Maurus*, a Moor, Mauritanian; Gr. *Mauros*], 1. a member of a Moslem people of mixed Arab and Berber descent living in northwestern Africa. 2. a member of a group of this people that invaded and occupied Spain in the 8th century A.D.
moor (moor), *n.* [ME. *more*; AS. *mor*, wasteland; akin to G. *moor* (< LG.); IE. base *mori-* or *mari-*, sea, as also in L. *mare*, sea, Eng. *marsh*, etc.; basic sense "swampy coast land"], [British], 1. a tract of open wasteland, especially in the British Isles, usually covered with heather and often marshy or peaty; heath. 2. a tract of land with game preserves.

A) Moors Sundry Act of 1790

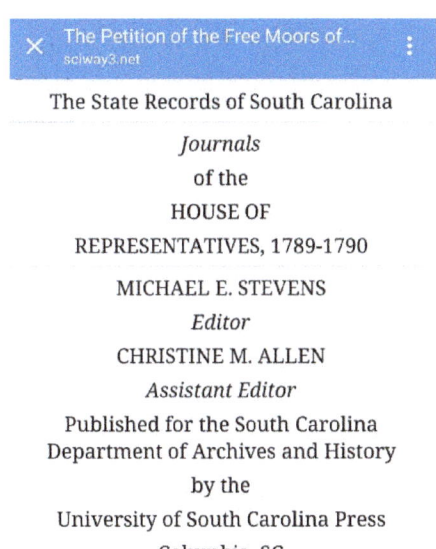

The State Records of South Carolina

Journals

of the

HOUSE OF

REPRESENTATIVES, 1789-1790

MICHAEL E. STEVENS

Editor

CHRISTINE M. ALLEN

Assistant Editor

Published for the South Carolina Department of Archives and History

by the

University of South Carolina Press

Columbia, SC

8557

Copyright ©1984 by the South Carolina Department of Archives and History

First Edition

Published in Columbia, SC by the University

A petition was presented to the House from Sundry Free Moors, Subjects of the Emperor of Morocco; and residents in this State, praying that in case they should Commit Any Fault amenable to be brought to Justice, that they as Subjects to a Prince in Alliance with the United States of America, may be tried under the same Laws as the Citizens of this State would be liable to be tried, and not under the Negro Act, which was received and read.

[The humble Petition of Francis, Daniel, Hammond and Samuel, (Free Moors) in behalf of themselves and their wives Fatima, Flora, Sarah and

(page) 364 House Journal 4 January 1790- 20 January 1790

Clarinda, Humbly Sheweth That your Petitioners some years past had the misfortune while fighting in the defence of their Country, to be captured with their wives and made prisoners of War by one of the Kings of Africa. That a certain Captain Clark had them delivered to him on a promise that they should be redeemed by the Emperor of Morocco's Ambassador then residing in England, in order to have them returned to their own Country: *Instead of which* he brought them to this State, and sold them for slaves. Since that period they have by the greatest industry been enabled to purchase their freedom from their respective Masters: And now prayeth your Honorable House, That as free born

For so-called African Americans to be a moor by ethnicity, they or their ancestors have to be a native of northwest Africa in the area of Morocco, Tunis, Algiers. They also have to be a mix of Arab and Berber blood. Some moors like to use the Moors Sundry Act of 1790 as proof of Americans being moors. However, upon reading the Act, There were only four families that were moors, and they were captives in Africa and sent to South Carolina as slaves. So unless you can prove that you are a descendant of those four families, you are not a moor by blood.

2. The Reason American Indians Were Erroneously Called Moors

Castillian ambassadors attempting to convince Moorish Almohad king Abu Hafs Umar al-Murtada to join their alliance (contemporary depiction from *The Cantigas de Santa María*)

The **Moors** were the Muslim inhabitants of the Maghreb, North Africa, the Iberian Peninsula, Sicily, and Malta during the Middle Ages, who initially were Berber and Arab peoples from North Africa.[1][2]

Moors are not a distinct or self-defined people,[3] and mainstream scholars observed in 1911 that "The term 'Moors' has no real ethnological value."[4] Medieval and early modern Europeans variously applied the name to Arabs, Berber North Africans and Muslim Europeans.[5] The term has also been used in Europe in a broader, somewhat derogatory sense to refer to Muslims in general,[6] especially those of Arab or Berber descent, whether living in Spain or North Africa.[7]

Negro, Black and Moor   81

In the latter part of the seventeenth century, then, the meaning of *moor* began to shift from black or non-white to Muslim, including Muslims of the East Indies. *Swart* began to be used more generally as a term for non-whites, embracing most of the peoples found from India through Indonesia as well as Africans and, occasionally, Americans. Since *moor* and *moren* had also been used for Americans (Antwerp, 1563, and Brazil, 1550s, 1640s), we can see a pattern where both *moor* and *swart* were flexible enough to embrace a broad range of brown to dark brown peoples.

AFRICAN-AMERICANS ARE THE AMERICAN INDIANS

When certain Europeans encountered the American Indians, they described them to have a brown hue similar to the Africans in Europe. Understandably, they called American Indians, moors. In conclusion, American Indians were only called moors because of their skin complexion. The following picture shows an American wearing the attire of a Moor to escape oppression in the United States.

Negro in Turban Tours South
Pastor Treated Like 'Visiting Dignitary'

New York, Nov. 17 (AP)

The Negro pastor of Holy Trinity Lutheran church in Jamaica, Queens, said yesterday he wore a rented purple turban during a recent visit to Mobile, Ala., and was treated like a "visiting dignitary."

Rev. Jesse Weyman Routte, 39, who speaks six languages and holds three college degrees, said in an interview with the Long Island Press that his "experiment" with the turban enabled him to meet white civic, social and political leaders during a week's stay in Mobile.

"I just told them I was an apostle of human relations seeing how other people lived," Rev. Mr. Routte said.

The pastor, who also is a singer and a pianist, said he rented the turban from a New York costumer and put it on in Washington, D. C., before boarding a white passenger car of a segregated train.

Thereafter, he said, he merely stared back at the quizzical, spoke with a "slightly Swedish accent," and ate in diners and restaurants for whites.

Rev. Mr. Routte said no one asked him if he were a Negro.

REV. JESSE W. ROUTTE

https://www.newspapers.com/clip/5434259/negro_in_turban/

AFRICAN-AMERICANS ARE THE AMERICAN INDIANS

3. American Indian Deny Being Called A Moor.

80 yr old John Sanders 1892 Times Article Philadelphia, PA about the (Delawares)

"I really don't know how we came to be called Moors. I have heard, though, that a good many years ago a family of genuine Moors settled somewhere in this part of the country, but I have never seen them, and never heard anything more about them. They certainly had no connection with our people, who are the ones usually known by that name. But if the story is true, the newcomers about here, whom I spoke of, may have got us confused with them, or attached their story to us. There are quite a number of families by the name of Moor or Moore living about here, and this village used to be called Moorton until a few years ago. But the Moore families are mostly white people and none of them have ever been connected with us in any way, and I never heard whether the village was so named on their account or ours. Probably it was on theirs, for the settlement, the original one, is a pretty old one and must have got its name long before we were ever called Moors, and while our descent was well known. In my young days we were called 'planters.' We belonged to the Delaware tribe of Indians, but I don't know what was the name of our clan, probably nobody does now. But I know that our last chief was buried somewhere in the neighborhood of Millsborough, in Sussex county, and I have heard that when they were building the railroad from Lewestown down to Snow Hill, in Maryland, they had to [...] the place where he was buried, [...]

John Sanders' house was found after a walk of about a mile over such perfectly level country as only Delaware can show. The old man was at home, and was glad to see visitors. He must have been a remarkably fine-looking man in youth, and has not yet lost all pretensions to good looks. Though he is 80 years of age, he walks as straight as ever; his eyes are clear and strong, his voice full, and his straight black hair, thick and heavy, is only slightly streaked with gray. Our modern American curse of baldness has passed him by, and he might easily pass for thirty years younger than he is. And his features were even more unlike a negro's than any we had yet seen; a lean face, broad forehead, high cheek-bones, and prominent but thin nose, with a downward curve which might have been termed "hooked."

"I'm afraid I can't tell you much about our people," he said, "but you are welcome to the little I know. No, we are not Moors, neither are we mulattos. We are Indians, and we belong to a branch of tha great Delaware Nation, which used to hold all this country from New York to Cape Charles. Down in Sussex county, on the backbone ridge of the Peninsula, the head waters of two rivers rise close together—one of them, the Nanticoke river, [...]

https://www.newspapers.com/newspage/52836993/

From the article, we learned that the Delaware Indians didn't know how they had come to be called moors, and the people who were moors were white (pale - skin Caucasian/European descent) people. They also said that they didn't have a connection with those people who were called moors, and they are proud to be called Indians.

Page | 252

4. Queen Isabella Knew The Difference Between A Moor & Indian

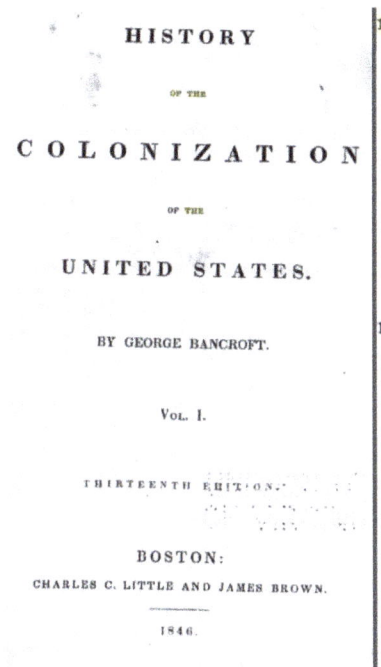

1500. The generous Isabella commanded the liberation of the Indians held in bondage in her European possessions.² Yet her active benevolence extended neither to the Moors, whose valor had been punished by slavery, nor to the Africans; and even her compassion for the New World was but the transient feeling, which relieves the miserable who are in sight, not the deliberate application of a just principle. For the commissions for making discoveries, issued a few days June 5 before and after her interference to rescue those whom and July Columbus had enslaved, reserved for herself and Ferdinand a fourth part³ of the slaves which the new 1501. kingdoms might contain. The slavery of Indians was recognized as lawful.⁴

The practice of selling the natives of North America into foreign bondage continued for nearly two centuries; and even the sternest morality pronounced the sentence of slavery and exile on the captives whom the field of battle had spared. The excellent Winthrop enumerates Indians among his bequests.⁵ The articles of the early New England confederacy class persons among the spoils of war. A scanty remnant of the

---
¹ Irving's Columbus, b. viii. c. v.
² Navarette, Coll. ii. 246, 247.
³ Esclavos, é negros, é loros que en estos nuestros reinos sean habidos é reputados por esclavos, &c.
⁴ Navarette, ii. 245, and again, ii. 249.
⁵ See a cédula on a slave contract, in Navarette, iii. 514, 515, given June 20, 1501.
⁵ Winthrop's N. E., ii. 360.

https://books.google.com/books?id=9mVTAAAAYAAJ&pg=PA168&lpg=PA168&dq=in+1500,+the+generous+isabella+commanded+the+liberation+of+the+indians+held+in+bondage+in+her+european+possessions&source=bl&ots=u1P0OXUPAc&sig=ACfU3U2UA-c1EvOKEPQkaqXjvL_xvjWBWg&hl=en&sa=X&ved=2ahUKEwjzmbSKqKPjAhXLc98KHTMLCXoQ6AEwBnoECAMQAQ#v=onepage&q=in%201500%2C%20the%20generous%20isabella%20commanded%20the%20liberation%20of%20the%20indians%20held%20in%20bondage%20in%20her%20european%20possessions&f=false

AFRICAN-AMERICANS ARE THE AMERICAN INDIANS

Chapter 22
YOU'RE A COTTON PICKER AND BE PROUD OF IT!

Many African Americans are insulted for being called a cotton picker. They were taught that they were the descendants of the weak stock of Africans brought to the Americas to be slaves and pick cotton for their European slave masters. The truth is cotton is indigenous to the Americas, and the American Indians have been cultivating cotton for thousands of years. The Americas have some of the oldest and most extensive variety of cotton species. There is nothing shameful about cotton picking. It's **OUR CROP**!

Cotton

文A ☆ ✏

For other uses, see Cotton (disambiguation).

Manually decontaminating cotton before processing at an Indian spinning mill (2010)

Cotton is a soft, fluffy staple fiber that grows in a boll, or protective case, around the seeds of the cotton plants of the genus *Gossypium* in the family of *Malvaceae*. The fiber is almost pure cellulose. Under natural conditions, the cotton bolls will tend to increase the dispersal of the seeds. [clarification needed]

The plant is a shrub native to tropical and subtropical regions around the world, including the Americas, Africa, and India. The greatest diversity of wild cotton species is found in Mexico, followed by Australia and Africa.[1] Cotton was independently domesticated in the Old and New Worlds.

The fiber is most often spun into yarn or thread and used to make a soft, breathable textile. The use of cotton for fabric is known to date to prehistoric times; fragments of cotton fabric dated from 5000 BC have been excavated in Mexico and between 6000 BC

Mexico

Cotton fabrics discovered in a cave near Tehuacán, Mexico have been dated to around 5800 BC.[10] The **domestication** of *Gossypium hirsutum* in Mexico is dated between 3400 and 2300 BC.[11]

Peru

In Peru, cultivation of the indigenous cotton species *Gossypium barbadense* has been dated, from a find in Ancon, to c 4200 BC,[12] and was the backbone of the development of coastal cultures such as the Norte Chico, Moche, and Nazca. Cotton was grown upriver,

Page | 254

THE

MISSIONARY HERALD,

FOR THE YEAR 1823.

VOL. XIX.

BOSTON:
PUBLISHED FOR THE BOARD BY SAMUEL T. ARMSTRONG.
Crocker & Brewster, Printers.

1823. Choctaw Mission:—Journal at Elliot. 115

About the 10th of December, Mr. Kingsbury arrived at Elliot to meet the agent of the United States, and confer with a dissatisfied chief, respecting the school. It is a subject of complaint with a part of the Choctaws, that boys are made to work when out of school, and punished for misconduct. With them, as with all untutored people, children grow up entirely free from restraint. It can hardly be expected, that, in the early stages of improvement, all difficulty and embarrassment from this source should be avoided. The missionaries have held but one language on the subject. They have uniformly declared, that children committed to their care must be subject to their authority;—must be docile and obedient in school, and trained to

Dec. 28. He was much gratified with the kindness of the people, and their disposition to receive instruction. He went to a village about 16 miles distant, and staid most of the time at the house of the chief. Within two miles of the house where he staid are about 20 families, and between 30 and 40 children of a suitable age to attend school, who now have little to do, and are wasting their time in idleness or play. There are three looms in this village;—one of them made by a Choctaw. The Indians raise corn, cotton, sweet potatoes, beans, &c. The women were generally at work, picking cotton, spinning, sewing, or cooking, while the men do little else than talk, sit, and smoke tobacco. The children appeared anxious to learn.

The Coronado expedition, 1540-1542
George Parker Winship, Smithsonian Institution, Bureau of American Ethnology

550   THE CORONADO EXPEDITION, 1540-1542   [ETH. ANN. 14

The men weave cloth and spin cotton. They have salt from a marshy lake, which is two days from the province of Cibola.[1] The Indians have their dances and songs, with some flutes which have holes on which to put the fingers. They make much noise. They sing in unison with those who play, and those who sing clap their hands in our fashion. One of the Indians that accompanied the negro Esteban, who had been a captive there, saw the playing as they practiced it, and others singing as I have said, although not very vigorously. They say that five or six play together, and that some of the flutes are better than others.[2] They say the country is good for corn and beans, and that they do not have any fruit trees, nor do they know what such a thing is.[3] They have very good mountains. The country lacks water. They do not raise cotton, but bring it from Totonteac.[4] They eat out of flat bowls, like the Mexicans. They raise considerable corn

https://books.google.com/books?id=sAcTAAAAYAAJ&pg=PA550&lpg=PA550&dq=coronado+saw+indians+raising+cotton&source=bl&ots=823E13jrWA&sig=ACfU3U2mIzrDXkscfGqTqYyWVcG2d6v6Jw&hl=en&sa=X&ved=2ahUKEwiiitS2q67jAhXBm-AKHXUEDZkQ6AEwCHoECAkQAQ#v=onepage&q=coronado%20saw%20indians%20raising%20cotton&f=false

Chapter 23

American Indians Are Not Hebrew Israelites

There has been a growing trend of African Americans calling themselves Hebrew Israelites. They claim that the American Indians are one of the lost tribes of Israel. Some of them will say that the African Americans plight correlates with some of the biblical stories, and that is another reason they claim the Hebrew identity. They also claim that their Hebrew ancestors came to the Americas during the transatlantic slave trade. In my opinion, all of these claims are false and suspicious. Some Hebrew findings in the Americas have proven to be fraudulent, and the American Indians claim to derive from no other place but the Americas. The Jews thought the whole world only consisted of Africa, Europe, and Asia, and the American Indians have their own creation stories. The American Indians didn't know of a Yahweh, Yeshua, Jesus, Elohim, or anyone from the Judaism or Catholic/Christianity belief system. If they knew of these Gods of their religion, then the Spanish and Portuguese wouldn't have forced the religion on them or documented that the American Indians didn't know their Gods. Things that make you go hmm.

HISTORY OF THE UNITED STATES.

PART I.
ABORIGINAL AMERICA.

CHAPTER 1.
THE RED MEN—ORIGIN, DISTRIBUTION, CHARACTER.

THE primitive inhabitants of the New World were the Red men called INDIANS. The name *Indian* was conferred upon them from their real or fancied resemblance to the people of India. But without any such similarity the name would have been the same; for Columbus and his followers, believing that they had only rediscovered the Indies, would of course call the inhabitants Indians. The supposed similarity between the two races, if limited to mere personal appearance, had some foundation in fact; but in manners, customs, institutions, and character, no two peoples could be more dissimilar than the American aborigines and the sleepy inhabitants of China and Japan.

The origin of the North American Indians is involved in complete obscurity. That they are one of the older races of mankind can not be doubted. But at what date or by what route they came to the Western continent is an unsolved problem. Many theories have been proposed to account for the Red man's presence in the New World, but most of them have been vague and unsatisfactory. The notion that the Indians are the descendants of the Israelites is absurd. That half civilized tribes, wandering from beyond the Euphrates, should reach North America, surpasses human credulity. That Europeans or Africans, at some remote period, crossed the Atlantic by voyaging from island to island, seems altogether improbable. That the Kamtchatkans, coming by way of Behring's Strait, reached the frozen North-west and

(41)

---

but most of them have been vague and unsatisfactory. The notion that the Indians are the descendants of the Israelites is absurd. That half civilized tribes, wandering from beyond the Euphrates, should reach North America, surpasses human credulity. That Europeans or Afri-

1. What The Hebrews Thought The World Consist Of

www.pinterest.com

1000+ images about Biblical - Noah and the Ark on Pinterest

AFRICAN-AMERICANS ARE THE AMERICAN INDIANS

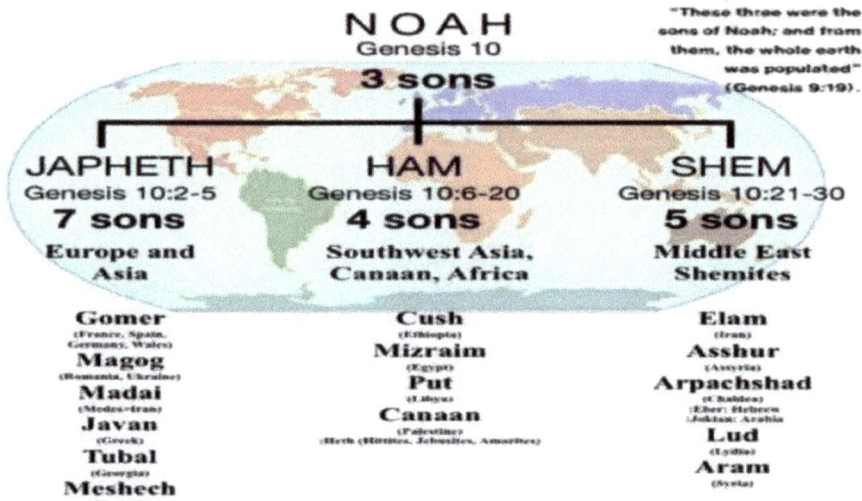

2. Hebrew Isn't A Race Of People

Hebrew (adj.)

late Old English, from Old French *Ebreu*, from Latin *Hebraeus*, from Greek *Hebraios*, from Aramaic (Semitic) *'ebhrai*, corresponding to Hebrew *'ibhri* "an Israelite." Traditionally from an ancestral name *Eber*, but probably literally "one from the other side," perhaps in reference to the River Euphrates, or perhaps simply signifying "immigrant;" from *'ebher* "region on the other or opposite side." The initial *H-* was restored in English from 16c. As a noun from c. 1200,

| Gen | ▾ | 14 | ▾ | Bible | ▾ |

went their way. ¹²And they took Lot, Abram's brother's son, who dwelt in Sodom, and his goods, and departed.

Abram Rescues Lot

¹³And there came one that had escaped, and told Abram the Hebrew; for he dwelt in the plain of Mamre the Amorite, brother of Eshcol, and brother of Aner: and these *were* confederate with Abram.

im·mi·grant
/ˈiməgrənt/ 🔊

noun

a person who comes to live permanently in a foreign country.
synonyms: newcomer, settler, migrant, emigrant,

Abraham the Hebrew

In this week's portion Abraham is referred to for the first time as "Abraham the Hebrew" (Genesis 14:13). The root of the Hebrew word for "Hebrew" (ivri) literally means "to cross over." Why does the Torah give Abraham this name? One opinion is that he gained this name because in coming to Israel he left his birth place in Ur Kasdim and crossed over the Euphrates, a major geographical demarcation line in the ancient world. Thus he was known as one who had "crossed over." In a more spiritual

3. Hebrew Artifacts In America Are Fraudulent

It certainly is true that John Emmert, the man who claimed to have found the Bat Creek Stone, was in the employ of the Smithsonian Institution at the time of its discovery. During this period, the Smithsonian hired an eclectic assortment of individuals with varying levels of expertise to conduct local operations on the Institution's behalf. Emmert appears to have been one of the lesser qualified excavators, and he was later fired because of questions about the quality of his work (Mainfort and Kwas 1991, 12). Even discounting the obvious questions about his competence, since Emmert excavated the stone in 1889, his methods could hardly be considered "modern" in any meaningful sense. Finally, since the archaeologists Robert Mainfort and Mary Kwas discovered the source used by the forgers of the Bat Creek inscription, conclusively demonstrating it to be a fraud (Mainfort and Kwas 2004), consideration of Emmert's qualifications is moot. It is clear now that Emmert either perpetrated the fraud himself or failed to detect the imposture because of his dodgy methods.

Figure 3. The Bat Creek Stone is one of a number of ancient artifacts found in North America bearing inscriptions in Old World scripts. All such artifacts have been shown to be fraudulent.

AFRICAN-AMERICANS ARE THE AMERICAN INDIANS

4. American Indian Origins

> The *Americans* can give but a little better Account of their firſt Original; and indeed it is no wonder, becauſe for want of Books they can relate nothing certain, but only what they have Regiſtred in their uſual *Quipocamagos*, which is not above four hundred years old. *Acoſta* asking what Original they judg'd they were of, and from what Countrey and People deriv'd? receiv'd no other Anſwer, but that *America* only was their native Countrey, and that they were deriv'd from no other elſewhere.

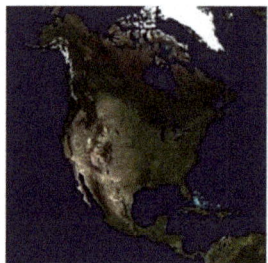

Satellite image of North America ("Turtle Island")

Turtle Island is a name for the Earth[1] or for land in North America (in whole or in part), used by many Native Americans and First Nations people and by Indigenous rights activists.

^ Lenape

The Lenape story of the "Great Turtle" was first recorded by Europeans between 1678 and 1680 by Jasper Danckaerts. The story is shared by other Northeastern Woodlands tribes, notably those of the Iroquois Confederacy.[2]

^ Iroquois

According to Iroquois oral history, "the earth was the thought of [a ruler] of a great island which floats in space [and] is a place of eternal peace."[3] Sky Woman fell down to the earth when it was covered with water, or more specifically, when there was a "great cloud sea.[1]. Various animals tried to swim to the bottom of the ocean to bring back dirt to create land. Muskrat succeeded in gathering *oeh-da* (earth),[1] which was placed on the back of a turtle. This earth grew into North America[4] or into the present planet Earth itself: "Hah-nu-nah, the Turtle, became the Earth Bearer."[1] According to Converse and Parker, the Iroquois faith shared with Hinduism and other religions the "belief that the earth is supported by a gigantic turtle"[1] In the Seneca language, the mythical turtle is called *Hah-nu-nah*,[1] while the name for an everyday turtle is *ha-no-wa*.[5]

https://en.m.wikipedia.org/wiki/Turtle_Island_(North_America)

Page | 262

MAN-BEING. Term for one of the many wise men some Indians believed came before everything else and created the earth and the gods. In most tribes this belief forms the basis of their mythology.

It would appear from the many legends that this once-powerful race of man-beings lived in a region above the sky. They all existed in peace and harmony in the beginning. However, these beings were not alike. Each one, as time ripened, became transformed more and more into what he later was to become. He had his own magic power by which he would perform his duties after the changing of all things.

Naturally these changing man-beings began to think differently, and unrest and discord arose among them. Then after commotion, collision, and strife the great change came about. The transformed man-beings were banished from their sky home to the earth where they assumed their proper forms. Some became trees, others plants, fish, rocks, animals, mountains—in fact they took the shapes of all things, even man.

The worlds were grouped into seven forms—a magic number among Indians. There was the east, west, north, south, upper world, lower world, and midworld. All these worlds were inhabited by man-beings in the forms of wind, sun, stars, the moon, and even storms. Winter, summer, fall, and spring—all were man-beings.

As all man-beings had magic powers, the Indian believed that mere man could not exist without the aid of man-beings around him. And, as some man-beings were good and others bad, the Indian thought it wise not to offend the bad ones.

Without knowing the Indian's belief in man-beings, the white man was at a loss to understand the Indian's religion. For each Indian selected his own man-beings to aid him in overcoming difficulties, after seeing them in dreams or visions, and often entire tribes would worship one or more man-beings.

The Mandan, for instance, placed a piece of cloth around one of the poles of his lodge as a gift to the God of Timber, believing it would keep this god from being angry at him for cutting down a tree to make a pole. The Navajo was always apologetic to the Earth when he removed clay to make pottery. The Menominee would not cultivate wild rice because in doing so he would have to disturb Mother Earth. See DREAMS, GREAT SPIRIT, MANITOU, MASKS, MEDICINE, MENOMINEE, ORENDA, SACRED BUNDLES, STARS.

Chapter 24

AMERICA : THE MOTHER

Many African Americans love talking about Africa and how they believe it's the motherland of man and woman. However, the Europeans gave the Out of Africa theory to them. In this chapter, we will reveal that North America is the oldest and how America has been taking care of Africa for a long time.

1. The oldest continent

largest modern continent still being pieced together; chunks of crust arrive from the south, riding on highly mobile tectonic plates. The African and South American continents aggregated from mobile cratons about 700 million years ago. North America, possibly the oldest continent, assembled from seven cratons around 2 billion years ago (Fig. 10), forming central Canada and north-central United States. Half a billion years ago, North America was a lost continent, drifting on its own, while most other landmasses combined into a supercontinent.

Continental collisions continued adding new crust to the growing proto–North American continent. A large portion of the continental crust underlying the United States from Arizona to the Great Lakes to Alabama formed in a surge of crustal generation unequaled in North America since. The assembled continent was stable and resilient, able to withstand a billion years of jostling and rifting. It continued to grow as bits and pieces of continents and island arcs adhered to its margins.

Large masses of volcanic rock near the eastern edge of the North American continent indicate that around 750 million years ago, the continent sat at the core of a supercontinent called Rodinia (Fig. 11), which is Russian

https://books.google.com/books?id=HnisTYtE2lYC&pg=PA13&lpg=PA13&dq=north+america+possibly+the+oldest+continent+assembled+from+seven+cratons&source=bl&ots=dDBhTyp73H&sig=ACfU3U3GnhaDfoGpDLeb7tb4Zge7AEHr0w&hl=en&sa=X&ved=2ahUKEwir4uWJ7O7jAhWPtVkKHfktAKoQ6AEwCnoECAcQAQ#v=onepage&q=north%20america%20possibly%20the%20oldest%20continent%20assembled%20from%20seven%20cratons&f=false

2. The oldest skull

COLLECTOR: FIND CHANGES EVOLUTION SCIENTISTS: 'SKULL FOSSIL' IS QUARTZ

By **RON DEVLIN, The Morning Call**
THE MORNING CALL

SEPTEMBER 28, 1986

Ed Conrad was poking around some old coal banks in northern Schuylkill County in June 1981, searching for fossils, when he came across an unusual rock.

The 47-year-old fossil collector was intrigued enough by its yellow claylike color and curved shape, which resembled the crown of a skull, to dig out the pineapple-size rock and take it home.

But the more Conrad looked at the rock, the more he thought he had unearthed a skull.

And after reading up on human anatomy, looking at scrapings under a microscope and having a portion of it X-rayed by a local dentist, he became convinced that what he had found was indeed part of a petrified skull - perhaps millions of years old.

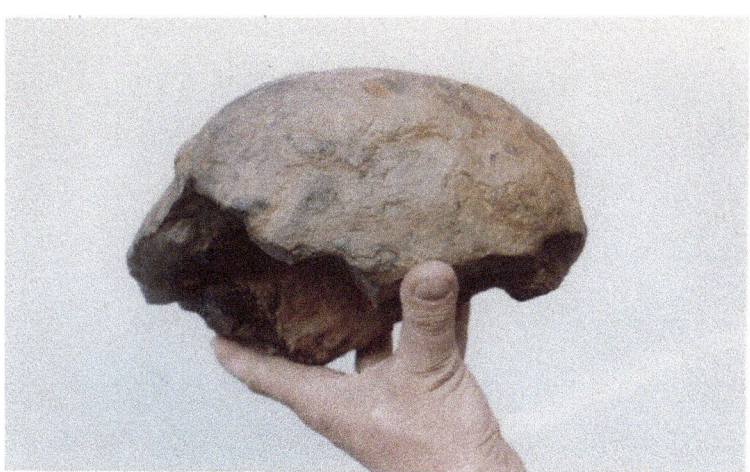

This is the specimen that both Wilton Krogman and Dr. Raymond A. Dart believed may well be a portion of a petrified human skull (a calvarium). It should be noted that the cellular structure of bone is plainly visible in microscopic study of this particular specimen and a CATscan had been done on it with favorable results.

It was a discovery that, although he did not realize it then, would have a major influence on his life.

Over the next few years, he would spend an estimated 15,000 hours of his spare time rigorously searching the coal banks, the remnants of decades of strip mining, for what he believes are important pieces in the evolutionary puzzle of the human species.

In the process, he has discovered what look like portions of two more skulls, three dozen artifacts shaped like parts of a primate jaw and thousands - perhaps 20,000 - of smooth bone-shaped rocks that he believes are the petrified bones of various species that inhabited the swampy region that was northeast Pennsylvania 300 million years ago.

https://www.mcall.com/news/mc-xpm-1986-09-28-2532363-story.html

AFRICAN-AMERICANS ARE THE AMERICAN INDIANS

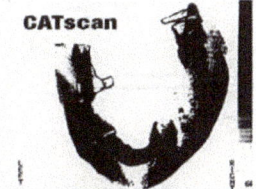

Oldest Human Skull

The late Wilton Krogman, author of "The Human Skeleton in Forensic Medicine," holds what he identified as "the world's oldest human skull." It was discovered by Ed Conrad between coal veins.

3. DNA older than Africans

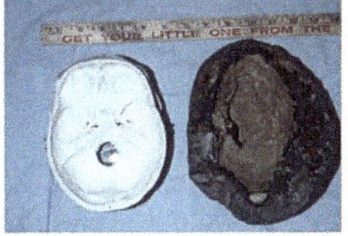

The father of all men is 340,000 years old

UNASSIGNED 6 March 2013

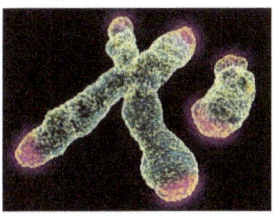

Dwarfed by the X chromosome, the Y seems more ancient than we thought

DNA: a Y chromosome so distinctive that it reveals new information about the origin of our species. It shows that the last common male ancestor down the paternal line of our species is over twice as old as we thought.

One possible explanation is that hundreds of thousands of years ago, modern and archaic humans in central Africa interbred, adding to known examples of interbreeding – with Neanderthals in the Middle East, and with the enigmatic Denisovans somewhere in southeast Asia.

Perry, recently deceased, was an African-American who lived in South Carolina. A few years ago, one of his female relatives submitted a sample of his DNA to a company called Family Tree DNA for genealogical analysis.

Geneticists can use such samples to work out how we are related to one another. Hundreds of thousands of people have now had their DNA tested. The data from these tests had shown that all men gained their Y chromosome from a common male ancestor. This genetic "Adam" lived between 60,000 and 140,000 years ago.

All men except Perry, that is. When Family Tree DNA's technicians tried to place Perry on the Y-chromosome family tree, they just couldn't. His Y chromosome was like no other so far analysed.

https://www.newscientist.com/article/dn23240-the-father-of-all-men-is-340000-years-old/

FYI: The eleven Cameroon Africans that they said Albert Perry was linked to, were unidentified. The reason they were unidentified is because they don't exist. They have to keep the out of Africa theory going even though it has been debunked for decades.

4. America (The Mother) civilizing Africa (The Child)

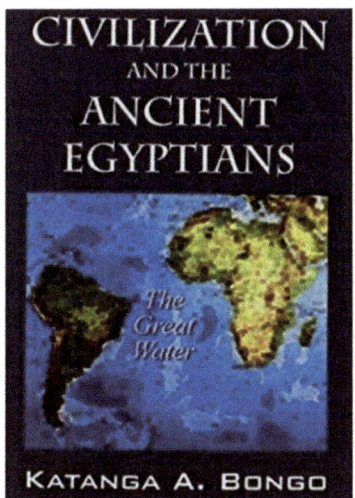

Katanga A. Bongo

West Africa-born Katanga A. Bongo is a historian who lives in the United States. His research in South America's influence on Africa was sparked by interest in the linguistic heritage of a relative, an 18th-century wanderer named Red Bird. Bongo's quest took him throughout the two continents to uncover the true history of the Ancient Egyptians. Civilization and the Ancient Egyptians is the first in a series unraveling the mysteries of Africa.

The idea that it was Europeans who introduced civilization to Africa is one of the biggest historical myths. In fact, evidence from archeology, oral history, traditional languages, and cultural practices strongly indicate that it was the South American Indians who introduced civilization to Africa some seven thousand years ago. Long before the Greek and Roman civilizations emerged, the South American Indians had introduced civilization to Africa, thereby making Africa the second continent in the world to become civilized. Spurred on by their South American Indian guests, the Africans built great empires that lasted for several thousand years at a time. Contrary to popular myth in

CIVILIZATION AND THE ANCIENT EGYPTIANS

ARCHITECTURE

The first novelty that the South Americans introduced to Africa was the art of house building. They built houses out of mud. To build a house, they took ordinary soil and poured water on it. They stepped on it for several minutes to transform it into mud. Next they rolled the mud into hand-sized balls. The wet mud balls were handed to a trained builder who stuck the mud balls one after another in a circle or a rectangle. When the circle or rectangle was completed, a second layer of mud balls were placed on top of the first layer. After three or four layers, the building was stopped and the structure was allowed to dry in the sun. House building was done in the dry season when there was a lot of sunshine and no rainfall. The next day another

CERAMICS

One of the most valuable works of art that the South Americans introduced to the Africans was the art of ceramics. The South American Indians pioneered the use of clay, and they had been making and using ceramic bowls, cooking vessels, and semi-closed water containers for several centuries before they came to Africa. There was an abundant supply of clay in North Africa 7,000 years ago. Clay work was the first major activity that the South Americans engaged in, alongside pyramid building and boat building. It was also one of the first artistic works that they taught the Africans. They showed the Africans how to use clay to mold circular bowls, cooking pots, and water containers. They also showed the Africans how to decorate the vessels. The decorations were made with red, black, or white paint. The finished products were burnt in fire for hardening. The pots were used as water containers and for cooking. The bowls were used as dishes. Clay figurines that were used as jewelry and for religious purposes were also quite common.

5. America (The Mother) Feeding Africa (The Child)

AGRICULTURE

Another often overlooked piece of evidence in the study of human civilizations is the agricultural similarity between South America and Africa. At the time that the South Americans first got to Africa, the Africans did not know anything about cultivation. It was the South American Indi-

64

CIVILIZATION AND THE ANCIENT EGYPTIANS

ans who introduced the idea of cultivation to Africa. The biggest change that the South Americans brought to Africa was the change in agriculture from foraging to cultivation. Not only did the South Americans introduce cultivation to Africa, but they also introduced a wide variety of crops to Africa. The land in North Africa at the time had amazing agricultural potential, but what was lacking was variety of agricultural crops. The wide variety of crops that the South Americans introduced to Egypt was one of the principal factors that led to the rapid rise in the prominence of ancient Egypt. Today more than ninety percent of the crop varieties that exist in Africa are South American Indian crops. All the root crops that are grown in Africa today are South American crops. Nearly all the vegetable varieties that are cultivated in Africa today originated in South America. Most African traditional dishes originated in South America. Among the crops that the South Americans introduced to Africa are pepper, kola nut, corn, millet, yam, sweet potato, cocoyam, pumpkin, squash, gourd, black-eyed peas, peanuts, okra, pineapple, cocoa, plantain, banana, tobacco, palm-nut, coconut, ginger, garlic, sugarcane, tomato, onion, and cotton. Gourds were used to make eating and drinking vessels. Tobacco was used only for smoking. The South Americans also introduced goat, hen, guinea hen, and dog to Africa.

Today, seven thousand years later, there is still a large overlap between indigenous South American agriculture and African agriculture.

https://books.google.com/books/about/Civilization_and_the_Ancient_Egyptians.html?id=44wtQCdCf70C&printsec=frontcover&source=kp_read_button

AFRICAN-AMERICANS ARE THE AMERICAN INDIANS

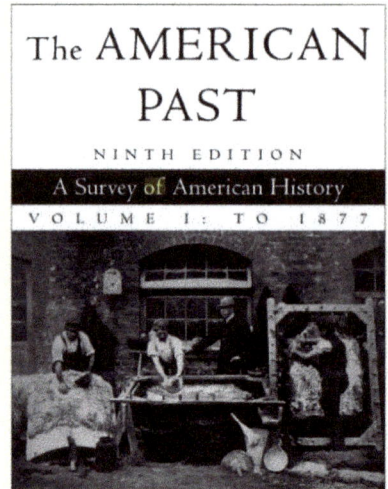

JOSEPH R. CONLIN

Feeding the World

America contributed few food animals to world larders, but American plant foods revolutionized the European, African, and Asian diet. Maize (Indian corn), an American native, astonished Europeans by the height of its stalks and the size of its grains. Cultivation of the crop spread to every continent, increasing the food supply and contributing to the runaway increase in population that characterizes the last five hundred years of human history.

The sweet potato became a staple in West Africa, where it was introduced by slave traders. (Yams, superficially similar to sweet potatoes, were already established there.) Beans, squash and pumpkins, peppers, strawberries (there was a European strawberry, but it was inferior to the American), vanilla and chocolate, wild rice, and tomatoes are American natives unknown in Europe, Africa, and Asia before 1492.

Of 640 food crops grown in Africa today, almost 600 originated in the Americas. Manioc (tapioca), also of American origin, is today a staple for 200 million people in the tropics. The white ("Irish") potato, a native of the Andes, provides basic subsistence for even greater numbers, from Ireland to China.

Many national cuisines today depend on foods of American origin for their zest, notably the tomato and the extraordinary variety of chili peppers that have been developed from Mexican forebears. Think of Hungarian paprika, of Italian sauces. These, as well as tobacco, were contributed to the Old World by New.

https://books.google.com/books?id=AbEIAAAAQBAJ&pg=PA22&lpg=PA22&dq=of+640+food+crops+grown+in+africa+today,+almost+600+originated+in+the+americas&source=bl&ots=KyJmNTOMlN&sig=ACfU3U1-9n5vdfn3Q9lPTvEpCyd5y-p-oA&hl=en&sa=X&ved=2ahUKEwiCmq6oye7jAhWmmOAKHZhqAOIQ6AEwAHoECAIQAQ#v=onepage&q=of%20640%20food%20crops%20grown%20in%20africa%20today%2C%20almost%20600%20originated%20in%20the%20americas&f=false

AND THAT'S WHY...

The **Maya** sages doubtless had reached similar conclusions, since they called their country **Mayach**; that is, "the land first emerged from the bosom of the deep," "the country of the *shoot;*" and the Egyptians, according to Herodotus, boasted that "their ancestors, in the 'Lands of the West,' were the oldest men on earth."

If the opinion of Lyell, Humphry, and a host of modern geologists, regarding the priority of America's antiquity, be correct, what right have we to gainsay the assertion of the **Mayas** and of the Egyptians in claiming likewise priority for their people and their country?

It is but natural to suppose that intelligence in man was developed on the oldest continent, among its most ancient inhabitants; and that its concomitant, civilization, grew apace with its development. When, at the impulse of the instinct of self-preservation, men linked themselves into clans, tribes, and nations, history was born, and with it a desire to commemorate the events of which it is composed. The art of drawing or writing was then invented. The incidents regarded as most worthy of being remembered and preserved for the knowledge of coming generations were carved on the most enduring material in their possession—stone. And so it is that we find to-day the cosmogonic and religious notions, the records of natural phenomena and predominant incidents in the history of their nation and that of their rulers, sculptured on the walls of the temples and palaces of the civilized Mayas, Chaldeans, and Egyptians, as on the sacred rocks and in the hallowed caves of primitive uncivilized man.

It is to the monumental inscriptions and to the books of the Mayas that we must turn if we wish to learn about the primeval traditions of mankind, the development of civilization, and the events that took place centuries before the dim myths recorded as occurrences at the beginning of our written history.

Historians when writing on the universal history of the race have never taken into consideration that of man in America, and the rôle that in remote ages American nations played on this world's stage, and the influence they exerted over the populations of Asia, Africa, and Europe. Still, as far as we can scan the long vista of the past centuries, the Mayas seem to have had direct and intimate communications with them.

https://books.google.com/books?id=7HwUAAAAYAAJ&pg=PR9&lpg=PR9&dq=the+mayas+sages+doubtless+had+reached+similar+conclusions,+since+they+called+their+country+mayach&source=bl&ots=6zY75ijp7W&sig=ACfU3U09cEUsrHOgC-JQLCbue-BG0XNitQ&hl=en&sa=X&ved=2ahUKEwj1v87a7-7jAhUszlkKHZLzC7gQ6AEwCnoECAkQAQ#v=onepage&q=the%20mayas%20sages%20doubtless%20had%20reached%20similar%20conclusions%2C%20since%20they%20called%20their%20country%20mayach&f=false

Cris Junior ▸ **African Americans Ain't Africans**
August 9 at 4:46pm

If Africa Is Our Motherland They Should Have 100 Michael Jordan's, Jackson's, Tyson's, Johnsons. Serena & Venus Williams, Tiger Woods, Peles, Simone Biles, Gabby Douglas's, etc. Africa Should Have 100 Stevie Wonders, Ray Charles's, James Browns, Aretha Franklins, Whitney Houstons, Mc Lytes, 2Pacs, Usain Bolts, Cherly Millers, Jackie Joyner Kerseys, Florence Griffith Joyners, etc. They Should Have a 100 Eddie Murphys' Richard Pryors, Dave Chappeles, Red Foxx's, Paul Mooney's, etc. They Should Be The Best Singers, Stand Up Comics, Rappers, Rock & Rollers, Guitarist, Pianists, Drummers, Have More Music Genres That Are Popular WorldWide Then Us In The AMericas That Gave The World, Negro Spirituals, Blues, Jazz, Rock & Roll, Country, R&B, Hip Hop, Reggae, Etc. They Should Have 100 George Washington Carvers, Madame CJ Walkers, etc. They Should Have More Pyramids Then The World. More Earthen Mounds Then The Rest Of The World. We Are Our Own People! We Should Be Biting Africa's Swag And So Should Everyone Else If That Is Our Motherland And The World's. If They Are The First And The Most Original And The Purest Of Man Why Would My Questions Not Be True? We Are The Soul People, That Eat Soul Food, Sing With Soul And Do Everything With Soul! AmeRicans The Soul Rich People! The Children Of The Sun And The Matriarch! People Around The World Imitate Us. Originals Create We Do Not Copy Or Imitate!

CONCLUSION

We have reached the end of this portion of the book. I provided overwhelming evidence proving that the people labeled African Americans are the descendants of the American Indians. I proved that reclassification was the cause of near extinction, utilizing census records, laws, school education, and the media. If you're an African American reading this book, I hope that you gained enlightenment and inspiration to learn more about America's history. There is a wealth of information that isn't in this book that I purposely left out because I want you to go on this journey with me. I hope that from reading this book, you'll investigate your family and find your exact truth in the Americas.

Your grandparents weren't lying to you when they told you that you have Indian blood in your family. It's the outsiders who lied by generalizing and telling you a false narrative that you're a descendant of an African slave brought to the Americas. The African slave trade narrative may be real for some because there were some Africans transported here, but that's an individual's journey to find out. I have talked to many African Americans, and they always say they were told that they were Indian from their relatives, and the African identity came from school or some scholar. If, after reading this far and you think I am crazy or ashamed of being "black" or African, then I apologize for wasting your time. You should delete this eBook or throw the physical copy in the trash. If this book resonates with you, keep reading because there is much to discuss.

> "A life that is not documented is a life that within a generation or two will largely be lost to memory. What a tragedy this can be in the history of a family. Knowledge of our ancestors shapes us and instills within us values that give direction and meaning to our lives."
>
> - Dennis B. Neuenschwander
>
> ancestry

SECTION 8: WHERE DO WE GO FROM HERE

Chapter 25
SOLUTIONS MOVING FORWARD

Now that we understand that the people labeled African Americans are the American Indians. The next question is, what should we do now? In this section, I am going to list things that we should start doing to preserve, progress, and strengthen us as a collective.

STOP CLAIMING "BLACK" AS AN IDENTITY

Many people labeled as African – American do not realize the problems of using black as a racial identity. I am going to list several reasons WHY the use of it as a racial classification should stop.

A) NO HUEMAN CAN BE THE COLOR BLACK

In elementary school, the first lesson we learn about the basic definition of the term black is that it is a COLOR. We also learned that it was an ADJECTIVE, the darkest color on the color spectrum, and used to describe the color of a noun. The teachers showed us a black dog and other black objects. If we are nouns as living beings and black is an adjective, how can we ever be black? That means you want to be an adjective and not exist.

AFRICAN-AMERICANS ARE THE AMERICAN INDIANS

Webster's Dictionary 1828

♦ Home   ≡ Menu

Dictionary Search

The KINGS BIBLE study tools >

Black

BLACK, *adjective*

1. Of the color of night; destitute of light; dark.

2. Darkened by clouds; as the heavens *black* with clouds.

 ad·jec·tive
/ˈajəktiv/

noun   GRAMMAR

a word or phrase naming an attribute, added to or grammatically related to a noun to modify or describe it.

From Oxford   Feedback

 noun
/noun/

noun   GRAMMAR

a word (other than a pronoun) used to identify any of a class of people, places, or things (*common noun*), or to name a particular one of these (*proper noun*).

From Oxford   Feedback

Black

This article is about the color. For other uses, see Black (disambiguation).

Black is the darkest color, the result of the absence or complete absorption of visible light. It is an achromatic color, a color without hue, like white and gray.[1] It is often used symbolically or figuratively to represent darkness, while white represents light.[2] Black and white have often been used to describe opposites such as good and evil, the Dark

Vantablack is made of carbon nanotubes[34] and is the blackest substance known, absorbing up to 99.965% of radiation in the visible spectrum.[35]

BLACK MAN

    Light skin black and dark skin black doesn't exist. Black is simply black. You can place a black crayon beside a person that is supposedly black, and the crayon would still be a darker hue than them. When you say "Black" man or woman, then that man or woman has to be the color black, and if they are not, then the term is being misused and doesn't apply. No "hue-man" can ever be the color black and shouldn't be called black.

AFRICAN-AMERICANS ARE THE AMERICAN INDIANS

B) THE CURSE WITH IDENTIFYING AS BLACK

When African Americans claim to be black, they take on the characteristics shown below. These behaviors can't be denied and have been seen regularly with our people. The word is cursed, so stop using it as a racial identity.

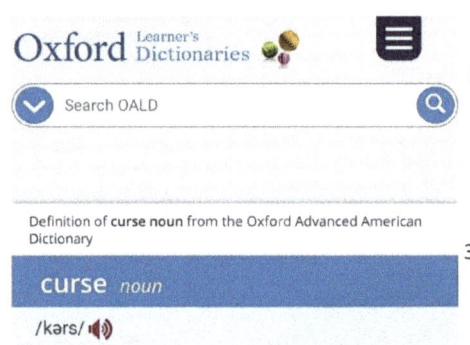

2 [countable] a word or phrase that has a magic power to make something bad happen
  • *The family thought that they were **under a curse**.*

3 [countable] something that causes harm or evil
  • *the curse of drug addiction*

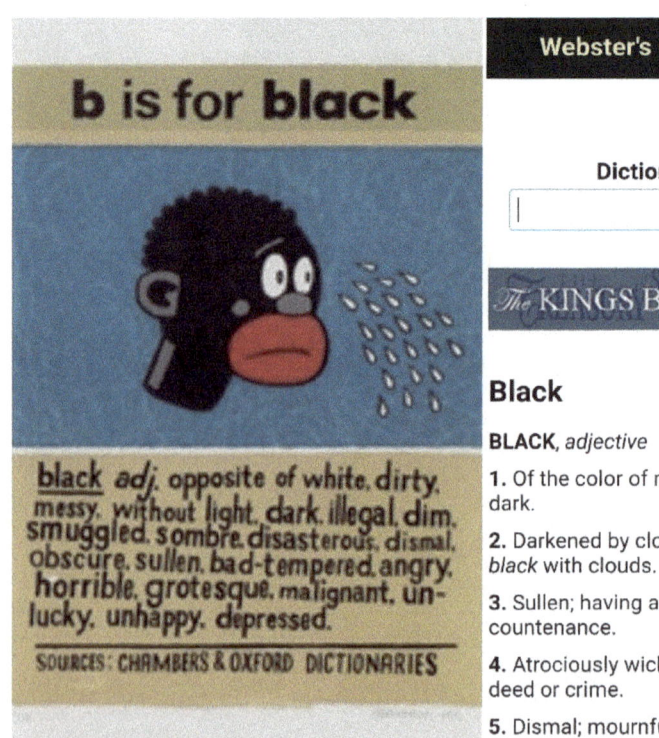

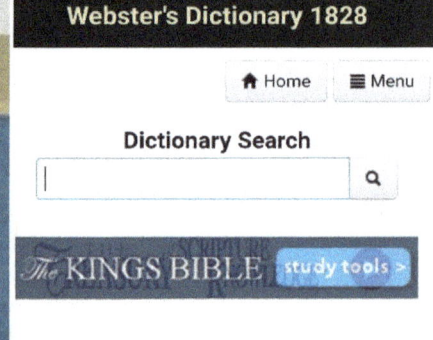

Black

BLACK, *adjective*

1. Of the color of night; destitute of light; dark.

2. Darkened by clouds; as the heavens *black* with clouds.

3. Sullen; having a cloudy look or countenance.

4. Atrociously wicked; horrible; as a *black* deed or crime.

5. Dismal; mournful; calamitous.

Page | 280

C) BLACK MEANS TO BLEACH & BECOME PALE

Many African Americans do not know that the term black means to bleach, lighten up, become pale and is partly the psychological reason why there is the issue of "black" people breeding with Caucasians and bleaching their skin. The continue use or the term enhances this behavior in some individuals.

 https://dictionary.cambridge.org › ...

ETYMOLOGY | definition in the Cambridge English Dictionary

etymology meaning: 1. the study of the origin and history of words, or a study of this type relating to one particular word: 2. the ...

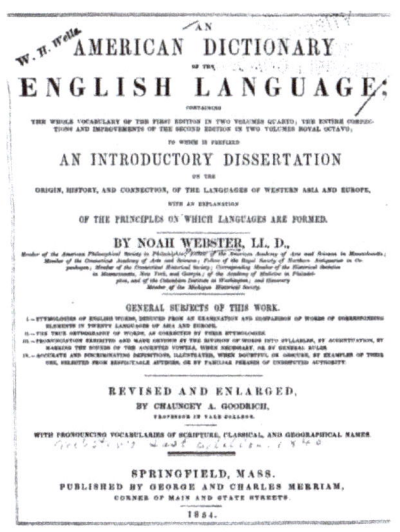

https://books.google.com/books?id=DqRHAQAAMAAJ&pg=PA126&lpg=PA126&dq=black
+bleak+and+bleach+are+radically+one+word&source=bl&ots=7dDjokCiLf&sig=ACfU3U1N
I3aMp71-
iFsR4lHSGS5B_IAsQ&hl=en&sa=X&ved=2ahUKEwiy6PWgjpjkAhVJmeAKHXyACyEQ
6AEwA3oECAQQAQ#v=onepage&q&f=false

BLACK IS WHITE; AN ARGUMENT FROM ETYMOLOGY.—The word *black* (Anglo-Saxon *blac, blæc,* bleak,) is fundamentally the same as the Old German *biach,* now only to be found in two or three compounds, as *Blachfeld,* a level or plain; *Blachmahl,* the scum which floats on the top when silver is melted, and *Blachfrost,* and it meant originally "level," "bare," and was used to denote blackness, because blackness is (apparently) bare of color. But the nasalized form of *black* is *blank,* which also meant originally *bare,* and was used to denote whiteness, because whiteness is (apparently) bare of color. The same word was used to denote the two opposite things. From which it would seem that *black is white.* To any one who shall point out a flaw in this etymological argument I shall endeavor to be grateful, provided he does not disturb the very satisfactory conclusion. This I should naturally resent. It may help him to a conclusion and serve as a further support to my contention to point out that *blác* in Anglo-Saxon actually means "white" as well as "black," so that it is not in its nasalized form only that the same word is employed to express opposite things. Why is this, unless that to the primitive mind both white and black appeared to agree in being bare or void of color, and for that reason to deserve the same name? And here I cannot help harboring a suspicion, suggested by the Old German *Blachfrost* (which appears to be nearly obsolete, or only used in some localities) that our "black frost" meant originally a frost bare of accompaniments, as hoar, rime, and it is a coincidence only that it should be black in color and blacken the vegetation. But we have long lost hold of the original meaning, and believe it to refer to the color.—*Notes and Queries.*

D) BECOMING BLACK FROM REPRODUCTION

BLACK, a. [Sax. *blac*, and *blæc*, black, pale, wan, livid; *blacian, blæcan*, to become pale, to turn white, to become black, to blacken; *blæc*, ink; Sw. *blek*, pale, wan, livid; *bleck*, ink; *bleka*, to insolate, to expose to the sun, or to bleach; also to lighten, to flash; D. *bleek*, pale; *bleeken*, to bleach;

Trevor Noah
South African comedian

OVERVIEW   MOVIES AND TV SHOWS

^ Early life

Trevor Noah was born on 20 February 1984 in Johannesburg, South Africa.[11][12] His father Robert is of Swiss German ancestry, and his mother, Patricia Nombuyiselo Noah, is of Xhosa ancestry. She converted to Judaism

^ Early life

Mariah Carey was born in Huntington, New York.[9][10] Her father, Alfred Roy Carey, was of African American and Afro-Venezuelan descent, while her mother, Patricia (née Hickey), is of Irish American descent. According to Mariah, her maternal grandparents were "from Ireland".[11] The last

AFRICAN-AMERICANS ARE THE AMERICAN INDIANS

Colin Rand Kaepernick is a former American football quarterback known for his political activism regarding police brutality and racism against African-Americans in the United States, and kneeling in protest during the National

Barack Obama

44th President of the United States

∧ Early life

Williams was born in Chicago, Illinois,[3] to Johanna Chase, a professional potter, and Reginald Williams.[4] Of mixed race, Williams has said his mother is Swedish and his father is African American, with some Seminole ancestry, from Georgia.[5][6] His two younger

∧ Early life

Kaepernick was born in 1987 in Milwaukee, Wisconsin, to Heidi Russo, who was white.[6][7] His birth father, who was African-American, separated from Russo before Kaepernick was born.[8][9][10] Russo placed Kaepernick for adoption with a white couple named Rick and Teresa Kaepernick. The couple who had two older children, son Kyle and daughter Devon.

Main article: Early life and career of Barack Obama

Obama was born on August 4, 1961,[6] at Kapiolani Medical Center for Women and Children in Honolulu, Hawaii.[7][8][9] He is the only president who was born outside of the contiguous 48 states.[10] He was born to a white mother and a black father. His mother, Ann Dunham (1942–1995), was born in Wichita, Kansas; she was mostly of English descent,[11] with some German, Irish (3.13%), Scottish, Swiss, and Welsh ancestry.[12] His father, Barack Obama Sr. (1936–1982), was a Luo Kenyan from Nyang'oma Kogelo. Obama's

Page | 284

E) BECOMING BLACK FROM SKIN BLEACHING

F) ORIGINAL BLACK PEOPLE ARE CAUCASIANS

The original "black" people are the pale-skinned Caucasians that many of us call "white" people. Even though they aren't white, The etymology of the term black applies to them and the reason you have some pale skin people identifying as black.

The *Chalk*-Asians are the *Cauk*-asians!

The whole of Europe, really is Chalk (white) Asia, Cauc-Asia

Europe is NOT a continent, despite what Albino dictionaries say. Europe is west Asia, thus the whole of west Asia is really Cauk-Asia or White Asia –not just the Cauc-asus mountains. Caucasia is named both, *after* the Whites themselves and the "cauk, calk, chalk" Other *Cauk* names include Chalcedon & Chalcis, ancient Greek (Albino) cities; and Chalcidice, a mountainous peninsula of Greece.

GOG too. The Cauk-Asians are the "Gog-Asians"

"Gog" sounds similar to "Cauk." The biblical, very white Land of Gog (also called the "Isles of the Gentiles") was to the North and included the Cauk-asus mountains

The "cauc" of CAUCasian is undoubtedly a variant of *cauk* (a word *removed* from dictionaries), *caulk, calk, chalk, chalc(edony), calc(ium)*; Middle English *cauken*; French *cauquer*; Latin *calx*; and Spanish *cauce, caucho*. All these words look similar, sound similar, and point to one thing: WHITEness. White substances. **The CAUC-asian is the *Cauk*-Asian, Caulk-Asian, Chalk-Asian –or chalky-white, caulky-white, calcium-white Asian!** "Calcium" and Caucasians are named after whiteness. Bones are essentially calcium, hence white. And yes, "cauc" is a major component of the Caucasus Mountains, which feature thousands of natural caves in its *limestone (cauk)* hills and slopes.² The **Cauk** caves of the **Cauk**-asus Mountains were the earliest homes of the **Cauk**-Asians for some 2000 years.³ Covering several hundred miles, these *Caverns of the Northern Caucasus*⁴ face north. Spanish *caucho* means *rubber*. What's the connection with whiteness? Natural rubber is milky white! The "caulk" you buy in stores is *rubber* –white or "colorless." Latin *calx* means chalk, lime, limestone –*calcium* in other words. It also means "heel bone" and "to tread." Again what's the white connection? Your heelbone, upon which you tread, is a large quad*angular spur*. Calcium loves to *spur* when it "calcifies," hence "calcspar." Stalactites & stalagmites are other forms of calcium /lime "spurs," spears. Yes "calc" is in *calculator* / *calculus*, for *stones* were early tools for "calculating," and a most common type of stone is the *mineral* CALCium; Greek *khalix* (pebble). Spanish *cauce* means *riverbed* –where *stones* are naturally abundant. *Elbrus*, apparently from the same root as *albino*, is the highest mountain in Cauc-Asia.

AFRICAN-AMERICANS ARE THE AMERICAN INDIANS

FLORIDA SHERIFF CALLS WHITE FAMILY BLACK
Barred from school because of broad noses, brown skins, Platts fight "Negro" label

OVERNIGHT, the Platts—free, "white" Americans—became Negroes. Whites all their lives, the Platt family crossed the racial borderline after Willis V. McCall, feared Florida sheriff and sometimes "anthropologist," found the broad noses and brown skins of some of the Platt children offensive to his sense of whiteness.

Perhaps the first white family to learn first-hand what it means to be a Negro—barred from the best schools because of a nose, ostracized because of the tint of the skin—orange picker Allen and Laura Platt termed their adventure a "tragic nightmare." Displaying documents that identified the family as white Americans of Irish and Indian ancestry, Allen asked sadly, "Why does it happen to us?"

Part of the answer lies in the brown skins of the Platts. This caused open wonder when the family settled in the little resort town of Mount Dora, Fla., last fall. The Platt children, however, attended white schools and were accepted as whites. Their troubles started when Denzell, the brownest of the Platts, was barred from a white Mount Dora theater. Then Sheriff McCall began his anthropological examination.

Accompanied by two armed deputies and a photographer, Sheriff McCall descended on the Platt household in the dark of night. The frightened, hysterical youngsters were lined up Gestapo-fashion and photographed. Earlier, Allen said, Sheriff McCall commented: "You know, Denzell favors a nigger." And, after a squint-eyed examination, the bespectacled sheriff pointed to Laura Belle, 13, and allowed: "I don't like the shape of that one's nose." Five of the Platt children then were barred from the modern white school. A little later, the Platts' landlady was threatened and the family moved, first to another house near Mount Dora and finally into neighboring Orange County, legally safe from McCall. As Allen appealed to the governor for "common justice," the search for non-white "whites" continued in McCall-run Lake County. Two part-Indian boys were barred from a white school in Eustis.

Continued on Next Page

AFRICAN-AMERICANS ARE THE AMERICAN INDIANS

CONCLUSION

STOP IDENTIFYING AS BLACK! Claiming it as a racial identity was the most significant trick played on our people in America. As soon as James brown influenced our people with the song and phrase "*say it loud, I'm black, and I'm proud*" to accept this derogatory term as an identity, it became one of the factors of our demise. It's the reason why supporting black businesses fails for us. You support and spend money with the real black people (pale skin Caucasians) and with brown-skinned immigrants because of similar skin complexion, but they spend your money with their people or send it back to their country instead of with your business. Identifying as black is one of the reasons why police officers avoid criminal charges of killing innocent "black" people. Black people don't exist according to the law, which governs the land. They're assassinating adjectives, and only nouns exist. Caucasians display all the behavioral attributes of black but are perceived as white and accepted. You chose to be the scapegoat by identifying as black.

STOP CLAIMING AFRICAN AMERICAN AS A RACIAL IDENTITY

Most people who claim to be African American don't have African ancestry and can prove it. For you to be a real African American, you were either; 1. Born in Africa and gained citizenship in the United States of America, 2. Parents or grandparents were born in Africa, and you were born in America or 3. You did actual genealogy research and traced your people back to a specific country in Africa (Ancestry DNA doesn't count because It's fraudulent in regards to ancestry). Examples of real African Americans are; Barack Obama, Nypsey Hussle & Akon. Identifying as an African American means that you're calling yourself an Immigrant in the U.S.A, even though you know your grandparents were American Indians.

GET YOUR MIND OUT OF AFRICA

Africa isn't your motherland and never was. Africans don't consider you to be African because they know the truth about America having original brown skin people. There isn't a transatlantic slave trade story passed down over there about their people being stolen or sold to the Americas. There isn't paperwork of any Europeans purchasing African slaves from kings to be brought to the Americas, and there isn't an African nation bringing up charges for reparations for the enslavement of their people. There isn't a real connection with Africans and us. Some Africans accept you because you are influential and adored across the world and others because you tend to be more African than the Africans themselves. While many of you want to be African, you never visited Africa or plan on moving there because something inside of you is telling you that you don't belong there and those aren't your people. They say very negative things about you in Africa and here in America. My God brother had to learn the hard way. He went to Africa and tried to open a business. They told him no because he wasn't African. I said to him," I told you, bro, they know their people, no matter how brown your complexion is." He also knows of his American Indian heritage. The colonizers have

AFRICAN-AMERICANS ARE THE AMERICAN INDIANS

romanticized you with Egypt, which has you wanting to be African, yet you can't trace your ancestry to those people. While you are in love with Africa, they are in love with America. I lived in Cape Town, South Africa, for three months and they adored me. They love our music and played it a lot in their clubs. They love our slang, the way we dress, talk, our celebrities, and our dances. It got to the point where I was upset because I wanted to hear African music and see their dances. If Africa is all that great, then tell me why so many Africans are coming to America? **GET YOUR MIND OUT OF AFRICA AND RESEARCH YOUR HOME IN AMERICA!**

REPORTS | APRIL 2012

Diverse Streams: African Migration to the United States

By Randy Capps, Kristen McCabe, and Michael Fix

Education

see more...

Black African immigrants represent one of the fastest-growing segments of the U.S. immigrant population, increasing by about 200 percent during the 1980s and 1990s and by 100 percent during the 2000s. This report,

https://www.pewresearch.org/fact-tank/2017/02/14/african-immigrant-population-in-u-s-steadily-climbs/

FEBRUARY 14, 2017

African immigrant population in U.S. steadily climbs

BY **MONICA ANDERSON**

Immigration from Africa surges since 1970

Total U.S. foreign-born population from Africa, in thousands

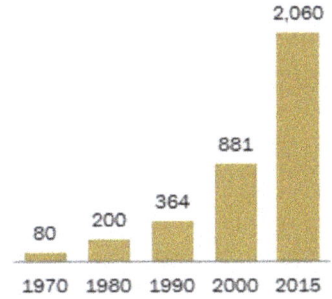

Note: Africa includes North African and sub-Saharan African countries as defined by IPUMS.
Source: Pew Research Center analysis of the 2015 American Community Survey (1% IPUMS). Trend data based on U.S. Censuses 1970-2000.

African immigrants make up a small share of the nation's immigrant population, but their overall numbers are growing – roughly doubling every decade since 1970, according to a new Pew Research Center analysis of U.S. Census Bureau data.

There were 2.1 million African immigrants living in the United States in 2015, up from 881,000 in 2000 and a substantial increase from 1970 when the U.S. was home to only 80,000 foreign-born Africans. They accounted for 4.8% of the U.S. immigrant population in 2015, up from 0.8% in 1970.

The growth is evident among recently arrived immigrants. When compared with other major groups who arrived in the U.S. in the past five years, Africans had the fastest growth rate from 2000 to 2013, increasing by 41% during that period. (Africans are also a fast-growing segment of the black immigrant population in the U.S., increasing by 137% from 2000 to 2013.)

Much of the recent growth in the foreign-born black population has been fueled by African migration. Between 2000 and 2016, the black African immigrant population more than doubled, from 574,000 to 1.6 million. Africans now make up 39% of the overall foreign-born black population, up from 24% in 2000.

https://www.pewresearch.org/fact-tank/2017/02/14/african-immigrant-population-in-u-s-steadily-climbs/

START IDENTIFYING AS AMERICAN INDIAN ON ALL DOCUMENTS

It's time to start cleaning up the mess that you, your parents and grandparents left you in. Select American Indians as your ethnicity on all your documents. Update your information with the social security office to correct your racial designation with SS-5 form. Go there and tell them that you want to correct your race in their database. Most of the time, it was left blank in their system. Have them change it, and then the federal government will be put on notice. At the same time, fill out and send the sf181-1 form to Washington D.C.

You want to start correcting your status all around so you can begin utilizing what your ancestors left behind. For many of us, our ancestors left us to land. For some, your ancestors were on the Dawes and other rolls, and you're entitled to land and money. As an American Indian, you're recognized in the eyes of the law, unlike black, colored, Moor, and Hebrew Israelite. You also can utilize the civil rights act of 1968.

sonoftheindigenous True. When I proclaim myself to be american indian or aborigine, I have no issues when dealing with commerce and law. When I decided to check African American I had to deal with a long drawn out process of paperwork and required explanations as to what my intentions were. Smh... I'm american aborigine and proud.

truthsetsusfree Exactly @sonoftheindigenous but alot of melanin rich people in america don't get it because they have been plagued with africa since grade school because they are being schooled by caucasians now... if we can get these 41 million people to start checking american indian on everything they do.. it will bring about a cause of action..but first we must wake them up from the africa spell and all these other confusing spells being cast on them...

SOCIAL SECURITY ADMINISTRATION
Application for a Social Security Card

Applying for a Social Security Card is easy AND it is free!

USE THIS APPLICATION TO APPLY FOR:
- An **original** Social Security card
- A **duplicate** Social Security card (same name and number)
- A **corrected** Social Security card (name change and same number)
- A **change of information** on your record other than your name (no card needed)

IMPORTANT: We CANNOT process this application unless you follow the instructions below and give us the evidence we need.

STEP 1 Read pages 1 through 3 which explain how to complete the application and what evidence we need.
STEP 2 Complete and sign the application using BLUE or BLACK ink. Do not use pencil or other colors of ink. Please print legibly.
STEP 3 Submit the completed and signed application with all required evidence to any Social Security office.

HOW TO COMPLETE THIS APPLICATION
Most items on the form are self-explanatory. Those that need explanation are discussed below. The numbers match the numbered items on the form. If you are completing this form for someone else, please complete the items as they apply to that person.

2. Show the address where you can receive your card 10 to 14 days from now.

3. If you check "Legal Alien **Not** Allowed to Work", you need to provide a document from the government agency requiring your Social Security number that explains why you need a number and that you meet all of the requirements for the benefit or service except for the number. A State or local agency requirement must conform with Federal law.

   If you check "Other", you need to provide proof you are entitled to a federally-funded benefit for which a Social Security number is required as a condition for you to receive payment.

5. Providing race/ethnic information is voluntary. However, if you do give us this information, it helps us prepare statistical reports on how Social Security programs affect people. We do not reveal the identities of individuals.

To **CHANGE INFORMATION** on your record other than your name, we need proof of:

- **Identity**, and
- **Another document which supports the change** (for example, a birth certificate to change your date and/or place of birth or parents' names).

AGE: We prefer to see your birth certificate. However, we can accept another document that shows your age if it is at least one year old. Some of the other documents we can accept are:

- Hospital record of your birth made before you were age 5
- Religious record showing your age made before you were 3 months old
- Passport
- Adoption record

Call us for advice if you cannot obtain one of these documents.

Form SS-5 (3-2001)   EF (3-2001)   Page 2

IDENTITY: We must see a document in the name you want shown on the card. The identity document must be of recent issuance so that we can determine your continued existence. We prefer to see a document with a photograph. However, we can generally accept a non-photo identity document if it has enough information to identify you (e.g., your name, as well as age, date of birth or parents' names). **WE CANNOT ACCEPT A BIRTH CERTIFICATE, HOSPITAL BIRTH RECORD, SOCIAL SECURITY CARD OR CARD STUB, OR SOCIAL SECURITY RECORD** as evidence of identity. Some documents we can accept are:

- Driver's license
- Employer ID card
- Passport
- Marriage or divorce record
- Adoption record
- Health insurance card (not a Medicare card)
- Military record
- Life insurance policy
- School ID card

AFRICAN-AMERICANS ARE THE AMERICAN INDIANS

U.S. Office of Personnel Management Guide to Personnel Data Standards	**ETHNICITY AND RACE IDENTIFICATION** (Please read the Privacy Act Statement and instructions before completing form.)	
Name (Last, First, Middle Initial)	Social Security Number	Birthdate (Month and Year)
Agency Use Only		

Privacy Act Statement

Ethnicity and race information is requested under the authority of 42 U.S.C. Section 2000e-16 and in compliance with the Office of Management and Budget's 1997 Revisions to the Standards for the Classification of Federal Data on Race and Ethnicity. Providing this information is voluntary and has no impact on your employment status, but in the instance of missing information, your employing agency will attempt to identify your race and ethnicity by visual observation.

This information is used as necessary to plan for equal employment opportunity throughout the Federal government. It is also used by the U. S. Office of Personnel Management or employing agency maintaining the records to locate individuals for personnel research or survey response and in the production of summary descriptive statistics and analytical studies in support of the function for which the records are collected and maintained, or for related workforce studies.

Social Security Number (SSN) is requested under the authority of Executive Order 9397, which requires SSN be used for the purpose of uniform, orderly administration of personnel records. Providing this information is voluntary and failure to do so will have no effect on your employment status. If SSN is not provided, however, other agency sources may be used to obtain it.

Specific Instructions: The two questions below are designed to identify your ethnicity and race. **Regardless of your answer to question 1, go to question 2.**

Question 1. Are You Hispanic or Latino? (A person of Cuban, Mexican, Puerto Rican, South or Central American, or other Spanish culture or origin, regardless of race.)
☐ Yes ☐ No

Question 2. Please select the racial category or categories with which you most closely identify by placing an "X" in the appropriate box. Check as many as apply.

RACIAL CATEGORY (Check as many as apply)	DEFINITION OF CATEGORY
✓ American Indian or Alaska Native	A person having origins in any of the original peoples of North and South America (including Central America), and who maintains tribal affiliation or community attachment.
☐ Asian	A person having origins in any of the original peoples of the Far East, Southeast Asia, or the Indian subcontinent including, for example, Cambodia, China, India, Japan, Korea, Malaysia, Pakistan, the Philippine Islands, Thailand, and Vietnam.
☐ Black or African American	A person having origins in any of the black racial groups of Africa.
☐ Native Hawaiian or Other Pacific Islander	A person having origins in any of the original peoples of Hawaii, Guam, Samoa, or other Pacific Islands.
☐ White	A person having origins in any of the original peoples of Europe, the Middle East, or North Africa.

Standard Form 181
Revised August 2005
Previous editions not usable

42 U.S.C. Section 2000e-16

NSN 7540-01-099-3446

[Print Form] [Save Form] [Clear Form]

https://www.gsa.gov/forms-library/ethnicity-and-race-identification

AFRICAN-AMERICANS ARE THE AMERICAN INDIANS

BLACK'S
LAW DICTIONARY

Definitions of the Terms and Phrases of
American and English Jurisprudence,
Ancient and Modern

By

HENRY CAMPBELL BLACK, M. A.
Author of Treatises on Judgments, Tax Titles, Intoxicating Liquors,
Bankruptcy, Mortgages, Constitutional Law, Interpretation
of Laws, Rescission and Cancellation of Contracts, Etc.

REVISED FOURTH EDITION

BY

THE PUBLISHER'S EDITORIAL STAFF

ST. PAUL, MINN.
WEST PUBLISHING CO.
1968

INDIAN TITLE. Claim of Indian tribes of right, because of immemorial occupancy, to roam certain territory to exclusion of any other Indians. Northwestern Bands of Shoshone Indians v. U. S., Ct, Cl., 65 S.Ct. 690, 692, 324 U.S. 335, 89 L.Ed. 985.

INDIAN TRIBE. A separate and distinct community or body of the aboriginal Indian race of men found in the United States. Montoya v. U. S., 21 S.Ct. 358, 180 U.S. 261, 45 L.Ed. 521.

INDIANS. The aboriginal inhabitants of North America. Frazee v. Spokane County, 29 Wash. 278, 69 P. 782.

"Persons" are of two kinds, natural and artificial. A natural person is a human being. Artificial persons include a collection or succession of natural persons forming a corporation; a collection of property to which the law attributes the capacity of having rights and duties. The latter class of artificial persons is recognized only to a limited extent in our law. Examples are the estate of a bankrupt or deceased person. Hogan v. Greenfield, 58 Wyo. 13, 122 P.2d 850, 853.

It has been held that when the word person is used in a legislative act, natural persons will be intended unless something appear in the context to show that it applies to artificial persons, Blair v. Worley, 1 Scam., Ill., 178; Appeal of Fox, 112 Pa. 337 ; 4 A. 149 ; but as a rule corporations will be considered persons within the statutes unless the intention of the legislature is manifestly to exclude them. Stribbling v. Bank, 5 Rand., Va., 132.

Holter, 19 Mont. 263, 48 P. 8. An Indian is a person, U. S. v. Crook, 5 Dill. 459, Fed.Cas.No.14,891; and a slave was

https://www.polskawalczaca.com/library/a.blackslaw4th.pdf

CONGRESSIONAL RECORD—SENATE. JANUARY 9,

politic composed of people and stic, and asserted for themselves ip and dominion as a race of veral States and in the United ese people, in the exercise of ursuance of law and that laws d regulate the electorate and to ers to conduct the Government.

The self-defining statement that "we, the people of the United States, do ordain this Constitution" referred to other inhabitants of the States and Territories who, at that time, were racially distinguished from the people of the United States. They were the negro race, who were then held in slavery, and were so recognized, in terms, by the Constitution, and Indian tribes, organized in separate but independent tribal governments; and Indians in the States who were not taxed.

The Navajos came to the Southwest millennia after the Tewas and call themselves Dine, sometimes spelled Dineh, which means "we the people." [2] Most Native American groups call themselves by names that mean "we the people." Like most societies they were ethnocentric - seeing their own culture as the yardstick of sound human behavior - and these names reflect that certainty.

Some names take note of physical characteristics of Natives. Thus British Americans called the Salish ("we the people") the Flathead Indians. The French called two groups of Indians "Gros Ventres," "big bellies," apparently derived from their name in Indian sign language. The French also renamed the Nimipus ("we the people") the Nez Perces, "pierced noses," because some of them wore nose pendants.

A few names were complimentary. On the east coast the British renamed the Lenape "Delawares." They didn't mind once the British explained that Lord De La Ware was a brave military leader. Lenape means - you guessed it - "we the people." [3] The most famous Arizona. Native people living in far northern Canada and Alaska call themselves Inuit - again, "we the people" - while the Crees to their southeast

https://books.google.com/books?id=zRtFAAAAQBAJ&pg=PA100&lpg=PA100&dq=the+navajos+came+to+the+south+west+millenia+after+the+tewas&source=bl&ots=mvDAYWP1MF&sig=ACfU3U2nZlwRpYisdvzb0KVBmH0hq1E4zw&hl=en&sa=X&ved=2ahUKEwivia7ep9PkAhVLvJ4KHd1YDsgQ6AEwAHoECAAQAQ#v=onepage&q=the%20navajos%20came%20to%20the%20south%20west%20millenia%20after%20the%20tewas&f=false

CIVIL RIGHTS ACT OF 1968

[Public Law 90–284, 82 Stat. 73]

[As Amended Through P.L. 113–4, Enacted March 7, 2013]

AN ACT To prescribe penalties for certain acts of violence or intimidation, and for other purposes.

Be it enacted by the Senate and House of Representatives of the United States of America in Congress assembled, That this Act may be cited as the "Civil Rights Act of 1968".

TITLE I—INTERFERENCE WITH FEDERALLY PROTECTED ACTIVITIES

SEC. 101. (a) [Amends chapter 13, civil rights, title 18, United States Code, by inserting at the end thereof a new section 245 (relating to federally protected civil rights activities).]

(b) Nothing contained in this section shall apply to or affect activities under title VIII of this Act.

(c) The provisions of this section shall not apply to acts or omissions on the part of law enforcement officers, members of the National Guard, as defined in section 101(9) of title 10, United States Code, members of the organized militia of any State or the District of Columbia, not covered by such section 101(9), or members of the Armed Forces of the United States, who are engaged in suppressing a riot or civil disturbance or restoring law and order during a riot or civil disturbance.

SEC. 102. [Amends the analysis of chapter 13 of title 18 of the United States Code by adding at the end thereof an item for the catchline of the section 245 added by subsection (a).]

SEC. 103. (a) [Amends section 241 of title 18 United States Code.]

(b) [Amends section 242 of title 18, United States Code.]

(c) [Amends section 12 of the Voting Rights Act of 1965.]

SEC. 104. (a) [Amends title 18 of the United States Code by inserting, immediately after chapter 101 a new chapter 102 (riots).]

(b) [Amends the table of contents to "PART I.—CRIMES" of title 18, United States Code.]

TITLE II—RIGHTS OF INDIANS

DEFINITIONS

SEC. 201. For purposes of this title, the term—

(1) "Indian tribe" means any tribe, band, or other group of Indians subject to the jurisdiction of the United States and recognized as possessing powers of self-government;

1

Sec. 202 **CIVIL RIGHTS ACT OF 1968**

(2) "powers of self-government" means and includes all governmental powers possessed by an Indian tribe, executive, legislative, and judicial, and all offices, bodies, and tribunals by and through which they are executed, including courts of Indian offenses; and

(3) "Indian court" means any Indian tribal court or court of Indian offense.

[25 U.S.C. 1301]

INDIAN RIGHTS

SEC. 202.[1]

(a) IN GENERAL.—No Indian tribe in exercising powers of self-government shall—

(1) make or enforce any law prohibiting the free exercise of religion, or abridging the freedom of speech, or of the press, or the right of the people peaceably to assemble and to petition for a redress of grievances;

(2) violate the right of the people to be secure in their persons, houses, papers, and effects against unreasonable search and seizures, nor issue warrants, but upon probable cause, supported by oath or affirmation, and particularly describing the place to be searched and the person or thing to be seized;

(3) subject any person for the same offense to be twice put in jeopardy;

(4) compel any person in any criminal case to be a witness against himself;

(5) take any private property for a public use without just compensation;

(6) deny to any person in a criminal proceeding the right to a speedy and public trial, to be informed of the nature and cause of the accusation, to be confronted with the witnesses against him, to have compulsory process for obtaining witnesses in his favor, and at his own expense to have assistance of counsel for his defense (except as provided in subsection (b));

(7)(A) require excessive bail, impose excessive fines, or inflict cruel and unusual punishments;

(B) except as provided in subparagraph (C), impose for conviction of any 1 offense any penalty or punishment greater than imprisonment for a term of 1 year or a fine of $5,000, or both;

(C) subject to subsection (b), impose for conviction of any 1 offense any penalty or punishment greater than imprisonment for a term of 3 years or a fine of $15,000, or both; or

(D) impose on a person in a criminal proceeding a total penalty or punishment greater than imprisonment for a term of 9 years;

(8) deny to any person within its jurisdiction the equal protection of its laws or deprive any person of liberty or property without due process of law;

(9) pass any bill or attainder or ex post facto law; or

153
DEPARTMENT OF THE INTERIOR,
COMMISSION TO THE FIVE CIVILIZED TRIBES,
IN THE MATTER OF THE ALLOTMENT OF THE LANDS OF THE
CHOCTAWS AND CHICKASAWS.
FREEDMEN.

CHOCTAW NATION.

Atoka Indian Territory, May 18, 1904.

TESTIMONY OF Sam Hall IN THE MATTER OF THE ALLOTMENT OF THE LANDS OF THE CHOCTAWS AND CHICKASAWS

To Patsy Hall

Sam Hall being first duly sworn, testifies as follows:

Q. What is your name? A. Sam Hall
Q. What is your post office address? A. Fort Towson I.T.
Q. For whom are you making this application? A. Patsy Hall
Q. Was the person for whom this application is made living on September 25th, 1902? A. yes
Q. Is she living now? A. yes
Q. Has the person for whom you make this application received or applied for an allotment of land in the Creek, Cherokee or Seminole Nation? A. no
Q. How do you represent this person? A. as her husband

Application is made for the following described land as an allotment:

Roll	No.	Subdivision	Sec.	Town.	Range	Area Acres 100	Appraised Value Dolls. Cts.	Cert. No.
Choctaw Freed	3773	NW¼ NE¼	25	6S	20E	40	130	24 88

Q. Have you been upon this land and examined it with a view to making this selection?
A. yes
Q. Are you fully informed as to the location of the same and the character of the soil? A. yes

GIVE JESUS, ALLAH AND THEM BACK, THEY AREN'T OURS

Christianity, Islam, and various other foreign religious systems were never our religions. Christianity was forced on us through violence if we didn't convert willingly. These religions have been used to subjugate and destroy our people. Give these eastern religions back to the colonizers.

THE INDIAN WARS of PENNSYLVANIA

An Account of the Indian Events, in Pennsylvania, of The French and Indian War, Pontiac's War, Lord Dunmore's War, The Revolutionary War and the Indian Uprising from 1789 to 1795

Tragedies of the Pennsylvania Frontier
Based Primarily on the Penna. Archives and Colonial Records

By
C. HALE SIPE

of the Pittsburgh and Butler Bars; Member of the Historical Society of Pennsylvania; Author of "The Indian Chiefs of Pennsylvania" and "Mount Vernon and the Washington Family"

Introduction by
DR. GEORGE P. DONEHOO, Former State Librarian of Pennsylvania

For Schools, Colleges, Libraries and Lovers of Informative Literature

THE TELEGRAPH PRESS
HARRISBURG, PA.
1929

Price $5.00, postpaid. Order from C. Hale Sipe, Butler, Pa.

The Pennsylvania Indians—Their Religion and Character

GO where we may, in Pennsylvania, we are put in remembrance of the American Indian by the beautiful names he gave to the valleys, streams and mountains where he roamed for untold generations, never dreaming that from afar would come a stronger race which would plant amid the wilderness the hamlet and the town and cause cities to rise where the forest waved over the home of his heart. The Wyoming Valley; the Tuscarora Valley; the winding Susquehanna; the blue Juniata; the broad Ohio; the Kittatinny Mountain; the Allegheny Mountains—these are but a few of the everlasting reminders of the Pennsylvania Indians. Until the new heavens arch themselves and until the new earth comes, our Pennsylvania valleys will lie smiling in the sunlight, our Pennsylvania streams will go singing to the sea, and our Pennsylvania mountains will lift their summits to the sky; and throughout the ages may succeeding generations of Pennsylvanians realize that the Indian loved these valleys, these streams, these mountains, with a love as strong as that hallowing passion which touched the Grecian mountain-pass of Thermopylae more than twenty-four hundred years ago, and has caused it to glow with never-dying lustre through the long night of centuries. It was love for the land of his fathers that caused the Indian to fight to the death for his home and hunting grounds.

A child of nature, the Indian knew not the God of revelation; but the God of the universe and nature he acknowledged in all things around him,—the sun, the moon, the stars, the flowers, the singing birds, the mighty oaks and sighing pines of the forest, the pleasant valleys, the babbling brooks, the dashing water-falls, the rushing rivers, the lofty mountains. Reverently he worshipped the Great Spirit, who created him, who governed the world, who taught the streams to flow and the bird to build her nest, who caused day and night and the changing seasons, who

18   THE INDIAN WARS OF PENNSYLVANIA

stocked the streams with fish and the forests with game for his Red Children. To the Great Spirit went up many a pure prayer from the Indian's dark bosom. He prayed when he went on the chase; he prayed when he sat down to partake of the fruits of the chase; he prayed when he went to war. And when he closed his eyes in death, it was in the firm belief that death was mere transition to the Happy Hunting Ground, where, with care and sorrow removed, he would pursue the deer throughout the endless ages of eternity.

https://books.google.com/books?id=_kUIAwAAQBAJ&pg=PA17&lpg=PA17&dq=a+child+of+nature,+the+indian+knew+not+the+god+of+revelation;+but+the+god+of+the+universe&source=bl&ots=RR9ARANSF3&sig=ACfU3U1vGy67WW8Zmaml9MvioiK_238yHg&hl=en&sa=X&ved=2ahUKEwi-spz7otTkAhWTHDQIHUjBCFEQ6AEwAHoECAMQAQ#v=onepage&q=a%20child%20of%20nature%2C%20the%20indian%20knew%20not%20the%20god%20of%20revelation%3B%20but%20the%20god%20of%20the%20universe&f=false

AFRICAN-AMERICANS ARE THE AMERICAN INDIANS

HISTORY

OF

TAZEWELL COUNTY

AND

SOUTHWEST VIRGINIA

1748-1920

BY

WM. C. PENDLETON

With Illustrations

1920
W. C. Hill Printing Company
Richmond, Va.

"Here, too, they worshipped, and from many a dark bosom went up a fervent prayer to the Great Spirit. He had not written his laws for them on tables of stone, but he had traced them on the tables of their hearts. The poor child of nature knew not the God of Revelation, but the God of the universe he acknowledged in everything around. He beheld him in the star that sank in beauty behind his lonely dwelling; in the sacred orb that flamed on him from his midday throne; in the flower that snapped in the morning breeze; in the lofty pine that defied a thousand whirlwinds; in the timid warbler that never left its native grove; in the fearless eagle, whose untired pinion was wet in clouds; in the worm that crawled at his feet; and in his own matchless form, glowing with a spark of that light, to whose mysterious source he bent in humble though blind adoration."

Moralists and scientists have tried in vain to fathom the depths of the moral and religious tenets of the untutored American aborigines. These simple children of nature, who were as ferocious as the beasts of the jungle when grappling with their foes, in the presence of the God whom they worshipped were as humble and reverent as the most cultured and devout expositors of the enlightened religions of the world.

The Indians as a race have rejected the great spiritual verities that Christ planted in his Church nineteen hundred years ago.

https://books.google.com/books?id=KiQSAAAAYAAJ&pg=PA66&lpg=PA66&dq=a+child+of+nature,+the+indian+knew+not+the+god+of+revelation&source=bl&ots=3Nksjxdf08&sig=ACfU3U09MPEMDUM2Ygonh_okvbUFs-OXA&hl=en&sa=X&ved=2ahUKEwie_9m7rtPkAhUTCjQIHTMNC60Q6AEwCXoECAgQAQ#v=onepage&q&f=false

THE *DIARIO* OF CHRISTOPHER COLUMBUS'S FIRST VOYAGE TO AMERICA
1492-1493

ABSTRACTED BY FRAY BARTOLOMÉ DE LAS CASAS
TRANSCRIBED AND TRANSLATED INTO ENGLISH
WITH NOTES AND A CONCORDANCE OF THE SPANISH, BY
Oliver Dunn and James E. Kelley, Jr.

Award Winner Thursday 11 October Trans

intelligent servants, for I see that they say very quickly everything that is said to them; and I believe that they would become Christians very easily, for it seemed to me that they had no religion. Our Lord pleasing, at

13v and another like those of mastic, and thus on a single tree [there are] five or six of these kinds, and all very different. Nor are they grafted, because one might say that grafting does it.² Rather, these trees are wild, nor do these people take care of them. I do not detect in them any religion and I believe that they would become Christians very quickly because they are of very good understanding. Here the fish are so

Page | 302

AFRICAN-AMERICANS ARE THE AMERICAN INDIANS

A sad feature of the early wars was the sufferings of those Indians who had listened to the preaching of Jesus Christ. In Massachusetts, during King Philip's war, the Christian Indians were treated no better than the "heathen savages." Some were hanged, some imprisoned, and some sold as slaves to the West Indies. At best, they lost their homes and improvements, and nearly perished of cold and hunger. In Pennsylvania, at Conestoga and Wyoming Valley, they were horribly murdered, and the peaceful Moravian Indians were butchered at prayer in their church, while no one dared say a word of protest except the Quakers.

https://books.google.com/books?id=OkxwDwAAQBAJ&pg=PA25&lpg=PA25&dq=a+sad+feature+of+the+early+wars+was+the+suffering+of+those+indians+who+had+listened+to+the+preaching+of+jesus+christ&source=bl&ots=bQCTA2ULJy&sig=ACfU3U38IVJday2i_K7F0uLttk4aegazLw&hl=en&sa=X&ved=2ahUKEwi_q4Oer9LlAhUmmuAKHYIcCpYQ6AEwAHoECAQQAQ#v=onepage&q=a%20sad%20feature%20of%20the%20early%20wars%20was%20the%20suffering%20of%20those%20indians%20who%20had%20listened%20to%20the%20preaching%20of%20jesus%20christ&f=false

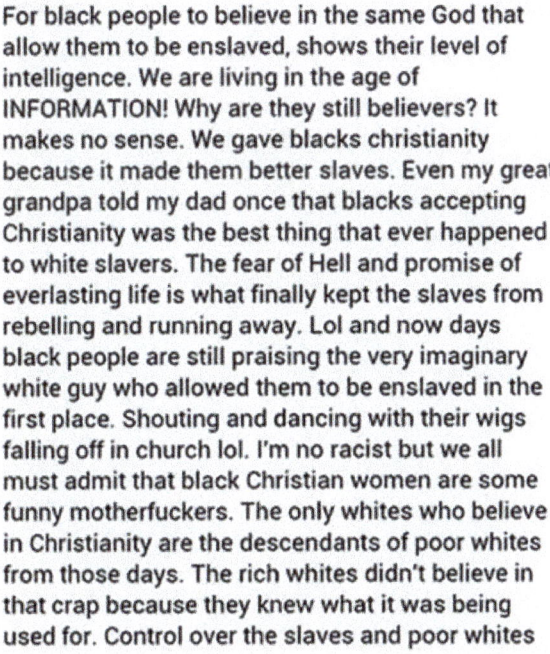

Tamara Tornado
8 hrs

For black people to believe in the same God that allow them to be enslaved, shows their level of intelligence. We are living in the age of INFORMATION! Why are they still believers? It makes no sense. We gave blacks christianity because it made them better slaves. Even my great grandpa told my dad once that blacks accepting Christianity was the best thing that ever happened to white slavers. The fear of Hell and promise of everlasting life is what finally kept the slaves from rebelling and running away. Lol and now days black people are still praising the very imaginary white guy who allowed them to be enslaved in the first place. Shouting and dancing with their wigs falling off in church lol. I'm no racist but we all must admit that black Christian women are some funny motherfuckers. The only whites who believe in Christianity are the descendants of poor whites from those days. The rich whites didn't believe in that crap because they knew what it was being used for. Control over the slaves and poor whites

DON'T FOLLOW "BLACK" LEADERS

There have always been so-called "black" leaders in our community working against the community either unknowingly or knowingly. Now that you have come to an understanding that you are American Indian, you have no reason to follow any "black" leaders. They are in place to keep the confusion going. Some Africanize you, keep you under a foreign religion, keep you under the spell of black, exploit your confusion for financial gain, mislead the collective, and never have your best interest at hand as a nation of people. Below are just a few modern-day "black" leaders who have damaged the community.

https://www.washingtonpost.com/archive/lifestyle/1978/05/09/the-father-of-kwanzaa/ec0fe360-c895-47d3-a5b6-0a1a09a471b1/?noredirect=on

AFRICAN-AMERICANS ARE THE AMERICAN INDIANS

Jesse Louis Jackson Sr. (né Burns; born October 8, 1941) is an American civil rights activist, Baptist minister, and politician. He was a candidate for the Democratic presidential nomination in 1984 and 1988 and served as a shadow U.S. Senator for the District of Columbia from 1991 to 1997.

Jesse Jackson

United States Shadow Senator from the District of Columbia

'African-American' Favored By Many of America's Blacks

By ISABEL WILKERSON, Special to the New York Times
Published: January 31, 1989

CHICAGO, Jan. 30— A movement led by the Rev. Jesse Jackson to call blacks African-Americans has met with both rousing approval and deep-seated skepticism in a debate that is coming to symbolize the role and history of blacks in this country.

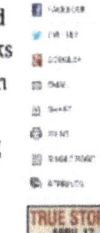

The term, used for years in intellectual circles, is gaining currency among many other blacks, who say its use is a sign that they are accepting their difficult past and resolving a long ambivalence toward Africa.

The term has already shown up in the newest grade-school textbooks, been adopted by several black-run radio stations and newspapers around the country and appeared in the titles of popular books and in the conversations of many blacks as they warm to the idea and speak of visiting Africa one day.

Our community adored this leader in the 80s, and that's when the ultimate blow was received. He led the charge in having our identity changed from black to a status that made us an undocumented immigrant in the United States. It started as just talk to convince the masses that it was our proper identity, but in reality, it wasn't. The label African American appeared on the census in the year 2000. When it was on official documents and various literature, institutions started applying this identity on the past and present public figures, activists and immediately began opening up African American museums to help solidify the false identity. This identity is still plaguing the community today.

AFRICAN-AMERICANS ARE THE AMERICAN INDIANS

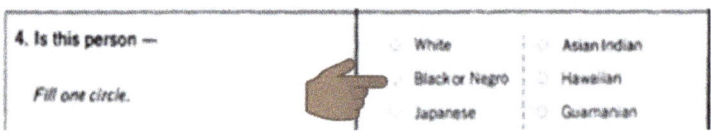

http://racebox.org/

AFRICAN-AMERICANS ARE THE AMERICAN INDIANS

Barack Hussein Obama II (/bəˈrɑːk huːˈseɪn oʊˈbɑːmə/ (listen);[1] born August 4, 1961) is an American attorney and politician who served as the 44th president of the United States from 2009 to 2017. A member of the Democratic Party, he was the first African American to be elected to the presidency. He previously served as a U.S. senator from Illinois from 2005 to 2008 and an Illinois state senator from 1997 to 2004.

Barack Obama

44th President of the United States

CNN.com › 2016/05/22 › politics

Obama blocks use of words 'Negro' and 'Oriental' in federal law - CNNPolitics

May 22, 2016 · U.S. President Barack Obama signed a bill Friday that modernizes the terms used for minorities. (CNN) The ...

Office Of Minority Economic Impact.—Section 211(f)(1) of the Department of Energy Organization Act (42 U.S.C. 7141(f)(1)) is amended by striking "a Negro, Puerto Rican, American Indian, Eskimo, Oriental, or Aleut or is a Spanish speaking individual of Spanish descent" and inserting "Asian American, Native Hawaiian, a Pacific Islander, African American, Hispanic, Puerto Rican, Native American, or an Alaska Native".

This leader was adored in 2008 when he secured the presidential election. He is considered the first African-American president, and this is true because he isn't a descendant of the American Indians/American Negro. Both of Obama's parents are from foreign countries. His mother is a European born American, and his father is an African. Our people were in love with him because of his skin complexion. Our community felt like they won, but in reality, we lost. He never did anything that directly aided or advanced the people labeled as African American. Some people argue that he tried to help us but was prevented every time. In my opinion, no president has ever aided in advancing our people. He wanted to hurt the community by removing negro and Indian off of federal documents. Removing these labels could potentially eliminate all treaties and work our ancestors fought for.

STOP CALLING THE COLONIZER "WHITE"

TOP DEFINITION

white is right

If you have a **white skin** color you are correct about anything **and everything** without **argument**

There isn't anyone on the planet, the color white. The word is a spell, and if we continue to call them white, it attaches the attributes to them. You will see them as innocent no matter how many wrongful murders are committed, believe them, no matter how many lies they tell to harm you (white is always right), free from guilt no matter how much they destroy the planet and animals, always see them as God and pure. Start calling them European – Americans, Cauc-asians (Caucasians), or Colonizers to remove the veil from your eyes and lift the spell.

AFRICAN-AMERICANS ARE THE AMERICAN INDIANS

REDUCE CPU, TV & CELL PHONE USE

It's time to reduce watching TV, using smartphones and computers. The government has been manipulating our thoughts with this technology. It is one way they're able to control how you think by influencing you to accept everything that is usually immoral to you. You are no longer a free thinker; you're a robot. **TAKE YOUR MIND BACK!**

US006506148B2

(12)	United States Patent	(10) Patent No.:	US 6,506,148 B2
	Loos	(45) Date of Patent:	Jan. 14, 2003

(54) **NERVOUS SYSTEM MANIPULATION BY ELECTROMAGNETIC FIELDS FROM MONITORS**

(76) Inventor: **Hendricus G. Loos**, 3019 Cresta Way, Laguna Beach, CA (US) 92651

(*) Notice: Subject to any disclaimer, the term of this patent is extended or adjusted under 35 U.S.C. 154(b) by 8 days.

(21) Appl. No.: **09/872,528**

(22) Filed: **Jun. 1, 2001**

(65) **Prior Publication Data**

US 2002/0188164 A1 Dec. 12, 2002

(51) Int. Cl.⁷ **A61N 2/00**; A61B 5/04; A61M 21/00
(52) U.S. Cl. **600/27**; 600/545
(58) Field of Search 600/9–27, 545; 313/419; 324/318; 378/901; 434/236

(56) **References Cited**

U.S. PATENT DOCUMENTS

3,592,965 A	*	7/1971	Diaz	313/419
4,800,893 A	*	1/1989	Ross et al.	600/545
5,169,380 A		12/1992	Brennan	600/26
5,304,112 A	*	4/1994	Mrklas et al.	434/236
5,400,383 A		3/1995	Yassa et al.	378/901
5,412,419 A	*	5/1995	Ziarati	324/318
5,450,859 A	*	9/1995	Litovitz	600/9
5,782,874 A		7/1998	Loos	607/2
5,800,481 A		9/1998	Loos	607/100
5,899,922 A		5/1999	Loos	607/2
5,935,054 A		8/1999	Loos	600/9
6,017,302 A		1/2000	Loos	600/28
6,081,744 A		6/2000	Loos	607/2
6,091,994 A		7/2000	Loos	607/100
6,167,304 A		12/2000	Loos	607/2

| 6,238,333 B1 | 5/2001 | Loos | 600/9 |

OTHER PUBLICATIONS

N.Wiener "Nonlinear problems in random theory" p.71–72 John Wiley New York 1958.
M.Hutchison "Megabrain" p.232–3 Ballantine Books New York 1991.
C.A.Terzuolo and T.H.Bullock "Measurement of imposed voltage gradient adequate to modulate neuronal firing" Proc. Nat. Acad. Sci, Physiology 42,687–94, 1956.
O.Kellogg "Foundations of Potential Theory" p. 191 Dover, 1953.
P.M.Morse and H.Feshbach "Methods of Theoretical Physics" p. 1267 McGraw-Hill New York, 1953.

* cited by examiner

Primary Examiner—Eric F. Winakur
Assistant Examiner—Nikita R Veniaminov

(57) **ABSTRACT**

Physiological effects have been observed in a human subject in response to stimulation of the skin with weak electromagnetic fields that are pulsed with certain frequencies near ½ Hz or 2.4 Hz, such as to excite a sensory resonance. Many computer monitors and TV tubes, when displaying pulsed images, emit pulsed electromagnetic fields of sufficient amplitudes to cause such excitation. It is therefore possible to manipulate the nervous system of a subject by pulsing images displayed on a nearby computer monitor or TV set. For the latter, the image pulsing may be imbedded in the program material, or it may be overlaid by modulating a video stream, either as an RF signal or as a video signal. The image displayed on a computer monitor may be pulsed effectively by a simple computer program. For certain monitors, pulsed electromagnetic fields capable of exciting sensory resonances in nearby subjects may be generated even as the displayed images are pulsed with subliminal intensity.

14 Claims, 9 Drawing Sheets

Page | 309

AFRICAN-AMERICANS ARE THE AMERICAN INDIANS

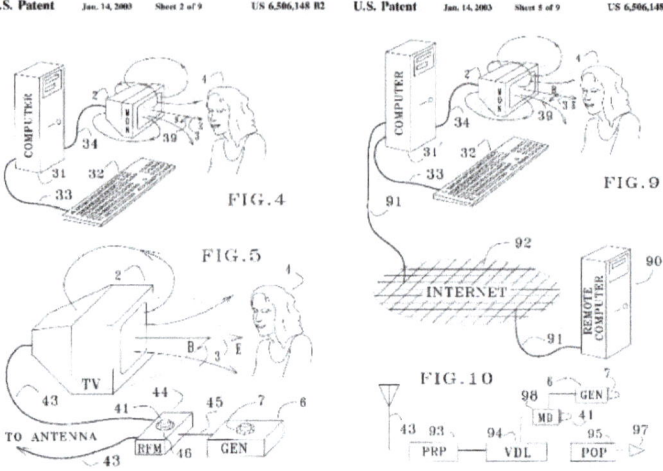

SUMMARY

Computer monotors and TV monitors can be made to emit weak low-frequency electromagnetic fields merely by pulsing the intensity of displayed images. Experiments have shown that the ½ Hz sensory resonance can be excited in this manner in a subject near the monitor. The 2.4 Hz sensory resonance can also be excited in this fashion. Hence, a TV monitor or computer monitor can be used to manipulate the nervous system of nearby people.

The implementations of the invention are adapted to the source of video stream that drives the monitor, be it a computer program, a TV broadcast, a video tape or a digital video disc (DVD).

For a computer monitor, the image pulses can be produced by a suitable computer program. The pulse frequency may be controlled through keyboard input, so that the subject can tune to an individual sensory resonance frequency. The pulse amplitude can be controlled as well in this manner. A program written in Visual Basic(R) is particularly suitable for use on computers that run the Windows 95(R) or Windows 98(R) operating system. The structure of such a program is described. Production of periodic pulses requires an accurate timing procedure. Such a procedure is constructed from the GetTimeCount function available in the Application Program Interface (API) of the Windows operating system, together with an extrapolation procedure that improves the timing accuracy.

Pulse variability can be introduced through software, for the purpose of thwarting habituation of the nervous system to the field stimulation, or when the precise resonance frequency is not known. The variability may be a pseudo-random variation within a narrow interval, or it can take the form of a frequency or amplitude sweep in time. The pulse variability may be under control of the subject.

The program that causes a monitor to display a pulsing image may be run on a remote computer that is connected to the user computer by a link; the latter may partly belong to a network, which may be the Internet.

For a TV monitor, the image pulsing may be inherent in the video stream as it flows from the video source, or else the stream may be modulated such as to overlay the pulsing. In the first case, a live TV broadcast can be arranged to have the feature imbedded simply by slightly pulsing the illumination of the scene that is being broadcast. This method can of course also be used in making movies and recording video tapes and DVDs.

Video tapes can be edited such as to overlay the pulsing by means of modulating hardware. A simple modulator is discussed wherein the luminance signal of composite video is pulsed without affecting the chroma signal. The same effect may be introduced at the consumer end, by modulating the video stream that is produced by the video source. A DVD can be edited through software, by introducing pulse-like variations in the digital RGB signals. Image intensity pulses can be overlaid onto the analog component video output of a DVD player by modulating the luminance signal component. Before entering the TV set, a television signal can be modulated such as to cause pulsing of the image intensity by means of a variable delay line that is connected to a pulse generator.

Certain monitors can emit electromagnetic field pulses that excite a sensory resonance in a nearby subject, through image pulses that are so weak as to be subliminal. This is unfortunate since it opens a way for mischievous application of the invention, whereby people are exposed unknowingly to manipulation of their nervous systems for someone else's purposes. Such application would be unethical and is of course not advocated. It is mentioned here in order to alert the public to the possibility of covert abuse that may occur while being online, or while watching TV, a video, or a DVD.

YOU'RE BEING MIND CONTROLLED!!

https://www.lens.org/lens/patent/US_6506148_B2

SLOWLY SEGREGATE

 Merriam-Webster › dictionary › seg...

Segregate | Definition of Segregate by Merriam-Webster

Segregate definition is - to separate or set apart from others or from the general mass : isolate. How to use segregate in a sentence.

The Civil Rights Act of 1964 is a landmark civil rights and labor law in the United States that outlaws discrimination based on race, color, religion, sex, or national origin. It prohibits unequal application of voter registration requirements, and racial segregation in schools, employment, and public accommodations. Wikipedia

Start date: July 2, 1964

BEFORE DESEGREGATION

Clark Campbell, left, and Theodore Campbell, seen in an undated photo from the Winston-Salem Transit Authority. The Safe Bus Company began business in Winston-Salem in 1926, thirteen years after the consolidation of Winston and Salem.

Photo Courtesy City of Winston-Salem

The state of North Carolina granted a charter to the company on May 24, 1926, and its buses operated on the streets in the city's eastern and northeastern sections. The fare was 5 cents, and most of its routes were short in populated areas.

Harvey F. Morgan was the company's first president. The company thrived in its first four years, earning enough money that it survived the depression of the 1930s. By 1935, Safe Bus transported 8,000 passengers daily, employed 75 people and had an annual payroll of $65,000.

The company published a pamphlet on its ninth anniversary in 1935.

"Each jitney owner had a designated area that he served," the company's history said. "If someone else came along and picked up passengers standing on a corner usually covered by someone else, it made some dangerous confrontations between the jitney owners."

Thirteen of the jitney owners contributed $100,000 to begin the Safe Bus Co. Inc. that served the black community during the Jim Crow segregation era in the city and throughout the South. The company was formed out of necessity.

Streetcars, which were owned by Duke Power Co., ran north, south, east and west, but didn't serve the entire black

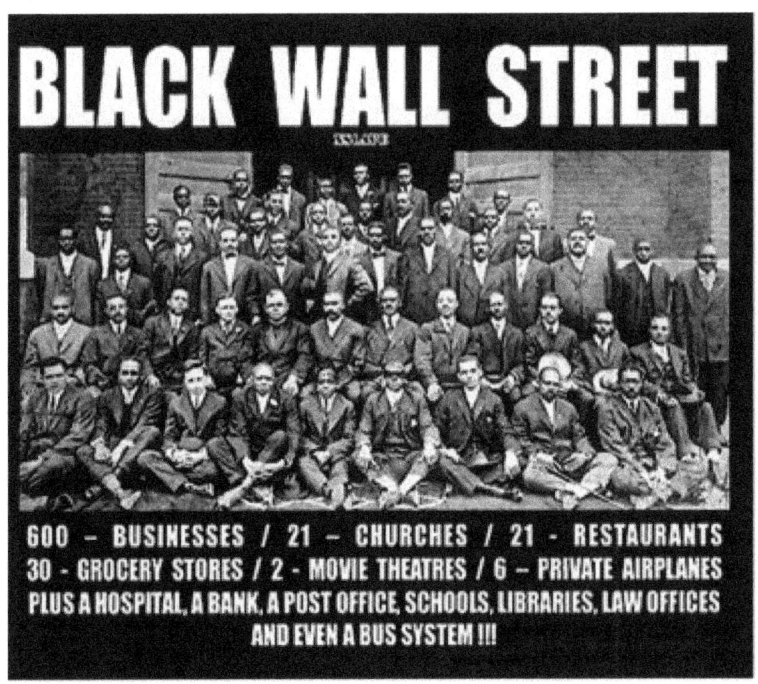

AFRICAN-AMERICANS ARE THE AMERICAN INDIANS

THE SILER CITY GRIT

A NON-PARTISAN FAMILY NEWSPAPER

Siler City, N. C., Wednesday, June 19, 1912.

Negro Race Has Billion in U.S.

Return of Colored People to Dark Continent is Impossible Owing to Material Progress Made by Them, It is Announced.

Kansas City, Mo.—Disfranchise the negro and send him back to Africa? Absurd. Impossible. More than a billion dollars' worth of United States real estate which he owns in his own name in the United States is not easily to be taken from him. Besides, the negro is not an African—he is an American. "African" is a misnomer. Why try to send him to a country which is not his own?

So says Dr. J. R. Hawkins of North Carolina, secretary and commissioner of education for the African Methodist Episcopal church, a delegate to the general conference, at the Allen chapel. Dr. Hawkins has made a study of the business status of his race in connection with his regular work as one of their foremost educators.

"It probably will startle the world when it realizes that we have acquired in the last 50 years over $1,000,000,000 in real estate," Dr. Hawkins said. "And that is only the beginning of the rapid forward march which the negro is making as a business man. The negro could not help being a business man. He was surrounded with it in the years of his slavery. He was taught how to drive a bargain in horses or real estate, even if his master didn't teach him how to read and write.

"There are 400 self-supporting newspapers, daily and weekly, owned and published by negroes in the United States; 3,000 physicians have been graduated from negro and white schools and are now practicing among their people; 2,000 lawyers have been admitted to the bar in the United States courts of justice and 380 authors are found among our race.

"We own 41 schools and colleges, representing an investment of $38,000,000, and $45,000,000 has been spent in church property for negroes. Negro men own and control 51 banks which are prosperous and flourishing, and $650,000 has been invested in negro libraries. And it is significant that in the southland negroes own 180,000 farms on which 50 years ago they toiled to the crack of the slave driver's whip.

"The negro is a born American and he feels it is his country. Africa has no call for him. It is as a fairy tale to him. Pestilence and disease are not uncommon in Africa, but America nurtures him and makes him strong and he likes it and intends to stay in it. That doctrine is being taught our 1,650,000 children in the public schools.

"The negro does not ask for any special legislation in his favor. He is willing to take his chance and is confident that he can bear his own burdent as well as the white man. And toward that end we are striving to educate our ignorant poor, make healthy the weak and to help more negroes to own their own homes and farms."

https://www.newspapers.com/clip/15632072/the_siler_city_grit/

AFRICAN-AMERICANS ARE THE AMERICAN INDIANS

BLACK INVENTORS AND THEIR INVENTIONS

INVENTION	INVENTOR	DATE	INVENTION	INVENTOR	DATE
Air-Conditioning Unit	Frederick M. Jones	7/12/1949	Lawn Sprinkler	J.W. Smith	5/4/1897
Auto Fishing Device	G. Cook	5/30/1899	Lock	W.A. Martin	7/23/1889
Auto Gear Shift	Richard B. Spikes	2/6/1932	Lantern	Michael C. Harvey	8/19/1884
Blood Plasma Bag	Charles Drew	Approx 1945	Lubricating Cup	Elijah McCoy	11/15/1898
Bicycle Frame	L.R. Johnson	10/10/1899	Mail Box	Paul B. Downing	10/27/1891
Baby Buggy	W.H. Richardson	6/18/1899	Mop	Thomas Stewart	6/11/1893
~~Cable TV Blocking Device~~	~~Joseph N. Jackson~~	7/25/2000	Motor	Frederick M. Jones	6/27/1939
~~Cellular Car Phone~~	~~Henry T. Sampson~~	7/6/1971	Peanut Butter	George W. Carver	1896
Chamber Commode	T. Elkin	1/8/1897	Record Player Arm	Joseph H. Dickinson	1/8/1918
Clothes Dryer	G.T. Sampson	6/6/1892	Refrigerator	J. Standard	7/14/1891
Door Knob	O. Dorsey	12/10/1878	Riding Saddles	W.D. Davis	10/6/1896
Egg Beater	Willie Johnson	2/5/1884	Rolling Pen	John W. Reed	1884
Elevator	Alexander Miles	10/11/1867	Shampoo Headrest	C.O. Bailiff	10/11/1898
Electric Lamp/Bulb	Lewis Latimer	3/21/1882	Spark Plug	Edmond Berger	2/2/1830
Eye Protector	P. Johnson	11/2/1880	Straightening Comb	Madam Walker	Approx 1905
~~Female Cycle Indicator~~	~~Joseph N. Jackson~~	2/8/2000	~~Stethoscope~~		Ancient Egypt
~~Female Cycle Predictor~~	~~Joseph N. Jackson~~	11/17/1998	Street Sweeper	Charles B. Brooks	3/17/1890
Fire Extinguisher	T.J. Marshall	10/26/1872	Stove	T.A. Carrington	7/25/1876
Gas Mask	Garrett Morgan	10/13/1914	Telephone Transmitter	Granville T. Woods	12/2/1884
Golf Tee	T. Grant	12/12/1899	Thermostat Control	Frederick M. Jones	2/23/1960
Guitar	Robert Flemming, Jr.	3/3/1886	Traffic Light	Garrett Morgan	11/20/1923
Hair Brush	Lydia D. Newman	11/15/1898	Tricycle	M.A. Cherry	5/8/1888
Insect-Destroyed Gun	A.C. Richard	2/28/1899	~~TV Remote Control~~	~~Joseph N. Jackson~~	3/28/1978
Ironing Board	Sarah Boone	12/30/1887	Typewriter	Burridge & Marshman	4/7/1885
Lawn Mower	J.A. Burr	5/19/1889	~~VCR Remote Timer~~	~~Joseph N. Jackson~~	10/14/1980

AFTER DESEGREGATION

BLACK INVENTORS AND THEIR INVENTIONS

INVENTION	INVENTOR	DATE	INVENTION	INVENTOR	DATE
Cable TV Blocking Device	Joseph N. Jackson	7/25/2000	TV Remote Control	Joseph N. Jackson	3/28/1978
Cellular Car Phone	Henry T. Sampson	7/6/1971	Typewriter	Burridge & Marshman	4/7/1885
Female Cycle Indicator	Joseph N. Jackson	2/8/2000	VCR Remote Timer	Joseph N. Jackson	10/14/1980
Female Cycle Predictor	Joseph N. Jackson	11/17/1998			

Page | 315

AFRICAN-AMERICANS ARE THE AMERICAN INDIANS

The company survived through decades until the Winston-Salem Transit Authority took it over in 1972.

A short documentary film, "The Legitimate Child" which portrays the Safe Bus Co., was shown in April at the 2013 RiverRun International Film Festival in Winston-Salem.

jhinton@wsjournal.com

(336) 727-7299

Clark Campbell, left, and Theodore Campbell, seen in an undated photo from the Winston-Salem Transit Authority. The Safe Bus Company began business in Winston-Salem in 1926, thirteen years after the consolidation of Winston and Salem.

Photo Courtesy City of Winston-Salem

AFRICAN-AMERICANS ARE THE AMERICAN INDIANS

Country	United States
State	Oklahoma
County	Tulsa County
City	Tulsa

Within five years after the massacre, surviving residents who chose to remain in Tulsa rebuilt much of the district. They accomplished this despite the opposition of many white Tulsa political and business leaders and punitive rezoning laws enacted to prevent reconstruction. It resumed being a vital black community until segregation was overturned by the Federal Government during the 1950s and 1960s. Desegregation encouraged blacks to live and shop elsewhere in the city, causing Greenwood to lose much of its original vitality. Since then, city leaders have attempted to encourage other economic development activity nearby.

Most people think by segregating, it's a step backwards, but in reality, it's a step moving forward to self-governing again. If you analyze our people's history before and after integration, you notice that we went from being the pioneers of the modern inventions, music, and intellect to being less innovative, creating fewer inventions and becoming the ultimate sidekick to the colonizers' dreams. We went from barely harming each other to killing each other at an alarming rate, from owning a plethora of real estate to becoming the biggest renters, from being efficient producers to the largest consumers. Our families were torn apart through programs such as welfare and section 8 that prohibited fathers from living in the home in exchanged for the government checks for women and children housing. We spend our money with every foreign nation that comes to our land instead of building our own.

http://m.amsterdamnews.com/news/2017/jan/12/dr-martin-luther-king-jr-i-fear-i-am-integrating-m/

STOP DRINKING ALCOHOL & FOLLOWING THE EUROPEAN COLONIZER'S INFLUENCE

SKETCHES

OF THE

HISTORY, MANNERS, AND CUSTOMS

OF THE

NORTH AMERICAN INDIANS.

BY JAMES BUCHANAN, Esq.

HIS MAJESTY'S CONSUL FOR THE STATE OF NEW YORK.

LONDON:
PRINTED FOR BLACK, YOUNG, AND YOUNG,
TAVISTOCK-STREET.

MDCCCXXIV.

Indians, which in all its discordant shapes rages with uncontrolled sway. "Their nations are split up into fragments; the son is arrayed against the father; brother against brother; families against families; tribes against tribes; and canton against canton. They are divided into factions, religious, political and personal; Christian and Pagan; American and British; the followers of Cornplanter and Sagoua Ha; of Skonadoi and Captain Peter. The minister of destruction is hovering over them, and before the passing away of the present generation, not a single Iroquois will be seen in the state of New York*."

Yet with all this guilt at our doors we call the poor Indians "savages,—barbarians." Yes, they have, indeed, become so since they were debauched and contaminated by the liquor and the example of European man. "*Our vices,*" says Heckewelder, "*have destroyed them more than our swords.*" I do not hesitate to say that, in my opinion, their ignorance of

* De Witt Clinton, p. 88, 89.

10 INTRODUCTION.

letters has been the only hinderance to their being, politically speaking, a most powerful people. With the faculty of circulating and improving their natural information, by means of literature, they would either not have been objects for the crafty arts of civilized man, or they would have been invulnerable to them, and never could have been driven from their territories. Their courage and warlike character, unaided by learning, are things but of inferior force. "Knowledge" says Bacon, "is power." How with

---

https://books.google.com/books?id=Q1JTAAAAcAAJ&pg=PA9&lpg=PA9&dq=yet+with+all+this+guilt+at+our+doors+we+call+the+poor+indians+%22+savages+--+barbarians%22&source=bl&ots=3gaCI42Tp0&sig=ACfU3U0uF1dnU7ZzTcR8agZLsBSoxNcDHw&hl=en&sa=X&ved=2ahUKEwi5hYmysazlAhVLvFkKHVcVAVUQ6AEwAHoECAkQAQ#v=onepage&q=yet%20with%20all%20this%20guilt%20at%20our%20doors%20we%20call%20the%20poor%20indians%20%22%20savages%20--%20barbarians%22&f=false

AFRICAN-AMERICANS ARE THE AMERICAN INDIANS

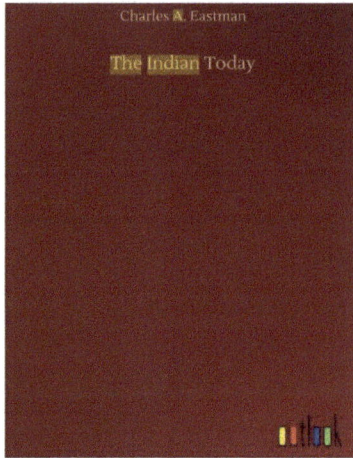

Practically all Indian wars have been caused by a few self-seeking men. For instance, a man may secure through political influence a license to trade among the Indians. By his unprincipled practices, often in defiance of treaty agreements, such as gross overcharging and the use of liquor to debauch the natives, he accumulates much tainted wealth. This he invests in lands on the border or even within the Indian territory if ill-defined. Having established himself, he buys much stock, or perhaps sets up a mill on Indian water-power. He gathers his family and hirelings about him, and presently becomes a man of influence in his home state. From the vantage point of a rough border town, peopled largely with gamblers, saloonkeepers, and horse-thieves, this man and his kind plot the removal of the Indian from his fertile acres. They harass him in every way, and having at last forced resistance upon him, they loudly cry: "Indian outbreak! Send us troops! Annihilate the savages!"

OSCEOLA AND THE SEMINOLES

The principal causes of Indian troubles in the South were, first, the encroachments of this class of settlers; second, the hospitable willingness of the Indians to shelter fugitive slaves. Many of these people had found an

https://books.google.com/books?id=OkxwDwAAQBAJ&pg=PA25&lpg=PA25&dq=practically+all+indian+wars+have+been+caused+by+a+few+self+seeking+men,+for+instance,+a+man+may+secure+through+political+influence+a+license+ro+trade+among+the+indians.+by+his+unprincipled+practice&source=bl&ots=bQCSx1ZFJA&sig=ACfU3U3G1y8qC1XLtzYT4ef7EBGUNnZWhw&hl=en&sa=X&ved=2ahUKEwjhodTAr6zlAhXGslkKHY8lB6cQ6AEwAHoECAEQAQ#v=onepage&q=practically%20all%20indian%20wars%20have%20been%20caused%20by%20a%20few%20self%20seeking%20men%2C%20for%20instance%2C%20a%20man%20may%20secure%20through%20political%20influence%20a%20license%20ro%20trade%20among%20the%20indians.%20by%20his%20unprincipled%20practice&f=false

Dictionary.com › browse › debauch

Debauch | Definition of Debauch at Dictionary.com

verb (used with object) to corrupt by sensuality, intemperance, etc.; seduce. to corrupt or pervert; sully: His honesty was debauched by the prospect of easy money. Archaic. to lead away, as from allegiance or duty.

"Negroes don't know the truth, you find a negro getting drunk, he doesn't know the truth, you find a negro taking dope, he doesn't know the truth, you find a negro lying and cheating, he doesn't know the truth, he's usually imitating the white man. Negroes get drunk because they see white people getting drunk, they smoke cigarettes because they see white people smoking cigarettes, they commit fornication and adultery because when they turn on the television all they see is the white man committing fornication and adultery. So and they want to be like the white man so they copy immoral social habit."

-Malcolm x

STOP RECREATIONAL USE OF MARIJUANA

Endocannabinoids control the production of neurotransmitters in the human brain. Neurotransmitters are chemical substances that facilitate communication between the brain and the central nervous system.

Endocannabinoids also relax our muscles, reduce inflammation, protect damaged tissue and regulate appetite and metabolism, among other beneficial functions.

Now here's where the problem lies. Because THC mimics endocannabinoids, the same physiological effects that arise from the normal application of endocannabinoids are triggered with the use of marijuana, especially in the brain.

This explains why marijuana smokers have memory-loss issues, feel higher levels of pain, have to cope with altered emotions and suffer movement control problems. In other words, THC screws the communication between the brain and the CNS.

One of the most deleterious effects of long-term weed use is loss of memory. This is because cannabis temporarily prevents the brain from creating new memories and learning new things. This type of memory los takes place in the hippocampus, the region o the brain that regulates short-term memory.

Heavy cannabis users are also at risk of developing false memories, even if these users haven't smoked pot for over a month, said a study published in journal Molecular Psychiatry.

https://www.msn.com/en-us/health/medical/long-term-effects-of-marijuana-on-brain-and-body/ar-BBVIXB1

Cardiovascular Health

Chemicals in marijuana called cannabinoids affect cardiovascular health. They can dilate blood vessels, raise resting heart rate and complicate heart pumping. According to a 2017 report by Harvard University, the risk for heart attack is much higher in the hour after smoking marijuana than it would be otherwise.

Respiratory Health

Cannabis comprises various toxic chemicals. Hydrogen cyanide and ammonia can affect the bronchial passages and lungs, which can impede breathing. A report published in the Journal of General Internal Medicine showed that the drug contains similar levels of tar as those in tobacco smoke, but marijuana has up to 50 percent more carcinogens.

Cognitive Health

Marijuana can lead to long-term cognitive impairment. According to the National Institute on Drug Abuse, the drug can affect thinking, memory and learning in people who began using cannabis during adolescence.

Researchers at Duke University contributed to a study that found that people who began heavily using marijuana as adolescents and had a marijuana use disorder lost an average of eight IQ points from ages 13 to 38.

Recent reports have also suggested that people who quit smoking marijuana after having regularly used the drug since adolescence did not fully restore their brain function.

A link between marijuana use and mental illness also exists. According to the National Institute on Drug Abuse, multiple studies indicate that cannabis use increases the risk for psychiatric disorders, including anxiety and depression. Using the drug can also exacerbate symptoms of schizophrenia.

https://www.msn.com/en-us/health/medical/long-term-effects-of-marijuana-on-brain-and-body/ar-BBVIXB1

    There is a continuous debate in regards to marijuana use. In my opinion, if it isn't being used for medicinal purposes to heal ailments, then it shouldn't be smoked or consumed. You read all of the problems marijuana use causes in an individual. On top of the issues above, marijuana also causes laziness, irresponsibility, short span mental retardation, and a lack of focus. I have a friend who was a chronic marijuana smoker and could never get his life together. He called me one day to tell me that he finally listened to me and stopped smoking, gained his focus and mental clarity back, cleared his criminal record and earned a six-figure income.

STOP EATING PROCESSED SUGARS, JUNK FOOD ETC.

1. Sugary Products

Sugar and sugary products are bad not only for your waistline, but for your brain function as well. Long-term consumption of sugar can create a wealth of neurological problems, and it can also interfere with your memory. On the other hand, sugar can also interfere with your ability to learn, this is why it is recommended to avoid pre-baked goods, sugar, corn syrup and products that are high in fructose.

2. Alcohol

Alcohol is known to harm your liver in the long run, and it also causes what is known as "brain fog". Like the name suggests, the term of brain fog refers to a feeling of mental confusion, it acts like a cloud that impacts your ability to think clearly, as well as your memory. Have you ever noticed that you cannot remember common item names, or you cannot recall certain events or you are not sure whether they were dreams or they actually happened? This might be influenced by the high alcohol intake which impacts the balance of the brain. Fortunately, these symptoms are reversible provided that you stop consuming alcohol, or you limit your intake to one or two drinks per week.

3. Junk Food

A recent study that was performed at the University of Montreal has revealed that junk food can change the chemicals in the brains, thus leading to symptoms associated with depression and anxiety. Besides, foods that are high in fat can also trigger some symptoms that are similar to the signs of withdrawal when you stop consuming them. These foods affect the production of dopamine, an important chemical that promotes happiness and an overall feeling of well-being. Moreover, dopamine also supports the cognitive function, the learning capacity, alertness, motivation and memory. This is why it is important to avoid all foods that contain excessive fat.

4. Fried Foods

Almost all processed foods contain chemicals, dyes, additives, artificial flavors, preservatives and such – these can affect the behavior and the cognitive functioning due to the chemical that causes hyperactivity, both in children and in adults. Fried or processed foods slowly destroy the nerve cells located in the brain. However, some oils are more dangerous than others – sunflower oil is considered to be among the most toxic ones.

5. Processed Or Pre-Cooked Foods

Just like fried foods, processed or pre-cooked foods also impact your central nervous system and they also increase the risk of developing a degenerative brain disorder later in live (such as Alzheimer's disease).

6. Very Salty Foods

Everybody knows that salty foods affect your blood pressure and they are very hard on your heart. However, as research suggests, foods that contain high amounts of salt (sodium) can affect your cognitive function and impair your ability to think. Otherwise stated, salty foods affect your intelligence!

As a matter of fact, the consumption of salty foods and nicotine have been shown to have the same effects as drugs, as they cause harsh withdrawal symptoms and cravings for salty foods.

9. Avoid Trans Fats At All Costs

Trans fats cause a series of problems, from heart-related issues to elevated cholesterol and obesity. However, they are bad for your brain as well, as they make your brain more sluggish, they affect your reflexes and the quality of your brain response – not to mention that they increase the risk of stroke!

Trans fats can also have other effects on your brain: if consumed for too long, they can result in a sort of brain shrinkage that is somewhat similar to the shrinkage caused by Alzheimer's disease. This brain shrinkage takes place due to the fact that trans fats slowly damage the arteries – you can prevent this and lower the stroke risk by simply limiting your intake of trans fats.

10. Artificial Sweeteners

When people try to lose weight, they tend to think that they will become slim overnight by simply replacing sugar with artificial sweeteners. It is true that artificial sweeteners do contain less calories, but they can actually do more harm than good! If used for an extended period of time, artificial sweeteners can cause brain damage and interfere with your cognitive capacity, especially if you use high amounts of sweetener.

https://kcallife.com/wellness/a77/

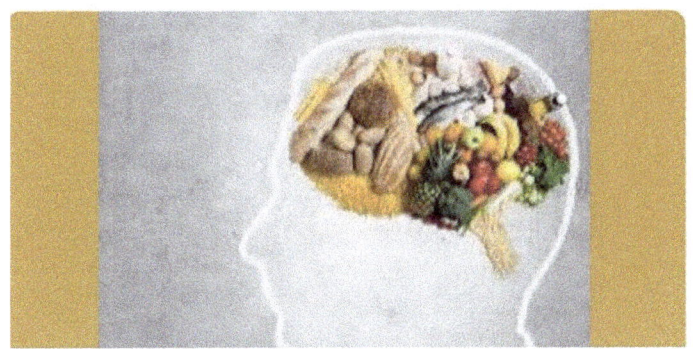

Put simply, what you eat directly **affects** the structure and function of **your** brain and, ultimately, **your** mood. ... Multiple studies have found a correlation between a **diet** high in refined sugars and impaired brain function — and even a worsening of symptoms of mood disorders, such as depression. Apr 5, 2018

Harvard University › health › blog

    Our diets are the main culprit in our decline in health. When I'm grocery shopping, I notice a lot of processed foods in people's grocery carts. Not only does process foods, sugars, and starches cause diabetes, high blood pressure, and multiple other ailments but a list of mental illnesses as well. There is no wonder why we can't get along with each other as a nation of people or solve significant problems plaguing our community. Drugs, artificial foods, and poisons have hijacked our minds. Many of us don't read the ingredients list to understand what we are putting into our bodies regularly. Eat more alkaline natural grains, fruits with seeds, and plants that assimilate with our bodies. It's time to get back on track to ascend our mind, body, and soul.

ABIDE BY THE FIRST LAW OF NATURE:
SELF PRESERVATION

self-preservation is the first law of nature

self-preservation is the first law of nature

1. *Proverb* All living things prioritize their own survival above all else and will do what is necessary to stay alive.

Every nation abides the self-preservation law except the erroneously called African Americans. Africans, Asians, Dominicans, Mexicans, Brazilians, Hindustani, and others bring their food, build their communities, establish schools, grocery stores, banks and produce political leaders to serve their needs when they come to the United States. Collectively, they preach and practice to refrain from intermingling and reproducing with our people to preserve their bloodline and traditions. We abide by the law of "everyone-else preservation," and it's time for a change. Here are some ways that we can get back on track.

1. Stop reproducing with the European colonizers

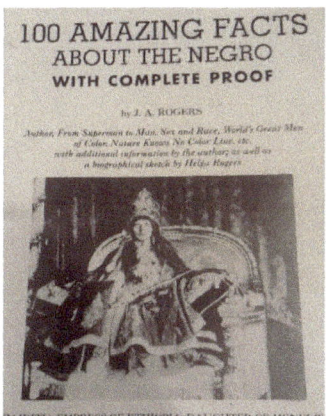

44. In 1787 while a party of 351 freed Negroes was aboard ship at Portsmouth, England, enroute to Sierra Leone, West Africa, the authorities brought on board sixty-two white women, prostitutes and others, whom they wished to get rid of, and married them to as many men, and sent them off to be the future mothers of the colony.

41. White American slave-holders used to induce white women to marry Negro slaves in order to hold the women slaves for life.

44. Utting says: "They sailed in 1787 from Portsmouth with 60 white women whom the Government wished to exile; the latter were made drunk, carried on board, and married to the Negroes without their consent being asked." (F. A. J. Utting: Sierra Leone, p. 81, London, 1931.)
Mrs. A. M. Falconbridge, who talked with these women in Sierra Leone says that they "were mostly of that description of persons who walk the streets of London and support themselves by the earnings of prostitution; that men were employed to collect and conduct them to Wapping where they were intoxicated with liquor, then inveigled on board ship and married to Black men whom they had never seen before." (Voyages to Sierra Leone in 1791-2-3, pp. 64-66.)

41. In Sept. 1664, Maryland passed a law that any white woman who married a Negro should serve the master of such slave "for life." Slave-holders took advantage of this law to induce the white women, some of whom were recent arrivals, to marry the Negroes. MacCormac says, "Instead of preventing such marriages this law enabled avaricious and unprincipled masters to convert many of their (White) servants into slaves." In 1681, the Legislature was forced to issue the following law: "Divers freeborn English or White women sometimes by the instigation, procurement, and connivance of their masters....and always to the satisfaction of their lascivious and lustful desires....do intermarry with Negroes and other slaves, be it enacted that if any master....having any freeborn English or white woman servant in their possession or property, shall by any instigation, procurement, knowledge, permission or contrivance," cause her to marry a slave she should be free at once and the master should pay a fine of "10,000 lbs. of tobacco." (Archives of Maryland, Vol. I, pp. 433-34, and Vol. III, pp. 203-04, also Johns Hopkins University Studies in Hist. & Pol. Science, No. 3 & 4.) What is true of Maryland was true of other states.

AFRICAN-AMERICANS ARE THE AMERICAN INDIANS

Rabbit-Proof Fence (2002)

Quotes / **Rabbit-Proof Fence**

- Film
- Quotes
- Trivia
- YMMV
- Create New

Notice, if you will, the half-caste child. Now, what is to happen to them? Are we to allow the creation of an unwanted third race? Should coloureds be encouraged to go back to the black? Or should they be advanced to white status and be absorbed in the white population?
—**Mr. Neville**, explaining his policies to the white audience.

I'm often asked by some white man: if I marry this Aboriginal, will our children be black? Here's your answer. (Turns on the next slide on the projector.) Half-blood grandmother, quadroon daughter, octoon grandson. The continuing infiltration of white blood finally stamps out the black color by the third generation. The Aboriginal has simply been bred out.
—**Mr. Neville**, during the same presentation.

Page | 330

Reproducing with Europeans over time has enabled them to take our birthrights and lay claim to an identity that doesn't belong to them. They have been using this tactic everywhere they go. They come in, mix with the natives, and then their offspring eventually govern the tribes. That is why you see Europeans as the chiefs of nearly every American Indian tribe. Some half-blood Indians reproduced with Caucasians, and their children reproduced with Caucasians until the Indian blood no longer existed but kept the benefits. That tactic made it possible for European-Americans to buy their Indian identity ($5 Indians) and claim our birthrights. Now it's more a political status than a racial one.

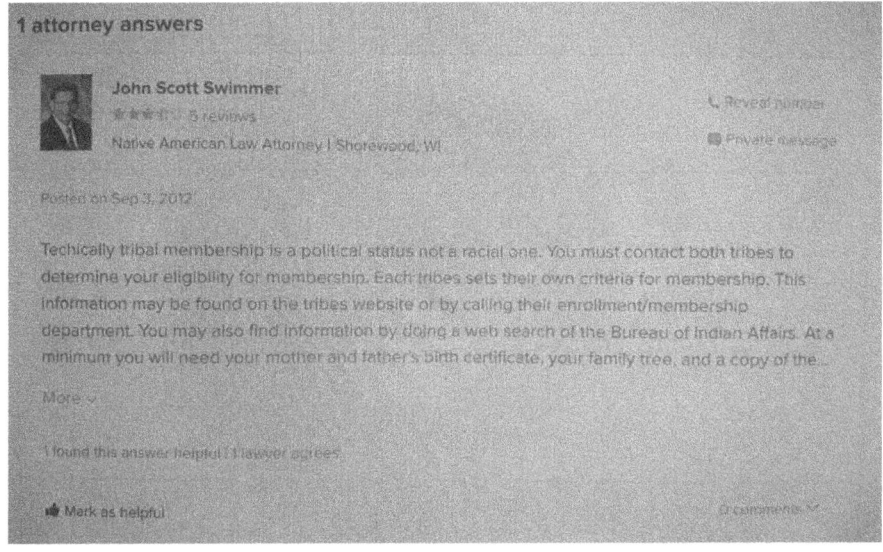

Reproducing with Europeans must cease. If today's mulatto children continue having offspring with Europeans, you can kiss your bloodline goodbye. If you currently have mulatto children, It would be wise to encourage them to have children with our people to keep the Indian blood alive here. Otherwise, you'll be the brown skin ancestor that quickly becomes extinct like in other countries in the Americas where they hide that ancestor.

AFRICAN-AMERICANS ARE THE AMERICAN INDIANS

Modern American Indian Family

Bigfoot Encounters
Bigfoot: Chief William Little Soldier, aka Bungard, Chief of the ...

AFRICAN-AMERICANS ARE THE AMERICAN INDIANS

The Cherokee were respected by the white man. They were people of high character, and were the first to own farms and accept the white man's schools. In 1825 it was recorded that forty-seven white men and seventy-three white women had married into the tribe. It was the gifted Sequoya, son of a white man and a Cherokee woman, who painstakingly created the first written Indian alphabet—an alphabet of the Cherokee language—so that his people could learn better the ways of the white man. It was the only case of the creation of a system of writing without the aid or prompting of the white man in the history of the Indian.

When gold was discovered in Georgia, the white man sought the

76

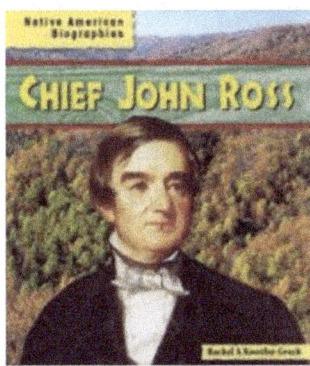

Chief John Ross of the Cherokee Nation - Legends of America
www.legendsofamerica.com › na-johnross

Chief John Ross of the Cherokee Nation would lead his people during a crucial and tumultuous time in their history. ... of business ventures, owned a 200 acre farm, and owned a number of slaves.

indiancountrytodaymedianetwork.com
New Choctaw Chief Gary Batton and His Council of Wisdom - ICTMN.com
Images may be subject to copyright.

Peter Pitchlynn
Chief

Peter Perkins Pitchlynn, or Hat-choo-tuck-nee, was a Choctaw chief of Choctaw and Anglo-American ancestry. He was principal chief of the Choctaw from 1864-1866 and surrendered to the Union on behalf of the nation at the end of the Civil War. Wikipedia

Born: January 30, 1806, Noxubee County, Mississippi, MS
Died: January 17, 1881, Washington, D.C.
Education: University of Nashville
Residence: Mississippi, Oklahoma

AFRICAN-AMERICANS ARE THE AMERICAN INDIANS

2. Only invest in our people

Every nation arrives here and establishes businesses for their people. We implemented this behavior in the past when segregation laws existed. It's time to spend money with our people again exclusively. If we have lost our way, let's take a look at the example below and pay attention to how foreigners operate when they arrive here.

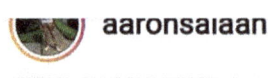 aaronsalaan

Last night I asked a Korean Beauty Supply owner how do they get loans to open businesses throughout our communities. I was wondering if they got special loans from the goverment. She put me on and respectfully told me that they do a money passing rotation where a group of 10 to 20 of them pool on average about 10 grand each. She said every 6 months each person gets about $100,000 out the pot to start a business. They must pay back into the pot when the business is established. She explained this is how they support and help each other. They only hire family and friends who all want to work for low wages til its their time to get theirs too. The plan is for all 10-20 of them to have a cleaning business, laundromat, restaurant, grocery store, beauty supply, clothing/shoes store or electronic store in our neighborhoods and build wealth for their families. She also admitted to me that we spend a lot of money with them. This is how they WIN! This is how most everybody besides us who build in our communities are winning. This is exactly what we need to do. If we start supporting each other we all could win. Some of you won't support anything with your own kind because your mind is too enslaved but you have to change your thinking if we are to all grow and leave wealth for our families instead of leaving

88 likes
aaronsalaah Damn

3. Buy and build our own cities

We should mimic our ancestors and build great cities. We should buy towns and start cultivating them like our ancestors of black wall street, rosewood, and various others cities.

Buy Buford, America's Smallest Town, For a Paltry $100K

APR 4, 2012.
BY SFIRSHEIN 4:30P

Now You Can Own the Hunger Games' District 12 For $1.4M

APR 4, 2012.
BY SFIRSHEIN 11:15A

Buy Entire Town of Scenic, South Dakota For Less Than $1M

BY SFIRSHEIN · JUL 26, 2011, 11:51A

Own an Entire South Dakota Town for Just $400K

BY SPENCER PETERSON

Entire Village of Pray, Montana, On the Market For $1.4M

BY SFIRSHEIN · FEB 27, 2012, 6:15P

4. Home school and build our own schools

It's time to start homeschooling and building schools for our youth. Only we have the best interest for the advancement of our people. The public educational school system is failing our children.

How do I start to homeschool my child?

To answer *"How do I start homeschooling?"* you'll need to:

1. **Review the homeschool laws for your state (or country).** Homeschooling laws vary by state (and it is illegal to homeschool in some other countries outside of the U.S.).
2. **Understand parent qualifications for your area.** Parents are not required to have a college degree to homeschool, but most states have a minimum education requirement (like a GED).
3. **Figure out your child's learning style.** Everyone learns differently and observing your child's learning style right from the start will save you time, money, and frustration.
4. **Choose a homeschool learning method.** There are many homeschooling methods like Charlotte Mason homeschooling, Montessori, unschooling, classical homeschooling, eclectic homeschooling and more. Understanding your homeschool method will assist you in choosing your curriculum or courses.
5. **Select curriculum or courses.** There are many options for homeschool curriculum and online courses that will assist you in home education.
6. **Deschool your child** (and yourself!).
7. **Find a homeschool support community.** When you're just starting out in homeschooling, it's easy to get overwhelmed. Having a homeschool community–online or in-person meetups–is extremely helpful.

https://homeschoolsuperfreak.com/how-do-you-start-homeschooling-your-child-today/

1 **Decide if the school will be for-profit or nonprofit.** Make this decision before deciding on any other academic aspects of your school. Nonprofit schools will be managed by a board of directors. For-profit schools, on the other hand, will be overseen by a proprietor (potentially yourself) or by a business partnership or LLC. One structure is not better than the other. It's simply up to you to decide how you want to manage and finance your school.[1]

- If you opt to run a non-profit private school, follow up by applying for 501(c)(3) nonprofit status with the IRS.

2 **Assemble a private school committee if your school is non-profit.** This committee will work together to make crucial decisions about the school's future, select a campus location, and hire faculty. The members will eventually become the core members of your board of directors. Committee members should be experts in different areas, including education, legal, accounting, business and construction.[2]

- If you aren't sure who to ask to become a committee member, reach out to other private schools in your area. Talk to their administration members, and find out who those schools used as committee members.

3 **Decide if you'd like to manage a day school or a boarding school.** Day schools function like typical public schools and send students home at the end of a 6- or 7-hour day. Boarding schools house students overnight. Boarding-school students typically stay at the school for an entire semester. Boarding schools take more financial input and more work, but the students tend to become deeply involved in their communities and to form close professional bonds with their teachers.[3]

- As another option, consider a Montessori school. Montessori schools are almost always private and offer children a discovery-based model of academic experimentation and learning.

4 **Determine the grade levels for your private school.** If you're inexperienced or want to start small, open a private grade school that offers grades K-5. A small school will be easier to run, require a smaller campus, and have lower enrollment.[4] Or, if you'd like to start a larger school, opt to offer grades K-12.

- Many private schools start with fewer and lower grade levels and add upper grades over time. For instance, you could begin by offering K-5. Then, after 3 or 4 years, you can add grades 6-8.

5 **Find a building to house your private school.** Plan to rent or lease a building in your community large enough—and in good enough repair—to house students.[5] Look around within residential or semi-residential areas within the community where you'd like to have your school. If no vacant school buildings currently exist, talk to city developer or commercial real-estate agents who may know of a viable school building.

- Unless you have a huge operating budget, do not plan to construct a new building for your school.

https://m.wikihow.com/Start-a-Private-School

http://classifieds.usatoday.com/blog/education/open-private-school/

STOP JOINING THE MILITARY & FIGHTING WARS THAT DON'T CONCERN US

Stop fighting in wars that don't concern us. We fight battles for the Europeans, return home, oppressed, and still called a nigger. Stop risking your lives and receiving the negative stigma that is affixed to the Europeans fighting as the American identity. The world has a problem with the European-Americans, not us. When they see your face with theirs, you're guilty by association and accessory to murder.

"My conscious won't let me go shoot my brother, or some darker people or some poor hungry people in the mud for big powerful America, and shoot them for what?? They never called me nigger, they never lynched me, they didn't put no dogs on me, they didn't rob me of my nationality, rape and killed my mother and father, shoot them for what? I gotta go shoot them, poor little black ppl, little babies and children and women, how can shoot them poor ppl, just take me to jail."

"I'm not gonna help nobody get something my negros dont have, if Imma die, I'll die now right here fighting you, if I want to die..you my enemy, my enemies are white people not Viet-kong or Chinese or Japanese.. you my opposer when I want freedom, you my opposer when I want justice, you my opposer when I want equality, you won't even stand up for me in America for my religious beliefs, and you want me to go somewhere and fight but you won't even stand up for me at home."

~ Cassius Marcellus Clay Jr. (Muhammad Ali)

EX MILITARY VETERANS SHOULD TRAIN THE YOUTH

If you're home from the military, start training the youth. Teach basic training and survival tactics that you learned at military boot camp. Take what you learned and bring it to your people to advance them as other nations do.

STOP SPENDING YOUR MONEY WITH IMMIGRANT BUSINESSES

Stop spending money with foreign businesses. They don't spend their money with you. They're getting rich off of your hard-earned money and send it back to their country or reciprocate with their people businesses here. If you date outside of your ethnic group, then they should pay when you eat at their ethnic groups' restaurant and vice versa. If you like Chinese food that much, learn how they make it. They make your style of fried chicken and sell it back to you in your neighborhood.

"Go into Japanese neighborhoods, you don't see negro stores. Go into China town, you don't see negro stores. Go into Jew town, you don't see negro stores. But come up here in black town and every kind of store is here but yours."

~ Malcolm X (speech; Cooperative economics)

BEWARE OF SAME SKIN FOLK THAT AREN'T OUR KINFOLK

We tend to accept everyone that shares a similar complexion with us and claim them as our people. That is a huge mistake because these people aren't from our genetic stock. They have their own ethnic identity, eat food from their homeland, have their customs and traditions. They come here and build their communities, work at places that are designed to oppress you, take advantage of the opportunities, and use the profits to help their people flourish. We need to be more aware of this moving forward. They aren't our kinfolk.

kin·folk

/ˈkinfōk/

noun

(in anthropological or formal use) a person's blood relations, regarded collectively.

Similar: relatives   relations   kin

- a group of people related by blood.
  "a set of kinfolk"

From Oxford   Feedback

Little Haiti
Neighborhood in Miami, Florida

Known for its creative global restaurants, colorful street murals and fruit stands, Caribbean-style Little Haiti also has a flourishing art scene centered on small, indie galleries. The Little Haiti Cultural Complex showcases Afro-Caribbean art, dance and theater, while the large covered Caribbean Marketplace sells produce and locally made handicrafts. The area's record stores and quirky dive bars draw a hip crowd.

Elevation: 7'

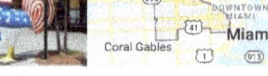

Little Havana
Neighborhood in Miami, Florida

Little Havana is Miami's vibrant Cuban heart, with Latin American art galleries and busy restaurants. Cafes with walk-up windows sell Cuban coffee to cigar-smoking patrons. On Calle Ocho (SW 8th Street), locals discuss politics over dominoes at Maximo Gomez Park, dubbed Domino Park by locals. The historic Tower Theater screens independent and revival films, while the area's clubs host live Latin music.

Little Ethiopia
Neighborhood in Los Angeles, California

Little Ethiopia is located in the Mid-Wilshire District of Central Los Angeles. It is known for its collection of Ethiopian restaurants, coffee shops, boutiques and thrift stores. The neighborhood is also home to The Little Ethiopia Cultural and Resource Center, located at 1037 South Fairfax Avenue. Wikipedia

https://www.themarshallproject.org/2015/06/03/nigerians-are-flocking-to-work-in-texas-prisons

https://en.m.wikipedia.org/wiki/Honoring_a_Father's_Dream:_Sons_of_Lwala

https://www.pv-magazine.com/2017/06/06/rapper-akon-lights-up-africa-with-solar/

GIVE FEMINISM BACK, IT'S NOT OURS

Feminism in our community has taken its toll on the relationship between our males and females. It only furthers the notion that women don't need men when, in reality, we need each other more than ever. Everyone serves a purpose in life, and both genders have their strengths and weaknesses. I was at a bar gathering for actors, and an elder actress of our ethnicity randomly apologized to me, and I asked why? She said, "One of the biggest mistakes we ever made was turning our backs on your guys during the civil rights era for the women's liberation movement." Feminism is a product of the European woman, and it had nothing to do with our community. Caucasian women were fighting with their men for rights and were front and center watching our men and women being hung, water hosed, and bitten by dogs.

FEMINISM

1ST WAVE FEMINISM
"We want to be equal to men"

2ND WAVE FEMINISM
"We don't need men"

3RD WAVE FEMINISM
"We are men"

AFRICAN-AMERICANS ARE THE AMERICAN INDIANS

"In 1964, government came in and pulled black women to the side, and they started to classify black women and women in general as minorities. In 1964, that's the first time they classified women as minorities, so they started to give them set asides and benefits and then they created the feminist movement. And alot of sistas branched off into that and that kinda created a riff because alot of sistas stop fighting for civil rights and started to fight for women's rights but women rights weren't being jeopardize in the black community our first priority, was racism, and we should've dealt with that first."

~ Tariq Nasheed

What did the women's movement gain from the civil rights movement?

The **civil rights movement** for justice and for economic equality actually influenced two **women's movement**, one in the 19th century, when the abolitionist **movement** inspired a **women's right movement** and suffrage **movement**, and then again in the 20th century, when **women** who had been member of the **civil rights movement**, the ...   Sep 2, 2013

 PBS › newshour › show › civil-right...

How the Civil Rights Movement Launched the Fight for LGBT ... - PBS

https://www.pbs.org/newshour/show/civil-rights-launched-the-fight-for-lgbt-women-s-equality

AFRICAN-AMERICANS ARE THE AMERICAN INDIANS

"We wanted to be free, we didn't need any boundaries, need no man to tell us what to do, well we hadn't had no man tell us what to do anyway you couldn't tell us what to do in slavery, so who ya know, we didn't really have no fight with you about that, that was the white woman's fight with her man, but we took it on, I wanna be free, ain't nobody gonna tell me what to do....so what happened was that movement and there never was a sisterhood in the women's liberation movement between the black woman and the white woman."

~ Shahrazad Ali

AFRICAN-AMERICANS ARE THE AMERICAN INDIANS

Elizabeth Cady Stanton

OVERVIEW   BOOKS   VIDEOS   QUOTES   ACC

Elizabeth Cady Stanton was an American suffragist, social activist, abolitionist, and leading figure of the early women's rights movement. Wikipedia

Born: November 12, 1815, Johnstown, NY

Susan B. Anthony was an American social reformer and women's rights activist who played a pivotal role in the women's suffrage movement. Born into a Quaker family committed to social equality, she collected anti-slavery petitions at the age of 17. Wikipedia

Born: February 15, 1820, Adams, MA

Lucy Stone was a prominent U.S. orator, abolitionist, and suffragist, and a vocal advocate and organizer promoting rights for women. In 1847, Stone became the first woman from Massachusetts to earn a college degree. Wikipedia

Born: August 13, 1818, West Brookfield, MA

RETURN TO A MATRIARCHAL SOCIETY

We always had that wise grandma that influenced everyone in the family. After all, it was women who ran the household and raised these great male leaders that you adore. Somehow we have strayed away from this part of our culture and started undermining and devaluing our women. We should start listening to them again. If they are confused, discouraged, or lost, then it is our duty as men to lead them back on the right path because through a woman, a nation is born. We must leave the patriarchal way of thinking and return to the matriarchal way of life.

Definition of **matriarch**. : a woman who rules or dominates a family, group, or state specifically : a mother who is head and ruler of her family and descendants Our grandmother was the family's **matriarch**.

(M-W) Merriam-Webster › dictionary › mat...

Matriarch | Definition of Matriarch by Merriam-Webster

WOMEN. Indian women were long thought of by the white man as hardly more than slaves or drudges of the men and the tribe in general. The term "squaw," which was a Narraganset Indian word for "woman," was early used by the white man and became the accepted term for an Indian woman, especially an Indian wife. Even Indians of other tribes on reservations throughout the United States adopted it. And usually the word brought to mind a poor, hard-working, burden-bearing woman, who was at the mercy of her husband, and without any rights of her own.

It is true that most Indian women had hard lives, but so did the men. Among the more highly organized tribes, such as the Iroquois, women had many rights. The child of the Iroquois woman always belonged to the mother's clan—in other words, descent was reckoned through the mother. Women selected the sachem, or chief of the clan. They could have this sachem removed from office if they were not satisfied with him. They could forbid their sons to go to war. They owned the tribal fields, the wigwams, and everything in these wigwams. They had the right of life and death over such prisoners as might become their share of the spoils of war. Thus women ruled the tribe, as the men who actually were the chiefs were representatives of the women—not of the men.

Among the Pueblo Indians much the same high position was given women. The husband came to live with the wife and she could get rid of him whenever she wanted to. The children belonged to the woman, or rather to her clan. Men helped the women with the heavier work, such as house-building and fuel-gathering; and even wove blankets and made moccasins for their wives, and worked in the fields.

Women on the Plains possibly had the hardest time. Before they had the dog or horse to drag the travois, they carried all the camp equipment. All hard work was done by them. Men killed the buffalo and left them where they fell. The women followed and skinned the buffalo, cured the hide, cut up the meat, and carried it to camp. They put up and took down tepees, did all the cooking and making of the clothing. Yet they were not without influence and power.

Women did not always remain in camp when their men went on horse-stealing expeditions or to war. The Piegan had a famous woman warrior named Running Eagle who went to war and led many horse raids. She was killed attempting to take horses from the Flatheads.

Women had their own dances and their own games. Some had their own "talk." There were women's societies in some tribes, too, such as the Goose Women, who guarded the corn, and the White Buffalo Cows, whose ceremonies were thought to lure the herds for the buffalo-hunters. In the South some women became rulers of their tribe, such as the Lady of Cofitachiqui, encountered by the Spanish explorer, De Soto. See BEADS, BLANKET, BRIGHT EYES, CLAN, COFITACHIQUI, COSTUME, DANCE, FEASTS, GAMES, HAIR, INDIAN LANGUAGE, INDIAN NAMES, MILLY, MINNEHAHA, MOCCASINS, MOTHER-IN-LAW TABOO, PAINT, POCAHONTAS, QUILLWORK, RIDDLE (TOBY), SACAJAWEA, SCALP DANCE, SONGS, SQUAW, SQUAW MAN, TATTOOING, TEKAKWITHA, TEPEE, TORTURE, TRAVOIS, WARD (NANCY). See illustration, page 328.

AFRICAN-AMERICANS ARE THE AMERICAN INDIANS

When Ahmad Simmons' (Brandon Hammond) diabetic grandmother, Josephine "Big Mama" Joseph (Irma P. Hall), falls into a coma during an operation to amputate her leg, it throws the Joseph family into chaos. Ahmad watches as his mother, Maxine (Vivica A. Fox), and aunts Teri (Vanessa L. Williams) and Tracy (Nia Long) struggle to adjust to the family matriarch's sudden absence, fall into old rivalries, share memories, and work to maintain the long-standing tradition of Sunday family dinners.

Life becomes complicated when Big Mama, the diabetic but wise and caring matriarch of the family and the glue that holds it together, suffers a debilitating stroke during an operation to amputate her leg. She slips into a coma, dying shortly after sharing a last word

FORGIVE OUT CENTRAL, SOUTH AND CARIBBEAN AMERICAN BRETHREN

Forgive our Caribbean, Central, and South American brethren. They don't know any better, like many of us don't. The Europeans colonized us with the English language, and Spain and Portugal colonized the rest of the Americas with the Spanish and Portuguese languages. Our American brethren were told the same lies but in a different language. They didn't see slave ships like we never saw any slave ships. I've talked to the locals in different parts of the Americas, and they don't know anything about their ancestors coming from Africa as slaves. They were very adamant about being where they are from originally. I bought a painting from a Panamanian local who spoke some English. I asked him about his ancestry, and he told me his people have always been in Panama. He knew nothing about a history of his ancestors arriving on slave boats from Africa.

DON'T EXPECT HELP FROM IMMIGRANTS

There is no reason for immigrants to ever come to your aid. They didn't have to ask you for permission to enter this country. The governing European-Americans granted them access here. Why would they risk deportation to assist people who hold no power of authority in their homeland? They don't thank our ancestors for taking the abuse that caused specific laws to pass that enabled them to reap the benefits. They only come here to seek a better life, escape poverty and oppression in their homeland. They don't respect us and could care less about us as a nation.

DON'T REPRODUCE WITH MULTI-ETHNIC PEOPLE

Multi-ethnic people are physically beautiful. However, reproducing with them causes psychological confusion for the offspring. Many of us are already confused about our heritage and busy trying to find ourselves. Imagine your confusion reproducing with someone who is two or more ethnicities, and you have to explain to your child about their heritage? What culture will they have that their ancestors passed down? If you're American Indian and you reproduce with someone who is Italian and Chinese, whose traditions, customs, and beliefs are they going to follow? I've talked to multi-ethnic people, and some claim that they are black or embrace European-American culture. Others don't speak the mother tongue of their various ethnicities or follow their ancestor's traditions. Reproducing this way is hazardous to our future.

START FARMING AGAIN

Farming is essential to being independent. If you produce your food, then it cuts down on your dependence on others. Our ancestors were master farmers and raised all crops. Everyone should have a garden where they live.

STOP LITTERING AND POLLUTING

Now that we understand that America is our home and motherland, it's time to clean it up and maintain it. If we live in project buildings or low-income neighborhoods, that doesn't mean we should pollute it. We should no longer litter and hold people accountable that litter in our faces. How would you feel if someone came into your house and threw trash on your floor? Carry that same energy for your country.

STOP LETTING PEOPLE SPEAK NEGATIVELY ABOUT US

Stop allowing people to mock and speak negatively about us. When you hear "***niggas ain't shit***" from foreigners, counter with "***NO!, our American men are great.***" When people say," ***American black women are difficult or bitches***," counter with" ***NO!, our American women are strong and beautiful.***" Stop letting different ethnicities belittle our people. If someone talked about your parents or siblings negatively, you would defend them, so keep that same energy for all of us.

LEARN A TRADE

Carpenters, Masons, Electricians, Plumbers, and other trades are always needed. We have strayed away from these and different ethnicities control this market now in our homeland. Everyone should add at least one of these to his or her skill set.

STOP LETTING OUR OWN PEOPLE DEPICT US IN A NEGATIVE WAY

Many foreigners' introduction to us is through movies, television shows, and social media. When people see constant negative depictions of us, they develop a belief that we are all like that. I understand that these negative stereotypes are present in all ethnic groups, but that shouldn't be the highlight of our American people. Our music should speak more about progression and productivity. Have you ever noticed that every other ethnic group's music doesn't degrade their women or talk about killing each other? So why should our music promote this majority of the time? When I was young, if you were behaving negatively in the community, an elder would discipline you and let your parents know. It is time to start having conversations with our people who depict us in a negative way to the world.

"We're the only people on this entire planet who have been taught to sing and praise our demeaning. I'm a Bitch. I'm a Hoe. I'm a Gangster. I'm a Thug. I'm a Dog. If you can train people to demean and degrade themselves, you can oppress them forever. You can even program them to kill themselves, and they won't even understand what happened." ~ Dr. Frances Cress Welsing

PRODUCE MORE PRODUCTIVE PROGRESSIVE CONTENT

We should start producing content that progresses our people. We should have movies that show us as the heroes, superheroes, and geniuses that we are. Too many people make billions off our stories and our abilities. The X-men comics were created from Martin Luther King Jr. (Professor x) and Malcolm X (Magneto) during the civil rights era. We should be the psychic detectives and the powerful telekinetic mutants. The saviors of the planet in movies should be us and not Europeans every time. We should produce more this type of content to inspire our youth.

RollingStone

Were you aware that Professor X is more like MLK, and Magneto is more like Malcom X? Was that a conscious projection there?
I think it was certainly an unconscious feeling, yeah. And I never felt Magneto was a hundred percent bad. I mean, there were reasons why he felt that way, but it was just up to Professor X to find some way to make him understand that he was on the wrong track.

And the whole civil rights metaphor that ended up being the defining metaphor of the X-Men, did that come along in the first few issues?
It came along the minute I thought of the X-Men and Professor X. I realized that I had that metaphor, which was great. It was given to me as a gift. Cause it made the stories more than just a good guy fighting a bad guy.

You probably didn't go into Martin Goodman and say, 'Hey, I have a great metaphor for civil rights here.' You said, 'The kids are gonna love this.'
He wouldn't have liked it, and he probably wouldn't have understood it.

https://www.rollingstone.com/culture/culture-features/stan-lee-dead-x-men-lost-interview-754889/

STOP PRAISING PEOPLE WHO APPROPIATE OUR CULTURE TO THEIR BENEFIT

We praise Europeans and other ethnic groups that can rarely sing or dance like us. We adore them but don't appreciate our own because these abilities are normal for us. In exchange, these different ethnicities make a lucrative amount of money because we accept them. We think they are unique because they train to talk, walk, emulate us, and benefit significantly from it. It happens so much that they teach our culture and abilities to their people and sometimes us.

Joyce Chang
Let's be real; black ppl made vine popular and everyone else hopped on that shit. There is no Asian American pop culture either. Asian bboys? Black culture. Asian rappers? Black culture. Is your eyebrows "on fleek?" You wanna twerk? You want good hair extensions? Also all borrowed from black culture.

AMERICAN pop culture in general is just black pop culture watered down for mass consumption.

Thursday at 3:42 PM · Unlike · 5 · Reply

Completely agree with this. "Black culture" is inherently "American Culture"

Thursday at 3:50 PM · Like · 1

STOP KILLING EACH OTHER & SPEAKING NEGATIVELY ABOUT EACH OTHER

Practice speaking positively about each other in our community and stop killing one another. During segregation, we didn't kill each other so often because we had a common adversary that was oppressing us. That enemy still exists, the oppression is still here, so the killing needs to stop. If we send out only positive vibrations towards each other, the healing of the nation starts taking place, and our perception begins changing from negative to positive. We'll seek to preserve our people.

TRAIN IN BOXING AND WRESTLING

We all should train in martial arts for self-defense. Train in boxing because we advance quickly, naturally, and are unmatched in that art. Study wrestling because many fights result in grappling immediately. If you don't choose one of these, at least learn other self-defense techniques and teach it to your children and community.

FOCUS ON NATION BUILDING INSTEAD OF POLITICS

Too many of our people focus on elections and politics. I can't name one politician or president that has ever done anything specifically for the progression of our people. We should focus more on nation-building. You have more power and political pull when you are a self-governing people with economic strength. Observe the behavior of other nations that come here. You don't see Chinese and Koreans complaining about voting or anything dealing with politics. They are too busy building and expanding their Chinatowns and Koreatowns across our soil. The very leaders we cherish Malcolm X, and Martin Luther King Jr. were Republicans. Here were are today, mostly voting democrat. Let's stop focusing on the entertainment of politics and work on building economic power.

AFRICAN-AMERICANS ARE THE AMERICAN INDIANS

https://books.google.com/books?id=IBvIFG6q4AkC&pg=PA51&lpg=PA51&dq=these+negroes,+they%27re+getting+uppity+these+days+and+thats+a+problem+for+us&source=bl&ots=umLhjPCoUu&sig=ACfU3U2UHD7cbX6m_GFulLo7aWsuMGXjrA&hl=en&sa=X&ved=2ahUKEwj6vJnh7-LlAhXIo1kKHRowDlcQ6AEwC3oECAYQAQ#v=onepage&q=these%20negroes%2C%20they're%20getting%20uppity%20these%20days%20and%20thats%20a%20problem%20for%20us&f=false

https://patriotpost.us/articles/44324-the-not-so-great-society-2016-08-17

AFRICAN-AMERICANS ARE THE AMERICAN INDIANS

<u>STOP COMMITTING CRIMES, SLAVERY NEVER ENDED</u>

Executive Mansion,
Washington, August 22, 1862.

Hon. Horace Greeley:
Dear Sir.

either to save or to destroy slavery. If I could save the Union without freeing *any* slave I would do it, and if I could save it by freeing *all* the slaves I would do it; and if I could save it b freeing some and leaving others alone I would also do that. What I do about slavery, and the colored race, I do because I believe it helps to save the Union; and what I forbear, I forbear

I have here stated my purpose according to my view of *official* duty; and I intend no modification of my oft-expressed *personal* wish that all men every where could be free.

Yours,
A. Lincoln.

https://www.nytimes.com/1862/08/24/archives/a-letter-from-president-lincoln-reply-to-horace-greeley-slavery-and.html

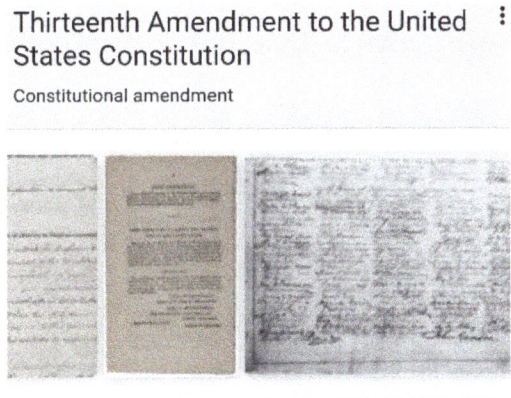

Thirteenth Amendment to the United States Constitution

Constitutional amendment

The Thirteenth Amendment to the United States Constitution abolished slavery and involuntary servitude, <u>except as punishment for a crime</u>. In Congress, it was passed by the Senate on April 8, 1864, and by the House on January 31, 1865. The amendment was ratified by the required number of states on December 6, 1865. Wikipedia

PARTICIPATE IN THE CENSUS

The census is critical in these times. One of the primary reasons why many African-Americans can't find their people is because they didn't participate in the census or register on the Dawes Rolls. We owe it to our future generations so that they can trace us. We should participate in every census identifying as American Indians, listing the specific tribes/nations of our bloodlines. The 2020 census is a very important and a chance for our people to preserve who we are in the United States. It is imperative that we, as a collective, participate.

NATIONAL

What You Need To Know About The 2020 Census

▶ LISTEN · 3:45   ...

March 31, 2019 · 9:05 PM ET
Heard on Morning Edition

 HANSI LO WANG

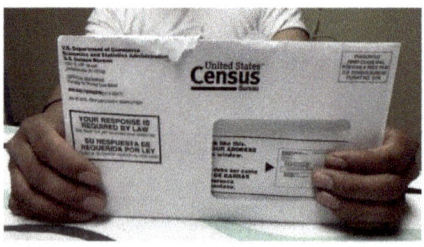

A Rhode Island resident holds an envelope he received for the 2020 census test run in Providence County.
Hansi Lo Wang/NPR

Why is the census important?

The census is required by the Constitution, which has called for an "actual enumeration" once a decade since 1790. The 2020 population numbers will shape how political power and federal tax dollars are shared in the U.S over the next 10 years. The number of congressional seats and Electoral College votes each state gets are determined by census numbers. They also guide how an estimated $880 billion a year in federal funding is distributed for schools, roads and other public services in local communities. The demographic data are used by businesses to determine, for example, where to build new supermarkets and by emergency responders to locate injured people after natural disasters.

When does the 2020 census officially start?

The head count is set to officially begin on Jan. 21, in Toksook Bay, Alaska — more than two months before Census Day (April 1), which is a reference date. Most households can start participating around mid-March, when letters with instructions are scheduled to be sent to 95 percent of homes around the country.

How is the census taken?

The 2020 count will be the first one to allow all U.S. households to respond online. Paper forms will still be available, and, for the first time, you can call 1-800 numbers to give responses over the phone. Census workers will make home visits to remote areas — including rural Alaska, parts of northern Maine and some American Indian reservations — to gather census information in person. Households in the rest of the U.S. that do not respond themselves by early April may start receiving visits from door knockers trained to conduct census interviews and collect responses using smartphones.

Who gets counted in the census?

The Census Bureau includes every person living in the U.S. — regardless of citizenship or immigration status. International visitors on vacation or work trips to the U.S. during the census are not included. Residents are counted at the address where they usually live and sleep. The Census Bureau has a detailed breakdown of how the 2020 census will count deployed troops, college students, incarcerated people, those displaced by natural disasters and other groups in unique living situations.

Can I refuse to answer a census question?

You can skip questions, submit an incomplete census form, and still be included in the head count. But you can be fined for refusing to answer a census question or intentionally giving a false answer, although the penalty has been enforced rarely in the past. Returning a partially filled-out questionnaire may result in a follow-up phone call or visit from a census worker.

What questions will the 2020 census ask?

Most of the questions will be similar to what census forms have asked for in recent counts:

- The number of people living or staying in a home on April 1, 2020.
- Whether the home is owned with or without a mortgage, rented or occupied without rent.
- A phone number for a person in the home.
- The name, sex, age, date of birth and race of each person in the home.
- Whether each person is of Hispanic, Latino or Spanish origin.

https://www.npr.org/2019/03/31/707899218/what-you-need-to-know-about-the-2020-census

CONCLUSION

I am not always right and far from perfect. I am not a racist or advocate any hatred towards any other ethnicities. I am not anti-African or anti-feminist. I may be a little blunt in my execution, so if this book offended you, I apologize. I love all people, but my first allegiance is to my people. I only listed SOME actions that I felt we should take to preserve and progress our people in the U.S. Only we can better our condition. I am not a professor or hold a doctorate in this field of study. I don't have the energy to debate, or compare your degrees and intelligence with my own. I am just a concerned individual who loves his people and wants them to thrive as everyone else wants for their people. Peace, and thank you for reading this book.

"I'm not saying I'm going to rule the world, I'm going to change the world. but I guarantee I will spark the brain that will change the world. And that's our job. It's to spark somebody else watching us. We might not be the one, but let's not be selfish. And because we're not going to change the world, not talk about how we should change it. I don't know how to change it. But I know if I keep talking about how dirty it is out here, somebody's going to clean it up!"

~Tupac Shakur

https://youtu.be/uijBebYpoto

ONE LAST THING TO THINK ABOUT

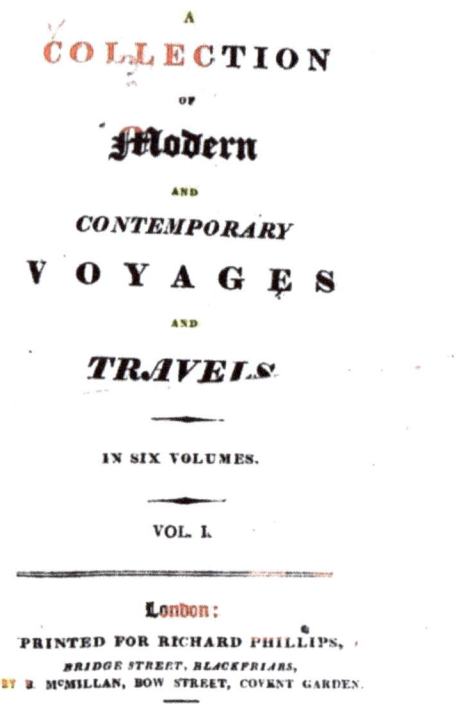

REMARKS ON SIERRA LEONE.   89

I shall add another reflection, of public utility. The Blacks are a kind of men destined by Nature to inhabit Africa and America; she has created them for burning regions: let us, therefore, take care not to oppose her views, or overthrow the barriers which she has established; but let us preserve their races in their natural purity, and not permit the Negroes to inhabit Europe. This mixture of black and white is dangerous to our population, and in time it may change, corrupt, and even destroy it.

https://books.google.com/books?id=PkROAQAAMAAJ&pg=PA89&lpg=PA89&dq=the+blacks+are+a+kind+of+men+destined+by+nature+to+inhabit+Africa+and+America&source=bl&ots=zyRX1mrMu8&sig=ACfU3U3c8Jb-wVAWL17wMm8MTLgnfUJPTg&hl=en&sa=X&ved=2ahUKEwjE6u_U3PXlAhUirlkKHVf4DAAQ6AEwAnoECAoQAQ#v=onepage&q=the%20blacks%20are%20a%20kind%20of%20men%20destined%20by%20nature%20to%20inhabit%20Africa%20and%20America&f=false

CALCUTTA JOURNAL
OF
NATURAL HISTORY:
AND
Miscellany
OF THE
ARTS AND SCIENCES
In India.

GEOLOGY AND ZOOLOGY,
CONDUCTED
BY JOHN M'CLELLAND, F. L. S.

Member Royal Ratisbon Bot. Soc.; Corresponding Member of the Zoological and Entomological Societies of London; Natural History and Philosophical Society of Belfast; Boston Society of Natural History, United States; Junior Member and Secretary of a Committee for the Investigation of the Mineral Resources of India; Bengal Medical Service.

BOTANY,
BY W. GRIFFITH, F. L. S.

MEMB. IMP. ACAD. NAT. CURIOS.; ROYAL RATISBON SOC.; ROYAL ACAD. OF SCIENCES, TURIN; CORRESPONDING MEMBER OF THE HORTICULTURAL SOCIETY OF ENGLAND, AND ENTOMOLOGICAL SOCIETY OF LONDON; ASSIST. SURGEON, MADRAS ESTAB.
Late Officiating Supdt. H. Co.'s Bot. Garden, Calcutta.

VOLUME V.

CALCUTTA:
W. RIDSDALE, BISHOP'S COLLEGE PRESS.
M.DCCC.XLV.

It cannot be questioned that physical diversities do occur, equally singular and inexplicable, as seen in different shades of color, varying from a fair tint to a complexion almost black; and this too under circumstances in which climate can have little or no influence. So also in reference to stature, the differences are remarkable in entire tribes which, moreover, are geographically proximate to each other. These facts, however, are mere exceptions to a general rule, and do not alter the peculiar physiognomy of the Indian, which is as undeviatingly characteristic as that of the Negro; for whether we see him in the athletic Charib or the stunted Chayma, in the dark Californian or the fair Borroa, he is an Indian still, and cannot be mistaken for a being of any other race.

https://books.google.com/books?id=76A5AAAAcAAJ&pg=PA120&lpg=PA120&dq=for+whether+we+see+him+in+the+athletic+charib+or+the+stunted+chayma,+in+the+dark+californian&source=bl&ots=fKyHaRzEoj&sig=ACfU3U051kJJeaUWecru4MhCFwy7T8BokA&hl=en&sa=X&ved=2ahUKEwiklYD0ttLlAhUhrlkKHX80Dz0Q6AEwA3oECAUQAQ#v=onepage&q=for%20whether%20we%20see%20him%20in%20the%20athletic%20charib%20or%20the%20stunted%20chayma%2C%20in%20the%20dark%20californian&f=false

About the Dawes Rolls

Officially known as The Final Rolls of the Citizens and Freedmen of the Five Civilized Tribes in Indian Territory, the Dawes Rolls list individuals who chose to enroll and were approved for membership in the Five Civilized Tribes (Cherokee, Chickasaw, Choctaw, Creek, and Seminole.) Enrollment for the Dawes Rolls began in 1898 and ended in 1906.

What kind of information will I find on the Dawes Rolls?
The Rolls list the individual's name, age, sex, blood degree, census card number and page, enrollment number, and tribe.

In most cases the ages indicated on the rolls are the age of individuals around 1902. Those listed as "newborns" and "minors" were born after the initial enrollment began in 1898, but before March of 1907.

Tribal association will be listed as "By Blood," "Intermarriage," or "Freedmen." Intermarriage indicates the person was married to a citizen of the tribe. You may also see the letters "I W" for Intermarried White. Freedmen were the former slaves of the Five Civilized Tribes and their descendants.

What information do I need before I search?
Basic information includes the name of a person who was alive and living in the Indian Territory during the enrollment period. If the individual was a married woman, you should look for her under her married name.

I cannot locate my ancestor in the index. What should I do now?
Look for your ancestor on the 1900 US census. If your ancestor did not live in Indian Territory, it is extremely unlikely they will be on the rolls. If they were living in Indian Territory check the available lists for rejected Dawes applications. Consider the possibility your ancestor belonged to another tribe or preferred not to be recognized as Indian.

For further information about tribal citizenship, contact the tribe directly.

di Drive, Oklahoma City, OK 73105 | 405-521-2491
om

The Dawes Commission required that individuals claim membership in only one tribe, although many people had more than one line of ancestry. Registration in the national registry known as the Dawes Rolls has come to be critical in issues of Indian citizenship and land claims. Many people did not sign up on these rolls because they feared government persecution if their ethnicity was formally entered into the system. People often had mixed ancestry from several tribes. According to the Dawes Commission rules, a person who was 1/4 Cherokee and 1/4 Creek had to choose one nation and register simply as '1/4 Cherokee', for instance. That forced individuals to lose part of his or her inheritance and heritage.[citation needed]

SUCCESS OR FAILURE DEPENDS ON INDIANS

The Ghost

Page | 364

FOR MORE INFORMATION

I don't have all the answers. There is a wealth of information on this topic that is surfacing everyday. It's important that we all help each other to advance our people. You can find more information and support below to help guide you on your journey.

Instagram: www.instagram.com/truthsetsusfree

Youtube:

www.youtube.com/truthsetsusfreetoday

www.youtube.com/theindigenous1

www.youtube.com/1000gohead

www.youtube.com/tyronest

www.youtube.com/abthalegend

www.youtube.com/phoenixmoon

Facebook: www.facebook.com/groups/africanamericansaintafricans/

Website: www.a4pure.com and www.a4live.com

EACH ONE, TEACH ONE!!

INDEX

Chapter 1: Christopher Columbus, **pg 5**

Chapter 2: The Transatlantic Slave Trade Exaggeration, **pg 15**

Chapter 3: Are The Europeans Really The African Slaves?, **pg 43**

Chapter 4: The Transatlantic Slave Trade Happened In Reverse. **Pg 64**

Chapter 5: The American And Their Complexion, **pg 75**

Chapter 6: American Indian Facial Features, **pg 89**

Chapter 7: American Indian Hair, **pg 95**

Chapter 8: They've Been Telling You, **pg 111**

Chapter 9: Doppelganger, **pg 151**

Chapter 10: From Indian To African Through Reclassification, **pg 181**

Chapter 11: African American Soul Food is American Indian, **pg 211**

Chapter 12: African American Holy Ghost Dance Is American Indian, **pg 214**

Chapter 13: Nigger, Jigaboo, Coon And Buck Mean American Indian, **pg 221**

Chapter 14: The "Black" People Of Black Wall Street Were American Indian, **pg 228**

Chapter 15: Roots is Fiction, **pg 229**

Chapter 16: DNA Test For Ancestry Are Fraudulent, **pg 233**

Chapter 17: "Native American" Mean European Not American Indian, **pg 237**

Chapter 18: American Indian Slave Masters Were The "Black" Slave Masters **pg 241**

Chapter 19: Maroons Are Aborigines Not Africans, **pg 243**

Chapter 20: (Afro) – American Doesn't Mean African, **pg 245**

Chapter 21: American Indians Are Not Moors, **pg 248**

Chapter 22: You're A Cotton Picker And Be Proud Of It!, **pg 254**

Chapter 23: American Indians Are Not Hebrew Israelites, **pg 257**

Chapter 24: America: The Mother, **pg 264**

Chapter 25: Solutions Moving Forward, **pg 277**